PELICAN BOOKS

CHINA: THE QUALITY OF LIFE

Wilfred Burchett was born in 1911 in Australia and is recognized as a specialist in Asian affairs. He spent nineteen years in South-East Asia and in China. During the war he was war correspondent for the *Daily Express* reporting for the Asian and Pacific theatres. In 1955 the Australian government revoked his passport because of his opinions on the Korean and Vietnam wars. Wilfred Burchett is a freelance journalist and author of twenty-three books which have been translated into thirty languages and sold all over the world. *My War with the C.I.A.* (with Prince Norodom Sihanouk, 1973) has been published in Pelicans. Wilfred Burchett speaks six languages and now lives in Paris with his wife and three children.

Rewi Alley was born in 1899 in New Zealand. A world renowned authority on China, a writer and poet, he has lived in China since 1927, working in many varied jobs, including that of Chief Factory Inspector of the Industrial Section of the Shanghai Municipal Council, and as Field Officer of the International Committee of Gung Ho. In 1972, Victoria University of New Zealand conferred a Doctorate of Literature on Rewi Alley both for his own voluminous writings and his translations of Chinese literary works.

2010) How did I get this book + should I keep it?
(moving)
I think my parents friend Gladys' Meyer, professor at Barnard College who got me into Horace Mann in 1940 — amazing woman, told

WILFRED BURCHETT with REWI ALLEY

CHINA: THE QUALITY OF LIFE

PENGUIN BOOKS

Penguin Books Ltd,
Harmondsworth, Middlesex, England
Penguin Books Inc.,
7110 Ambassador Road, Baltimore, Maryland 21207, U.S.A.
Penguin Books Australia Ltd,
Ringwood, Victoria, Australia
Penguin Books Canada Ltd,
41 Steelcase Road West, Markham, Ontario, Canada
Penguin Books (N.Z.) Ltd,
182–190 Wairau Road, Auckland 10, New Zealand

First published 1976
Copyright © Wilfred Burchett, 1976

Made and printed in Great Britain by
Hazell Watson & Viney Ltd,
Aylesbury, Bucks
Set in Linotype Times

CONTENTS

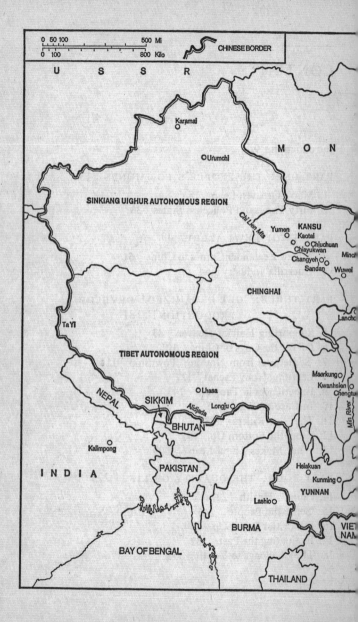

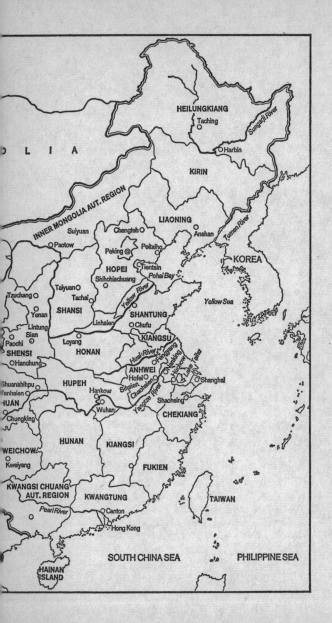

INTRODUCTION

In the Introduction to my other book on China,[1] written over twenty years ago, I excused myself for 'having produced a book after only six months' stay in People's China', giving as a pretext for rushing into print that 'there is as yet no other record of contemporary developments', and that the book 'was intended to answer the questions of people in the West who are being pressured to take up arms against People's China'. (The book was turned down by established publishers in my native Australia and was eventually published with great difficulty by my father and a few friends in Melbourne. Written in 1951 at the height of the Korean War, it was bound to have a difficult birth!)

In the two decades since, hundreds of books have been written about China, some by writers who have never set foot there, others by those who skipped in for a few days or weeks and were later billed as 'specialists'. There were a few excellent works of people with deep knowledge of China and its problems who conscientiously tried to plumb the lower depths.

In the Introduction to that earlier book, I promised it would be followed by another, 'dealing with aspects of the Chinese Revolution not touched on in the present work'. The book that follows, written in collaboration with the New Zealand poet, writer, educator and engineer Rewi Alley, the most knowledgeable of all who write on China today, represents a belated fulfilment of that pledge.

If I felt diffident in writing that first book and waited another twenty-odd years before tackling the follow-up, and if Rewi Alley waited almost a quarter of a century after first setting foot in China to write his first book, *Yo Banfa! We Have a Way!*, it

1. *China's Feet Unbound*, World Unity Publications, Melbourne, 1952,

is because we were both conscious of our responsibilities in presenting a valid, authentic picture of revolutionary changes that embrace one quarter of humanity.

How could one generalize on the basis of even relatively sound knowledge of a few areas when there are twenty-nine provinces and autonomous regions in China, each with an average population of over 25 millions – a total equalling almost double that of the populations of the United States and Soviet Union combined? How relevant are the changes which affect the majority Han people for the 50 millions of the national minorities? In portraying the swift-moving drama of China's continuing revolution, what moment should we seize on which would remain valid for a whole period ahead?

What follows represents a synthesis of results of independent travels and investigations carried out in a planned and co-ordinated way by Rewi Alley and myself in the summer of 1973. This is grafted on to the unique experience of Rewi Alley in forty-six years of almost unbroken residence, work and travels in China, as well as intermittent residence and frequent travels by myself for over thirty years.

The idea of pooling our experiences in book form was born some twenty years ago. Concrete projects were postponed several times, partly for the reasons mentioned above, partly because of my preoccupation with questions of war and peace in the perimeter areas, and later by the Cultural Revolution, which temporarily obscured a clear view of the future. Finally we have got down to it.

Except for two chapters devoted to something of the life, work and times of Rewi Alley (included despite his most strenuous objections, but which he grudgingly agreed to check for accuracy), the editorial 'we' form has been used throughout. This does not mean that Rewi Alley and I were together during all our material-gathering activities. More often than not we were apart, but we were working to an agreed plan and method. While I was visiting the newly developed oilfield at Taching for instance, Rewi Alley was visiting the older fields at Yumen in the north-west – an area he has known for well over thirty years. Although we both visited Szechuan in the south-west, Rewi Alley visited the capital, Chengtu, and the rugged Tibetan minority areas further west, while I visited the Kuomintang wartime capital of Chungking, where I had been based thirty years earlier, continuing east by boat through the fabulous Yangtze gorges. Some places, like the famous Tachai agricultural brigade, we both visited, but at different times, whereas other places such as the Taoyuan brigade we visited together in 1973, Rewi Alley having been there several times previously.

The historical references, and the rich material on life in the north-western areas and the minority regions in the south-west, are among Rewi Alley's priceless contributions to the book.

Our central interest has been to measure the changes that have occurred in recent years in China and to set them in perspective against what we knew of old China. We tried to under-understand also how ordinary Chinese citizens conceive that much-bandied-about term: 'quality of life'. Their concepts were bound to be different from those who measure human progress by the 'gross national product' – a point of view badly shaken in many countries by the 'energy crisis' in the latter part of 1973. The chapters that follow record the essence of what we discovered.

WILFRED BURCHETT, Paris, 15 January 1974

PART ONE

THE PEOPLE'S COMMUNES

CHAPTER ONE

MAO'S GREATEST LEAP

Of all the leaps into the future that Mao's China has made, the formation of People's Communes in 1958 was one of the most decisive, the most controversial, the most audacious in bringing together the 'struggle between two lines' inside the country and polarizing China's position within the socialist camp. 'Is Mao rushing madly on to get China's communism ahead of the Soviet Union's?' was the question being passionately debated at the time among European communists and indeed in the Soviet Union itself. The setting-up of the communes, which placed more power than ever before in the hands of the peasantry, marked a point of no return in the social, economic and administrative organization of China, which is now the responsibility of committees elected by the peasants, each commune embracing several villages.

Basing the main force of the revolution on the peasantry, rather than on the industrial proletariat, was as unorthodox as basing military affairs on guerrilla rather than on classical warfare. The speed with which the whole thing was done was remarkable. For anyone who remembers the tremendous upheavals occasioned when Stalin began setting up collective farms in the Soviet Union, or the long and painful process of collectivization in some of the eastern European countries, it was especially impressive. After a quarter of a century of Communist Party rule, Poland still had only a little over 20 per cent of her farmers in co-operatives. Within four months of the formation of the first People's Commune, all of China's more than half a billion farmers were reorganized without any interruption in production. (Later the number of communes was increased because some of the units formed were too big and in many areas of the national minorities communes were formed much later.) This radical transformation between the harvesting season of one year and the planting season of the next could not have taken place unless the farmers wanted it to. There is no force in China that could have imposed it on the peasantry, and not even the prodigious prestige of Mao Tse-tung could have brought it about by administrative measures from above.

We watched this revolutionary transformation from the beginning and have followed it ever since in every province of China (with the exception of Taiwan and some parts of Tibet), having visited five or six hundred communes over a period of fifteen years. We were convinced at the time – and this conviction has been borne out by events – that the formation of the People's Communes corresponded to an urgent necessity of the farming community and was a logical development of what had been going on in the countryside since the setting-up of the People's Republic, and before that in the Liberated Areas.

A typical case of the cell-like growth from embryo to full-fledged adult is that of the pioneer Hsin Fa commune, at the approaches to Harbin City. It was an area liberated in April 1946 – much earlier than the rest of the country. Land reform had been carried out as soon as the People's Liberation Army entered the area; land, implements, livestock and houses belonging to the landlords were distributed immediately to the poor and landless peasants.

'The typical thing in our area,' explains Pai Chen-hua, now a member of the farm's management, whom we have watched develop from a slow-moving, slow-thinking cautious peasant to an alert, brisk worker, 'is that the heavy soil here requires three horses to pull one plough. But no family that benefited from land reform got three horses – the average was one per household. Not all had ploughs – they are bigger and more expensive than in other areas. So there was a spontaneous tendency right from the start for three or four households to get together, pool their horses and plough each other's land in turn. There were a few bigger groups forming two ploughing teams. There were others who were suspicious and tried to get by on their own in that first season after liberation. These were labour-exchange teams which lasted during the ploughing season and harvest and were dissolved in between, but it was the beginning of a scattered and uneven collective initiative. Those who tried to work individually the first season saw the results and sought out work partners for the following season.'

This sort of thing happened wherever land reform was carried out, because it was so clearly the best thing to do. At the Harbin farms in the extreme north it happened in 1946; in Chekiang, far to the south, work-exchange teams were formed only in 1950, as liberation worked its way south. The movement was based on a spontaneous initiative sparked by Mao Tse-tung's famous 'Get Organized' appeal to the peasantry in November 1943, which encouraged them to generalize the practice of mutual-aid teams. These were a slight advance over the labour-exchange teams. Mao insisted, however, that they should be formed only if the peasants wanted them and where there was clear mutual benefit for those taking part.

'Two types of mutual-aid teams were formed around here,' continued Pai Chen-hua, 'those that continued to pool their resources only for the busy seasons and those that pooled for work all the year round. They were still on average made up of only four to six households, but some of the more advanced started forming bigger units. One of the difficulties at first was that, as it was the custom for the person whose land was being tilled or harvested to provide a meal for those taking part, and as each wanted to outdo the other in generosity, it was costing everyone more than he could afford in food. But the results were still better than they were even for the lower-middle peasants who were working on their own.

'The pooling of several work-teams paved the way for a new development in 1952, when there was a "land-pooling" campaign in which thirty to fifty households pooled their land, implements and cattle, forming agricultural co-operatives and planning production according to an overall state plan. A careful record was kept of what each member had contributed in terms of land, implements and draught animals, and part of the payments for the year's collective earnings were based on that.

Also, if anyone wanted to pull out at the end of the year, he could take his implements and draught animals with him and be given an equivalent piece of land elsewhere. There were practically no such cases, but members felt secure because they were not risking anything by joining the co-op. The benefits were so clear that no one in our area thought of going back to the old ways.

'After a few years of collective work, the political consciousness of members changed. They no longer thought of their own bits of land, as they did in the days of the mutual-aid teams, because now it was the crop from the whole area that counted. Before, each wanted to have his bit of land worked the best; also there was always a question of whose land was ploughed first, and harvested first, as this could have an important effect on crop yields. But the poor and lower-middle peasants who constituted the majority of members were not happy about retaining the payments according to land etc. contributed. They worked very hard for a little, while some who had contributed much land but did not work so hard in the fields got a much bigger share of the profits. This was the basis for a new move in 1956 to forget about what everybody had contributed and to base payments exclusively on the labour contribution. Thus it was decided by a very big majority to form a socialist-type co-operative, in which the socialist principle of "to each according to his work" was applied. This had a big effect the following season – everyone pulled his weight to boost the year's profits, with payments according to work done. The per-hectare yield went up from 1·3 tons to 1·9 tons.'

Pai Chen-hua said that most members, including himself, felt they had gone as far as they could go at that time in the direction of socialist agriculture. They did a lot of work on small irrigation canals, and improving compost fertilizer and seed selection.

'The only way to improve production radically was by more irrigation,' he continued, 'and the Sungari river was the obvious source of more water. But to bring water to our co-op from the Sungari meant cutting a channel through several neighbouring farms. We held meetings with them, pointing out the benefit for everybody, but we could not get agreement, because the extent of the benefit was very unequal. For some farms it would have meant taking a lot of land out of production, whereas they already had sufficient water for irrigation. But when we heard of the formation of the first commune, without waiting for the call from the Central Committee we had a meeting with seven other neighbouring advanced co-ops and decided to put them all together and form one of our own. Everybody agreed that, from labour-exchange teams onwards, the experience was that the bigger the unit, the better the yields.'

The movement to form communes had started a month or two earlier with groups of farms in scattered provinces joining together to form what they then called 'federations'. The motive was almost always the same – to tackle water conservancy works too large to be handled by individual co-operatives. These imposed hardships on some through whose lands the big irrigation channels would have to pass, thus violating the principle of 'clear mutual benefit'. Mao Tse-tung, as is his custom when something new is afoot, went on an inspection trip and liked what he saw. On a visit to Peiyuan in Shantung province on 9 August 1958, in which he talked to poor and middle peasants in the fields, Mao 'learned that they were planning to join their co-operatives into a big farm' and is quoted as having said: 'It would be better to set up a People's Commune. Industry, agriculture, trade, education and military affairs can be combined there and administrative work will become easier. That would be a great advantage.'[1]

Mao pushed through a resolution supporting the formation of People's Communes at a Central Committee meeting at the seaside resort of Peitaho, and on 29 August 1958 the call went out to combine groups of neighbouring socialist-type co-operatives into People's Communes. The communes should be large enough to merge co-operative management with local government at township level and to absorb local industry.

'We were able to go right ahead with the irrigation project,' continued Pai Chen-hua, 'and within the next three years we built 20 kilometres of trunk irrigation canals as well as many

1. *Peking Information*, No. 37, 16 September 1968.

subsidiary channels. We could go in for levelling the fields and preparing them for mechanized ploughing and harvesting. We became quite a big concern, with 5,700 households totalling 28,600 people with 9,000 acres of cultivable land. The workforce was split up into ten production brigades and fifty-two work teams.'

The growth from labour-exchange teams to People's Communes represents a vivid example of the speed at which a project gathers momentum in China if it is what people want. It took six years at Hsin Fa to move from labour-exchange and mutual-aid teams to a basic type of co-operative; four years to move up to socialist-type co-ops; and only two more years to take the most radical step of all, forming the People's Communes.

In China's 'Short March' of agricultural development from co-operation between four to six households to co-operation between four to six thousand households, the constant feature was that every step forward solved some old problems but created new ones, the solution of which made a new step forward inevitable if there was not going to be stagnation. Each new step forward involved acceptance at an even higher level of priority for the collective, as opposed to individual interest.

The decisive breakthrough and change in mentality of the peasants came in 1956, when private ownership of land, implements and draught animals was relinquished. This could take place only because, firstly, the poor and lower-middle peasants constituted the overwhelming majority of co-operative members; secondly, they had hardly any property anyway, their chief contribution being their labour, and so they had nothing to lose; and thirdly, their political consciousness had been raised greatly during the previous years, as had their educational level, and they were thus able to speak for themselves.[2] It was clear that these various steps were not made without resistance from the former upper-middle and rich peasants, as we found out in some co-ops and communes we visited at the

2. During the early period of the co-operatives, the more articulate peasants usually succeeded in imposing their views.

time of their formation, and this resistance was reflected in sharp fights within the top leadership of the Communist Party, as the storms of the Cultural Revolution illustrated all too clearly. This was one of the reasons why Mao vigorously resisted the idea that class struggle ceases with the consolidation of socialist power.

Hsin Fa was not a particularly advanced commune – grain production had moved up from 2·3 tons per hectare to 3·2 tons between 1957 and 1972, well below the yield for neighbouring farms – but Pai Chen-hua explained that this was because, as the commune was close to Harbin, they had concentrated on producing vegetables, eggs and meat etc. for the city while growing enough grain for their own needs. 'When we were at the labour-exchange period we did not have any of these things to eat ourselves,' he said, 'but last year we supplied Harbin with 32,000 tons of vegetables, 4,000 tons of potatoes, 60 tons of eggs, 150 tons of powdered milk, 100 tons of poultry, 90 tons of fish and 5,000 slaughtered pigs, for a total value of 9·85 million yuan.[3] We were able to do this because the setting-up of the commune brought with it irrigation for nearly half of the cultivable land, the levelling of the ground and a fair degree of mechanization. The farm has forty-one tractors and twenty trucks for taking our produce to market. We paid for them out of our accumulation fund. Each year we invest in new equipment; in 1970 we sunk some sixty-eight wells and invested in electric pumps at 20,000 yuan each; in 1971 we bought plastic material for fifty acres of hot-houses which we built that year; last year we invested in rotary sprinkler systems; for this year we shall decide only when the accounts' department tells us what the profits are.'

The powdered-milk plant had been started with hand-operated machinery but was gradually mechanized by equipment made by commune technicians. The milk was sprinkled through jets onto the heated surface of rotating cylinders, producing a granulated powder of 3·5 per cent butter-fat content. Instantly soluble in hot or cold water, packed in plastic bags

3. At that time, 2 yuan equalled roughly 1 dollar. There are 10 mao in 1 yuan and 10 fen in 1 mao.

and neatly labelled cans, Hsin Fa's 'Peacock' brand of powdered milk was up to international standards in all respects, including packaging. Year-round average daily production was half a ton. Apart from that there were oil-pressing and grain-processing mills and a machine shop for truck and tractor maintenance – nothing to compare with the sophisticated factories in communes further south.

A higher elementary school with 2,400 pupils – about one hundred of them boarders – and twelve primary schools with 4,700 pupils catered for the educational needs of commune children. All but sixty-four of the 300 school-teachers were provided by the state, the rest coming from among the one hundred or so young people from the commune who had graduated from university. At the time of our visit there were twenty commune students at university.

One of the very first communes we visited was the Chung-Pao Yu-i (China Bulgarian Friendship) commune on the outskirts of Peking. It had been set up at the end of August 1958 by combining co-ops with a total population of 40,000. To our question why a commune was necessary and why at that time, Yang Min, the local Communist Party secretary, whose functions in those days corresponded to those of the later chairman of the revolutionary committee, replied:

'A big water-conservancy programme was mapped out earlier in the year. But even the biggest of the advanced co-ops didn't have enough man-power to handle what was proposed. Then there was the question of getting the correct levels for the irrigation canals, which could only be settled by agreement with the neighbouring co-ops. This was impossible to get. When we started reading about the combining of co-ops to form bigger units, the solution was there in front of our eyes. Regular water supply means bigger crops, and one big master canal could serve a much bigger area than individual ones could. We held a meeting with the co-ops which had not agreed on building a master canal. The decision was virtually unanimous – to merge and form a commune.'

We visited the same commune a year later. Grain yields had jumped 25 per cent in the first season to just under 1 ton per acre. Average household income increased in that first year from 479 yuan to just over 600. Fourteen years later the grain yield was running at 2·2 tons per acre, with proportional increases in yields of fruit and vegetables for the Peking market. A small plant built in 1959 which produced concrete posts for use in supporting grapevines had blossomed out into a plant for producing concrete piping up to 20 inches in diameter for deep underground irrigation channels – in case of bombing. The piping in various calibres was also exported to neighbouring communes.

This sort of specialization was very typical. Communes concentrated on different products necessary for the whole county – the next highest administrative and economic-planning level after the commune. Even in the very early days you found one commune making the wooden chassis of farm carts, another the steel axles and wheels – from castings made from their own little blast furnaces and forges – and still another making the rope reins which replace their leather counterparts in the Chinese countryside. The components were exchanged among the communes on a fixed-value barter basis. Later there was a merging process similar to that which took place in the move from labour-exchange groups to communes whereby all the processes would come under one roof, one commune specializing in farm carts, another in ploughs, harrows, and even small tractors, later on, in some areas. But from the early days each commune set up its own repair and maintenance shop with an adequate supply of lathes and other machine-tools, and small factories for processing their own products and servicing their own activities. The Chung-Pao Yu-i commune for instance inherited a carpet-weaving factory, so they added a small plant to make their own dyes from a wood-alcohol base. Like many others it also had its own brick kiln for commune construction needs.

As the initiative for forming the communes came from the grass-roots, there was no standard set of rules. Members made their own. So many people had suffered so much in the not very distant past that the idea of having communal restaurants where you ate your fill and sold what was left over to the state – after having paid the 15 per cent agricultural tax – was obviously tempting. We visited a newly established commune in the Peking area where the main activity was rearing the very special birds so much appreciated by all visitors to the capital's famous Peking duck restaurants. We watched girl apprentices sitting on stools like milkmaids, ducks between their knees, force pellets of concentrated food into the hapless birds, stroking the long necks to ease the passage. The aim was to produce a six-pound duck within seventy days of hatching. Once released from the duckmaid's nimble fingers, the creatures literally staggered off to rest.

In the part of the communal kitchen which we were shown, some excellent maize bread was being cooked, together with lots of vegetables, but in the background there was the un-mistakable, nose-gripping odour of roast duck.

We asked our guide if the principle of free feeding did not entail the risk of eating up the profits. He looked a bit em-barrassed and mumbled: 'After all, a man's only got one stomach' – and it was left at that. But who could blame the peasants if they were eating their fill for the first time in cen-turies? This was precisely the reaction of Mao Tse-tung when critics raised the point. The free restaurants had to be closed simply because people ate too much. The restaurants remained in many of the communes, but there was a strict accounting for consumption, so that the socialist principle of 'to each according to his work' was observed.

Later on some loose codified guide-lines for the communes were worked out, based on what the majority had themselves adopted as their working rules.

The economic relationships between the communes and the state would drive any cost-accounting economist out of his mind. The American economist Kenneth Galbraith in a visit to China in the early summer of 1973 almost whooped with triumph when he found that prices for tomatoes and other perishable fruit and vegetables in the Peking street markets dropped towards the end of the day if there were large unsold stocks. The immutable law of supply and demand was brought into play, he observed, even in People's China, whose economics he admittedly found bewildering. He would have been still more bewildered had he been with us, at about the same time, in Peking's 'Evergreen' commune, where we were delving into the same question.

'We work under contract to the Peking Vegetable Company,' explained Chia Chun-ling, the chairman of the revolutionary committee. 'Prices are set by the state and remain very stable. They are sometimes unfavourable to the state, because the prices paid to us are not subject to supply and demand. For instance the state pays us 7 fen per pound of tomatoes, but they are sold in Peking for 3 to 4 fen per pound.'

'But if the season is unexpectedly good,' we asked, 'and you are stuck with production above your contracted quota?'

'We are encouraged to over-produce and we are paid at the standard contract price, except for grain, for which we are paid 30 per cent more than the contracted price for all above-quota production.'

The 'immutable law of supply and demand' was manipulated somewhere at the top in a way that benefited both consumer and producer, whereas the 30 per cent price-rise for above-quota grain production – operative throughout the country – was an obvious material incentive for maximum efforts by the grain-growers. Not only that but the state encouraged above-quota production, according to our investigations, in another way – that is by reducing the estimates for the following season's crop submitted by the communes at the end of each season. By allotting a somewhat lower quota the state almost guarantees an extra 30 per cent price bonus for a percentage of the crop.

The way agricultural tax is handled would also bother ortho-dox economists – not to mention tax collectors. In pre-liberation days anything up to 50 or 60 per cent of a peasant's earnings went in rent to the landlords and taxes. When the communes were formed a set sum was fixed as an agricultural tax – usually about 15 per cent of the 1958 harvest. Production jumped so quickly after the formation of the communes that the sum – not the proportion – was revised upwards three years later, but has remained stable ever since. As production increased and various sidelines developed, the proportion paid in tax obviously decreased. In the 'Evergreen' commune it had dropped to 2·8 per cent by 1973, a little below the nationwide average, which was around 4 per cent.

Agricultural tax varies according to location and the special assistance available from the state. A commune in the poorer hinterland would pay less, one on rich, well-served land more. If drought, flood or natural disaster hits a commune, the tax is remitted. Let us take the Chentsun commune near Shihchiachuang in Central Hopei. From 1965 to 1972 the agricultural tax stood at 8,300 yuan, though the commune's gross output shot up from 1·7 million yuan to 3·9 million during the same period. In 1972 the tax took up no more than 4 per cent of the commune's grain output.

The state also purchases a limited amount of grain from the team, which is fixed according to the area sown, total output and actual consumption and reserve of the team. The state pays 30 per cent above the set prices for anything which the team sells above its quota. The whole commune sold 3,200 tons of grain in 1973. This was 2·5 times the state quota.

At each of the three levels of commune organization, the team, the brigade and the commune itself, management is elected by assemblies of the total membership at each level. The elected organ at team level is known as the 'leading body', and at brigade and commune level as the 'revolutionary committees'. The basic unit – the team – is a work-group specializing in one or another of the activities of the commune – field work, pig-raising, machine maintenance, tractor-driving and so on. It is the basic accounting unit on most communes, drawing up its own production plan and allotting payments by work-points. Members of the 'leading body' work in the fields and are paid by work-points like everybody else, with work-points for time given to administrative work allotted on a scale decided by the members. The brigade usually corresponds to a former advanced-type co-operative, and it carries out tasks beyond the capacity of individual teams – small irrigation and flood-control works benefiting the teams under the brigade. It also manages rice mills, food-processing plants and machine maintenance stations and looks after primary schools and small clinics. Members of the 'revolutionary committee' are virtually full-time farm workers.

At the top of the pyramid is the commune revolutionary committee, the competence of which goes far beyond economic management. On the economic side it handles tasks beyond the capacity of the brigades, managing the tractor and heavy machinery stations, farm-machinery and hydro-electric plants, fertilizer factories and pumping stations. It also looks after administrative matters, security and military affairs; it runs secondary and technical schools – with a high proportion of teachers supplied by the state, but paid by the commune on the work-point system – and clinics able to handle basic surgery. Members of the commune revolutionary committee are obviously almost full-time administrative workers, but they must spend a minimum of sixty days a year working as ordinary commune members – an insurance against them developing into bureaucrats. Their annual salaries are assessed by the same criteria as apply to rank-and-file members.

The system of commune management is designed to prevent the emergence of a privileged managerial caste. The management is elected democratically, and management members whose performance is regarded as unsatisfactory may be replaced at any time. Everything is done to prevent the emergence of a privileged or self-generating bureaucracy. The peasants really feel they are running their own affairs, as indeed they are.

It is difficult to disagree with the formula expressed in the January 1972 issue of *China Reconstructs* – that the People's Commune represents 'a basic unit of China's socialist society and of proletarian political power in the countryside ... in short, the People's Commune is a brand-new social organization unifying leadership of politics, economy, military affairs and culture'. Doctrinaire Marxists may quarrel with the term 'proletarian political power'; Soviet theoreticians place the peasantry in the category of the 'petty bourgeoisie'. In China, however, the overwhelming majority of peasants were not landowners or property-owners in the real sense of the term. They

lived by selling their labour to the landlords.[4] After the formation of the socialist-type co-operatives, when payment was
exclusively based on labour and the co-op members directed
their own political affairs, the term 'proletarian political power'
seems correct.

When the drastic step was taken to renounce any further
rights in land, draught animals and implements, or the earnings
from them – the real death blow to the individualism of peasant
small-holders – it was in exchange for a most detailed system
of work-points. There were keen debates to decide how work-
points were to be allotted. A scrupulously fair method of ensuring that an honest day's work earned an honest allotment of
work-points was needed. In general the average for an eight
hours' day of work was set at ten points; if you exceeded the
allotted task, you could earn twelve or more points; if you
didn't you might get eight or less points, or work some extra
hours to make up the difference. On some communes we visited
there were up to 150 categories of tasks, each carrying its agreed
number of points, earnings being calculated each evening. Obviously there were adjustments as time went on: there were
allowances for the special problems of women, for work in
helping and training younger members and so on.

Each new form of social organization yielded parallel

4. When the Agrarian Reform Law was passed on 30 June 1950, the
categories of the various social strata in the countryside were carefully
defined. The poor peasants – the majority – were described as those who
'have to rent land for cultivation and are exploited by others in the form
of land rent, loan interest or hired labour.' Farm labourers or landless
peasants were those 'with neither land nor farm implements ... who depend wholly or mainly on the sale of their labour power for a living'.
Middle peasants, later described as 'lower-middle peasants', were those
who 'depend wholly or mainly upon their own labour for a living. In general they do not exploit others. Many of them are themselves exploited
on a small scale by others in the form of land rent and loan interest.' The
well-to-do, or 'upper'-middle peasants – whose land was not touched
during the land reform – were those who lived mainly off the exploitation
of hired workers, but also worked themselves, whereas the 'rich' peasants
and landlords lived entirely by exploitation. It was essentially the properties of the landlords which were expropriated under the Agrarian Reform Law.

economic progress, and this made the advance, and the speed of the advance, from labour-exchange teams to communes possible. Many of those who had been most suspicious in the early days of co-operation were later in the vanguard, pushing for higher forms of organization when they saw the leap in perhectare yields which followed each move. Although this leap was blunted somewhat during the three years of natural disasters which followed hard on the heels of the formation of the communes, it was the unanimous opinion in communes we visited in the 1959–62 period that without the great irrigation and water conservation works started in 1958 the extent of the losses would have been infinitely greater.

A striking aspect was the general uniformity of the way things worked, whether it was around Harbin in the extreme north-east, in Peking the capital, or around Chungking in Szechuan, the south-west. The changes of course were all the more spectacular in the remotest parts of the country.

At the Hua Chi (Flower-river) commune, on the opposite side of the Yangtze river from Chungking, we found the chairman of the revolutionary committee, Yeh Yun-chen, looking more like a university freshman than the manager of a farming community of 32,500 people and 7,310 households. The commune had been set up in October 1958 by the merger of nine socialist-type co-ops. Set in the typical, rolling Szechuan hills, it covered 3,500 acres of cultivable land, about 1,500 acres of which was for grain, the rest for fruit and vegetables, medicinal herbs and other sidelines for the Chungking market. 'The typical features of our province,' explained Yeh Yun-chen, 'are the hills and mountains, with the natural difficulties which these present for irrigation. But since we formed the commune, which vastly increased the financial resources and man-power at our disposal, we have been able to irrigate 70 per cent of our land and grow two crops of rice instead of the traditional single crop. In the old days, although we are close to the Yangtze, we were always short of water – there was drought in nine out of every ten years. We were able to put in pumping stations to bring water up from the Yangtze to where we could deal with it, and we have also dug out 119 ponds in the valleys. We have a permanent water-storage capacity now of 2·8 million cubic metres, and thirty main irrigation canals covering 16 kilometres, which is a lot in this sort of country.'

Over the years since it was formed the commune had invested 1·2 million yuan in setting up fifty-one big pumping stations, as well as fifty-five mobile pumping units which could draw on the reserves in the ponds.

'Thus,' continued Yeh Yun-chen, 'although we had a drought of unprecedented severity in 1972, we got slightly over three tons of rice per acre.' (1972 was one of the driest years in China for over a century, with the drought spread over almost the whole country – except the north-east – in varying degrees of severity.) 'With all the water we have tapped we have put in hydro-electric stations, producing enough power to supply electricity to all houses and processing plants, leaving a surplus which we sell to the state. Households pay 30 to 80 fen a month for electricity according to the number and wattage of bulbs used. In the pre-commune days, there was one highway which cut through this area. We have laid down 25 kilometres of roads which radiate out from the centre to each of the twelve brigades.'

Shops at the brigades which we visited carried very much the same variety of goods as one might find in a Peking department store – and at the same prices. They were run by the Chungking city commerce department, except that the service personnel were paid by the commune. For medical care, a commune member paid 5 fen for registration and an annual levy of 1·50 yuan per head of family members. For private consultations they paid half of the doctor's fee of 28 fen, the commune paying the rest as well as the bulk of medical costs from its welfare fund. At commune level there was a fifty-bed hospital, a clinic at every brigade level and a team of 'barefoot doctors[5] and a first-aid station at team level. The commune hospital was equipped to perform many types of operation.

On family planning the commune was doing better than the national average. Natural increase of births over deaths in 1972

5. The popularization of medical care in China and the role of the 'barefoot doctors' is dealt with on pp. 231–3.

had been only 1·6 per cent and it would be still lower in 1973. Contraceptives were free and women wanting abortions, and men or women wanting sterilization – fairly popular in some parts of China – could have free operations with paid post-operational leave. (The national average increase of births over deaths is officially given at around 2 per cent.)

Having both spent much of our youth on dairy farms, we were not too impressed by the commune's dairy herd of nearly 300 black and white Frisian-type cows, but they supplied 375 tons of milk annually to children in crèches and kindergartens and to local factories where workers have become newly conditioned to drinking milk. More impressive were the ponds which had been intended as reserves of water in case of drought, but which had been turned into fish farms. The fish had been conditioned to nourish themselves on fresh or dried grass and would rise to the surface in numbers which made the water fairly boil when one of the fish-farm hands threw in armfuls of freshly cut grass. The annual yield was between half a ton and one ton of fish per acre of ponds. Apart from furnishing a much-appreciated food item for commune members, 75 tons of fish were supplied yearly to the Chungking market. The two grass-eating types bred were carp and another firmer-fleshed fish, the gastronomic excellence of which we were able to confirm at lunch on the day of our visit. Weight of fish-per-acre was something which had not entered into our agricultural experience and we had no comparative data on the subject, only subjective appreciation of the quality of grass-fed fish. In winter they were fed on grass hay.

'Dig deep and store' was one of the national slogans at the time, a succinct version of Chairman Mao's original formulation: 'Prepare against war; prepare for natural disasters. Serve the People'. At the Hua Chi commune we found that the total storage of grain reserves – the accumulation of stocks at commune, brigade, team and individual household level – was 1,150 tons, added to yearly. The grain was poured into fat silos which were tapped from the bottom for current supplies, so that the reserves were constantly topped up with fresh stock. This represented a good six months' reserve in case of an unprecedented (and unthinkable) zero harvest due to natural or man-made disaster. The Hua Chi commune was already getting two crops a year and planning a third – one of wheat sandwiched between two of rice – but in areas where there was only one crop a season, at Harbin and other places, we found the grain reserves were sufficient for one year.

Hua Chi, like some of the other advanced communes we visited in 1972–3, had abandoned the work-points system and the time-consuming daily assessment of work done in favour of payment by work-days, assessed every three months. This decision must have produced sighs of relief from the accounting section. Mutual confidence had been built up over the years that every working member did his best to 'pull his weight'. An assessment was still made based on work-days contributed, because some women had to devote part of their time to household duties, some young people put in a few hours after school, older people worked half days, etc. Payment on days, rather than points, represented another step along the road of putting collective above individual interests.

Mao's leap into the communes was no leap into the dark. It was based on real faith in the peasant masses and not just on demagogic slogans. Had the latter been the case, China's agriculture would have been plunged into the most terrible mess long ago.

CHAPTER TWO

FIFTY THOUSAND
POLICELESS STATES

The overwhelming majority of Chinese – over 600 million out of the 750 million usually considered to be the present total population – live in the People's Communes.[1] Although the communes have a certain degree of autonomy, they become increasingly important links in the total state structure. They pay an annual agricultural tax, sell their annual grain quota to the state and through the county organizations in which they are integrated they have the contacts necessary to complete each year's production plan in accordance with the overall state plan. But in a way they are something like 50,000 states within a state.

Their economic role was well defined by the British economist Joan Robinson, when she wrote after several tours of investigation that: 'The basic characteristic of the Chinese economy is that 80 per cent and more of the population, organized in communes, is responsible for feeding and housing itself. The surplus provided by the communes feeds the rest of the population and provides raw material (particularly cotton) to industry.'[2]

They represent almost the ultimate in decentralization of state power – short of the actual 'withering away of the state' – which is essential to Mao Tse-tung's philosophy and was anathema to that of Liu Shao-ch'i and his top-level supporters. The latter believed in a tightly centralized super-state, operating through a structurized hierarchy with its hands on everything, literally, down to individual households. One thing that strikes even a casual visitor is the absence of the normal attributes of

1. Hsinhua, the Chinese official news agency, reported on 20 September 1973 that the population 'exceeded 700 million'.

2. *Economic Management: China 1972*, Anglo-Chinese Educational Institute, London, March 1973.

state power. Although there is a People's Militia, there is no army, no police and no courts or gaols. For communities of often 30,000 to 40,000 people, this is astonishing, to say the least.

When we asked about crime on our commune visits, we would often be told: 'As long as class society exists, crime will exist and there are still elements of the old exploiting class in the communes. But . . .' And it always turned out that serious crime was virtually non-existent.

When we raised the subject at the Chung-Pao Yu-i commune a year after its formation, the reply was: 'The only cases we have had were a few petty thefts of government property and some cases of ill-treating animals. There have been no crimes of violence at all.' At the Hua Chi commune near Chungking, visited in the summer of 1973, we were told: 'Crime is not, and never has been, a problem since the commune was set up. Occasionally someone has stolen someone else's bike. But everybody knows everybody else here, so it's impossible to get away with a thing like that. Team-members are curious if someone turns up with a bike when he never had one before. They will look it over, admire it, ask how much it cost and where he bought it. Then if the word gets around that somebody's bike had been stolen, people would guess straight away who was the culprit.'

'What would happen then?'

'There is a public security committee at brigade and commune level. The person who lost the bike would have reported the loss to the brigade public-security committee, giving the details and registration number. Other security committees within the commune would first be contacted, and those in neighbouring communes if the case could not be settled locally.'

'And when the culprit was discovered?'

'He would be severely criticized at a meeting of his brigade members. He would have to make a self-criticism, promise not to do such a thing again, and pay for any damage to the bike.'

We asked what would happen if there was a serious crime – murder for instance.

'We have never had such a thing. In the very early days, there were a couple of cases of arson – by class enemies who had been lying low. Those responsible were immediately identified by their neighbours. They were arrested by members of the commune security committee and handed over to the county authorities, where they were tried. But the principle we use for dealing with all petty offences is that of re-education within the community.'

Apart from public-security committees, there are also 'social-affairs' committees at team level, as well as at brigade and commune level. 'They try to head off problems before they become serious,' explained Yeh Yun-chen, head of the commune's revolutionary committee. 'For instance in the Kwangming brigade an elderly couple suddenly fell out. For weeks there was nothing but quarrels and fights in their house. One day they distributed their belongings – each putting his and her share outside the house – and announced they were getting a divorce. People from the social-affairs committee went to reason with them, individually at first, then at a long session with both of them together. They found that most of the sources for the quarrel were misunderstandings which could not be brought out in their quarrels, but came out in the discussion. Things were cleared up and they have lived in harmony ever since – for more than four years now.'

We were interested to discover at what point the state could enter the commune precincts – for instance in search of a commune member who had committed a crime in the county town or elsewhere outside the commune. It was a hypothetical question – none of the communes where we talked about crime admitted to having had such cases. 'If such a case arose,' we were informed, 'county public security officials would approach the commune public-security committee with the facts. The person accused would be investigated by the commune committee and if it was not a serious offence he would be dealt with by public criticism; if it were a serious offence he would be handed over to the county where he had committed the offence.'

It seemed clear at the many scores of communes at which we raised the question that crime simply was not a problem. The managing personnel usually looked rather astonished that after a serious discussion on their real problems – production, management, irrigation, housing, etc. – we would suddenly move to a subject which for them was without the slightest interest. It was also clear that the social pressures generated by people living and working together as one family was a powerful factor in favour of social morality, not to mention that the economic base for crime had largely disappeared with food, clothing and housing – even if at a modest level – no longer a problem. It was the principle of 'common law', based on 'common sense', that prevailed when things went wrong.

A good example of this in practice was the occasion when the son of a friend of ours knocked down an elderly commune member with his bike. A gust of wind had suddenly blown his straw hat over his eyes as he was speeding home and he hit the old chap as he was crossing the road, breaking his leg. Passersby helped him to carry the old man back into the commune clinic – it was in the Peking outskirts. A meeting was immediately held by the public-security committee to decide what was to be done. Clearly the incident was not deliberate, but it was considered the young man had been careless – and there was an old member with a broken leg as a result. Nobody even thought of calling the police, however.

While the old man's leg was being set at the commune hospital the public-security committee deliberated and came up with the sentence which the young chap cheerfully accepted:

'The old man lives on his own, so you had better move in and look after him until he gets well. You can cycle to work from here.' So the lad moved in with the old man, and bought and cooked his food for him. Apart from the fact that the old man liked meat while the young chap was vegetarian, they got on famously together. When the leg was mended they parted but have remained fast friends ever since. Throughout the communes one finds such examples of common law in action – people settling their own affairs without interference by the 'law' as it is understood in most societies.

It is in the communes in the countryside and the street committees in the cities that one senses a degree of social cohesion, and the morality that goes with it, which is something very special to China and which we think has some origins in age-old traditions which came to their fullest flowering under the present social system. The commune retains and develops the spirit of group values which has never been lost in China. From the early stages of primitive communism, through slavery and feudalism, during the anti-Japanese and civil wars, values of group and co-operative life among the poor, who have always been the overwhelming majority, have managed to survive. This was despite ferocious onslaughts against these values by landlord, warlord and other ruling forces of the day. Physical survival of a community often depended on co-operative efforts and the functioning of a social conscience. The experience of Rewi Alley in organizing co-operatives during the war against Japan[3] was decisive in proving that Chinese people wanted to work together and liked working together, the moment they saw the practical possibility of doing so. The type of individualism that is often held up as a model in the West and was indulged in by the old Chinese ruling class has always been thought little of by the working folk of China. The first native products of capitalism in China were the 'compradores' (still a dirty word there), individualists who acted as the go-betweens for the Western traders, who had forced China's doors with the barrels of their cannon, and the local merchants. They were despised by virtually all strata of society as violators of social values, making fortunes from what came to be known as foreign imperialism.

Perceptive observers in China have remarked on this emphasis on group values, which is an integral part of Chinese culture. Thus Dr Joseph Needham, the noted bio-chemist, historian and orientalist,[4] in a series of articles written for the Japanese newspaper *Mainichi* in June 1971, makes the following point: 'Perhaps nowhere is the nuclear family life, and all that it entails, more valued than in China. The sense of responsibility is extended towards grandparents and the aged, who are cared for with respect and understanding, and beyond them to-

3. See Chapter 3.
4. Dr Needham is Master of Caius and Gonville College, Cambridge University, and author of the monumental seven-volume work, *Science and Civilization in China.*

wards society as a whole.' (Many communes in China have 'Homes of Respect for the Aged' where elderly people who have no immediate relatives to look after them are cared for under apparently good and very humane conditions. (Clearly defined relationships between people were stressed by the forces that made for national liberation and therefore the role of the Chinese Communist Party became all important in continually educating the ordinary working folk of factory and farm, so that everyone felt his responsibility towards others – making the slogan of 'Serving the People' one that carried a daily meaning in practice, and thus breaking down many old barriers.

We raised the question of crime at the Hung Chiao commune, one of 197 communes in the Shanghai area, thinking that, as in the old days Shanghai used to compete with Chicago for the sinister distinction of being the world's most crime-ridden city, we might get some meatier data. With a population of over 26,000 living on 3,300 acres of land, the problems of making a decent living must have been acute.

'Crime?' said the burly chairman of the revolutionary committee, Liu Hsiao-chen, a former market gardener. 'It's practically non-existent, because people have been educated away from bourgeois ideology. If anyone stole something he'd be criticized and that's the worst sort of punishment. If he continued in anti-social activities, he would be sent to the county authorities to be dealt with. But there hasn't been a case of that for years.'

We asked if there had not been problems with the former landlords of the area. What had happened to them, anyway?

'Ah! That's different,' replied chairman Liu. 'In this area there were formerly forty-three landlords. We re-educated them – in other words they had to work like the rest of us and reform their ideology through labour. They were paid like everybody else according to their work. Nineteen of them developed well and became full members of the commune when it was formed; another ten were comparatively good and have been accepted as "limited members" (they had no voting rights); the other fourteen are still being remoulded – we have to step up our efforts a bit with them. In other areas, the dictatorship of the proletariat was exercised severely on those who had committed major crimes – such as having killed their hired hands – and a few were executed. But here it was a case of remoulding them through work and making them see the error of their past ways. They realized very quickly that, with their economic base gone, they had no standing in the community.'

Another element in the social cohesion and stability one finds inside the commune is the fact that the children are not uprooted by having to get their basic education outside the community. They are educated on the spot and if they go on to higher education later – having spent a preliminary period working on the commune – they will usually return to find jobs awaiting them which can absorb the specialities for which they have been trained. The teachers, even those provided from outside by the state, are integrated into the commune and paid under the work-points system like other commune members. The children grow up among the problems which their education is aimed to solve. There are primary schools at brigade level and secondary schools at commune level. Teachers from outside are immediately made to feel at home and treated with that respect for learning which the ordinary folk have always shown in China.

In a commune in Chekiang province, for instance, we met a woman teacher from Huchow, a fairly big city alongside the Taihu lake. She felt she would like to go into the countryside because one of her three children had been crippled by polio. She admitted that she left the city for an unknown village with great misgivings.

'But when the boat edged into the jetty at the little village, with mountains reaching up to the sky behind, the whole school and half the children's parents had turned out, with banners and drums, to meet me,' she said. 'It was really moving. Then, that evening, the brigade members came round and asked just how I would like the school to be. They cleared an old grave area and built the school – in a few days – just as I wanted it. Three big classrooms, and two smaller rooms in front for myself. They brought me everything I needed in the way of cooking implements; some of the school-children took on the job of bringing me water; others carried my polio-stricken son into the classroom every day. I was surrounded by love and affection from the very first day and I have never had such attentive pupils, such satisfaction in teaching. My husband is also a school-teacher. He comes to see me quite often to try to persuade me to go back to the city. I explain that I am integrated into a community where I feel I belong. I have become a part of the progress of the children and will never go back to the city. I had been half afraid of the countryside before – it represented the unknown. I came because I felt it was a duty, and also because I thought the unpolluted air would be better for my polio-crippled son. But I have never felt happier or more useful in my life than since I have been here.' We heard many similar expressions of satisfaction from teachers who came in from outside.

The fact that secondary and technical secondary educational facilities are inside the commune solves the acute problem of the drift from rural areas to the cities, a nightmare in many developing – and developed – countries. In most developing countries, the type of education now available in China's communes can only be had in the nearest big town, and even if the students would like to settle in their local communities there are usually no outlets for the talents and skills they have acquired. Together with the taste for city life acquired during their secondary-school studies, the result is the steady drain of young people to the cities to take any jobs that will permit them to stay. On the communes, the community gets a full return for its investment in education.

Secondary-school graduates, on the communes as elsewhere, go to work for two or three years before going on to higher education. Application for university entrance has to be accompanied by a recommendation from the unit where the student has been working, based partly on his attitude towards work and fellow-workers. By the time a student goes off to university, his or her roots will have been sunk deep into the soil of the community and the specialities chosen are almost certainly those needed 'back on the farm'. They are usually longing for the day when they return as specialists in genetics and agronomy, or as hydraulic, electrical or mechanical engineers, forestry experts, doctors, school-teachers, accountants, etc., to contribute to raising the scientific and technical level of brigade activities. The young people remain integrated in their own communities and help to diversify the constantly expanding activities of the commune so that each becomes as self-reliant as possible. There are jobs to cater to everyone's tastes and appetites. Life is exciting – there are always 'new heights to scale', as they say these days.

Secondary technical schools on the communes have well-equipped laboratories and workshops, and experimental work is tried out on the adjacent fields and in the brigade workshops. Young people are encouraged to master several specialities. A tractor-driver should not only be a first-rate mechanic as well, but perhaps a lathe-worker and seed-selection expert too. Commune members should become interchangeable, as far as possible, where skills are concerned.

At the Hung Chiao commune we found that, out of the total population of 26,340 people, 9,600 children were enrolled in the commune's fifteen primary and six secondary schools. Working in the various teams and brigades were no less than 206 university graduates from the commune itself, forty-two of whom were Western-type doctors attached to the commune hospital and the clinics of the sixteen brigade clinics. The home-grown university graduates had been reinforced by 430 'educated young people', as revolutionary committee chairman Liu Hsiao-chen referred to them, who 'had responded to Chairman Mao's call to come to the countryside and receive education from the peasants', during the Cultural Revolution. Some had later been recommended to go back to university studies, others had settled down and become tractor-drivers, technicians, doctors and teachers. 'The poor and lower-middle-class peasants,' explained Liu Hsiao-chen, 'regard such educated young people as their own children.'

This treasury of home-grown and imported intelligentsia had produced striking results. The commune was fitted out with twenty-one large underground pumping stations, each set in solid concrete pits, which sent water for irrigation pulsing along 130 kilometres of underground concrete pipes, served by 216 electric pumps to force the water out at ground level so that the fields of the entire commune could be watered at will. Why were the pumps underground? The usual answer was: 'Chairman Mao said we should prepare against war.' Apart from the impressive underground irrigation system, there were five small factories making farm implements or repairing tractors and pumps, a plant for insecticides and another for canning surplus fruit and vegetables.

We visited one of the repair shops, where there were 230 workers in half a dozen well-spaced buildings, housing fifty-seven machine-tools – everything necessary, the head of the workshops assured us, to take care of any repairs to trucks, tractors or electric pumps, including the making of spare parts. He pointed to some specialized lathes designed by some of the university graduates and manufactured by a Shanghai factory with which the commune had special links. (Where geography permits, every commune has such links with a higher educational establishment and a factory, where they can send students from their own schools to take short study courses or work at the factory benches.)

'The direct contact between our commune members and the educated young people works both ways,' explained Liu Hsiao-chen. 'We learn from each other. The young people learn from our simple life and direct way of doing things, as well as from our practical experience of agriculture; we learn from their theoretical and technical knowledge. Once confidence is established, our farmers raise all sorts of problems that stand between us and increased production. The young people put their brains and learning together to solve these problems. The fact that our grain yields have moved up from an average of just under one ton per acre for this general area in pre-liberation days, to over 5 tons in 1971, by far the biggest increase being since the Cultural Revolution, is largely due to their good work.'

In the remote back-country regions the communes have brought spectacular changes. One of the wildest, most backward regions used to be the Maerkung region of eastern Tibet, the crossing of which was one of the most perilous episodes in the 'Long March'. Ed Snow, in *Red Star over China*, describes how the Queen of the Mantsu tribespeople had an implacable hatred of all things Chinese and obviously made no distinction between 'Reds' and the 'Whites' who were pursuing them. At her orders the Mantsu tribespeople harassed the 'Long Marchers' where they could, and otherwise withdrew with their herds and flocks to the mountains from where they rolled down huge boulders which swept away many Red Army men and their animals. In order to survive, one of the cardinal principles of the Red Army – to pay for whatever supplies they needed – had to be violated. They had the money, but there was nobody to accept it. They were forced to take what was necessary – sometimes fighting battles for a few sheep, reaping green grain in the fields. Mao Tse-tung was later to tell Ed Snow: 'Some day we must pay the Mantsu and the Tibetans for the provisions we were obliged to take away from them.'[5] Formation of communes in the minority areas has been one way of paying the debt.

This area now forms part of the Apa Tibetan Autonomous Region, in which is included the Chiang Autonomous County – the Chiang people being those who were formerly known as the Mantsu. Capital of the Apa region is Maerkung, formerly a small opium-trading post and scene of the historic meeting of the main part of the Red Army under Mao Tse-tung with the North Szechuan Fourth Front Army under Chang Kuo-tao. In the old days there were no highways – only tracks cut around the sides of cliffs, and swaying bamboo rope suspension bridges spanning the steep ravines. Transport of goods was by poverty-stricken porters who staggered along under incredible loads. A backward, savage area where three major Tibetan lords and a myriad of minor ones were continually fighting each other at the cost of their slaves and serfs.

These days there is a modern highway along which we drove from Kwanhsien, where the Szechuan plain ends and one enters an area of magnificent snow-capped mountains, majestic forests and rushing streams, to Wen Chuan county and on to Maerkung, crossing the Min river over a new suspension bridge, built to accommodate the heavy truck traffic of the region. From

5. *Red Star over China*, Gollancz, London, 1937.

Maerkung, with its modern brick buildings, assembly hall, hospital, factories and shops set out along the bend of a tempestuous river, we crossed the river on another suspension bridge to visit a brigade of the Aidi commune. Leaders of the brigade were awaiting us at the head of the bridge, surrounded by a lively bunch of children, and we were introduced to a matronly Tibetan woman as the brigade leader. Because of language problems, and to save time in translating, an account of the brigade development was given by one of her Chinese-speaking deputies. Of the 150 acres of valley land which the brigade's ninety-two families now farmed, 110 in the old days had belonged to the lamas and landlords, leaving about one tenth of an acre per head of the 402 people (eighty-two families) who lived there in 1950 when land reform took place.

'One of the lords,' continued the account, 'named Pan Kwan, owned 16 acres of the best land and had it tilled by slaves. He had eighteen mules and horses and fourteen slaves. In the few years prior to liberation seventeen families in this area died out completely; the list of those who had been killed, who starved to death or ran away was 149. Everyone from the poor families had to do Ula service – compulsory, unpaid labour for the local lords. Loans were easy to get in a bad season from the lamas at 20 per cent interest, but if it were not repaid by the end of the year the borrower, or an able-bodied member of his family, had to be given up as a slave. The total grain harvested in the year before liberation was 55 tons, whereas in 1972 it was 322 tons from the same acreage. That year, after sales to the state, the rest was divided up on an average of 520 pounds per head (including babies and children) plus 135 yuan in cash for brigade members. Grain reserves amount to 58 tons.' These dry statistics could hardly convey the changes in people's lives. A look inside the solid stone, fortress-type houses in which Tibetans like to live provided a glimpse of what these entail. Electricity in every house, transistor radios, a sewing machine in the home of the brigade leader – and she assured us many other houses also had one – a hand tractor in a shed outside, a horse and cow for every family. Most of the families had cash in the bank and the brigade had its own reserve fund of 104,000 yuan.

At Wen Chuan county, we had spoken to Ma Chen-hsing, one of the leading cadres in the Autonomous Chiang county – a former hired hand of Chiang nationality. He was eager to explain some of the changes:

'In pre-liberation days we had to exchange with the traders from the plains 80 pounds of grain for 1 pound of salt; 22 pounds of pepper for one length of homespun to make a gown. Now with the fair prices we get for our grain and pepper and cheap salt and cloth, the equivalent is 1 pound of grain for 1·7 pounds of salt; a length of much better cloth for less than 3 pounds of pepper. In one of our villages in the old days, of the forty-two families, the able-bodied members of thirty-two of them had to work as porters for eight months of the year – they could grow enough grain for only four months. Now there are fifty-five families, and they earned 11·5 tons of grain between them in 1972, plenty for all to eat and some to sell. With two other commune brigades they dug an irrigation channel nine miles long, and crops will be better than ever this year. Every house has electricity – no more pine shavings for lighting.'

Not all the communes in the Apa Autonomous Region are self-sufficient in electricity, but the drive is on to attain this objective as soon as possible. There are already 434 small hydro-electric plants of between 30 and 1,000 kw. capacity operating. Regional and county industry, as elsewhere in China, has been developed to service the communes of the area.

From Apa in West Szechuan, we went to West Kansu along the Old Silk Road. A place we would have liked to visit there was Su Nan county on the upper slopes of the Chilien mountains, in the Yuku Autonomous District of Kansu province, but it was too impossibly high up. However, as the visiting Mahomets could not go to the mountain, the mountain came to us in the shape of some Tibetans and Yukus from the leadership of the Huangseng and other communes of Su Nan county. The spokesman was Heichiming, a forty-seven-year-old Tibetan, ruggedly built and forthright, who talked to us in Chinese. His was a pastoral commune without a brigade, just sixteen production teams. At the time of liberation, the combined farms in the area had a total of 20,000 head of stock. Now there were

160,000, of which 100,000 were good wool-producing cross-bred sheep. 'It was difficult to get the girl shepherds to learn how to do artificial insemination at first,' recalled Heichiming, 'but now they take it as a matter of course.'

In the county as a whole, we learned that, in the twenty years which had preceded the end of Kuomintang rule, flocks and herds had been reduced to 270,000, but by 1968 they had been built up to 600,000 head of better stock – thanks to artificial insemination – and had been levelled off at that figure, which is the amount the pastures could support.

Heichiming, who had been in the leadership of co-operatives and the commune for eighteen years, spoke of how members had learned the importance of giving the pastures a rest; of periodically sowing them to better strains of grass and giving a dose of fertilizer; of how they had learned to store snow in shaded valleys, for melting at the height of summer. In his county, drought was something to be feared more than the worst blizzards.

Education was not as good as elsewhere, because families are dispersed, especially in the summer months, following the sheep and cattle around the grazing grounds. Only 78 per cent of the children got regular schooling, but this situation was being remedied by setting up a network of 'horseback teachers' who would make the rounds of the grazing areas. Most of the children galloped in on their own ponies to schools set up in the summer grazing encampments, but the 22 per cent who eluded the educators were from encampments too remote to make the twice-daily pony ride.

'Have things got better for us?' Heichiming treated the question with a short laugh. 'In the old days we had to pay a sheep for one brick of tea. Now we get eight bricks for a sheep.' (Brick tea is a staple food in these remote areas. Boiled tea mixed with barley flour, known as 'tsamba', is an essential item of diet for the Tibetans and other mountain peoples.) 'Before we set up the commune, we lost livestock every winter. We soon built up reserves and invested 300,000 yuan in building winter quarters for the sheep and cattle. We've had no losses since. We have seven tractors and other farm implements, plenty of draught cattle and horses. We've got everything we need, plenty of food and clothing, good housing, medical care, transport.'

As the long shadows started creeping down the valleys, Hei-chiming abruptly looked at the sky, and with a few words of farewell the little group took off for the mountains in their long robes and that slightly bent-forward lope of people who spend most of their lives in the saddle or climbing steep mountains.

In one essential sense, wherever we looked the picture was the same – of people running their own lives within the commune precincts, without interference from the outside and progressing steadily towards prosperity – very modest progress by Western standards but enormous by their own.

The military aspect of the role the communes play in national defence, with virtually every able-bodied person of both sexes enrolled in the well-equipped People's Militia and their organic links with the People's Liberation Army, will be touched on elsewhere. It is clear however that the existence of 50,000 such economic units, encouraged by diversification of agriculture and other activities to be as economically autonomous as possible, transforms China into an unsinkable battleship because of the multi-cellular construction of the base. Damage to one cell need not affect its neighbours, and it is clear that they are self-renewing even if heavily damaged. The principle of maintaining months or years of grain reserve at every level, from commune to individual households, tallies with Mao's concept that survival by non-starvation would be a decisive factor in any new war. The engineering capacity in every commune, if called upon to produce weapons or repair them, would also be a vital factor in any land war in China.

PART TWO

REWI ALLEY

CHAPTER THREE

A NEW ZEALANDER COMES TO CHINA[1]

Among a tiny handful of foreigners in China whose seemingly impossible dreams have come true with the continuing drama of the Chinese revolution, and who have worked hard and well to make them come true, is Rewi Alley.[2] Born in 1897 at Springfield on the rolling Canterbury plains, some forty miles west of New Zealand's second largest city, Christchurch, there was nothing in his background, boyhood or education to hint that he would become a passionate and most articulate defender of the Chinese revolution, or that he would develop into one of the world's foremost experts on China.

His father, a school-teacher with a love of farming, took the public platform in favour of farming co-operatives, as did my own preacher-journalist father, who also had a penchant for farming, in Australia. Alley senior wrote pamphlets extolling the virtues of 'factory farms' for the future. It would be stretching the point to suggest that this idea was filed away in the back of the mind of Alley junior, to spring forth later in impassioned advocacy of China's 'factory farms', better known as People's Communes.

Alley junior grew up as much as he could in the out-of-doors, dog, gun and fishing rod always close at hand. He acquired a feeling for nature and a distaste for city life that he has never

1. To include the following two chapters, I had to overrule strong objections from my collaborator on the grounds that a sketch of his life and works had little to do with 'quality of life' in China. My view is that it is precisely his unique, unrivalled experiences during forty-six years of work and travels in China that have made it possible for us to judge and measure the changing quality of life and present it in proper perspective.

2. Rewi's unusual first name is perhaps due to his father's sneaking regard for a great Maori chieftain, Rewi Maniopoto, who in the 1860s led his people in heroic battles against the British invaders.

lost. At seventy-six, he is still awkward in city clothes, but very much at home in shorts and open-necked shirt. He was not happy with formal studies and was the only one of the four Alley sons not to enter university, vaguely toying with the idea of a military career.

Having helped to make the world 'safe for democracy' in eager response to the 'call of Empire' in the First World War, and twice wounded on the battlefields of France, Rewi Alley made a leisurely return to New Zealand to take up sheep-farming. After six years or so he left the farm to his partner and, practically penniless, left New Zealand to look again at the great world outside.

He took a third-class passage to Sydney and a job in a ferti-lizer factory; worked a passage on a ship to Hong Kong and then on to Shanghai as a 'wireless watcher', having picked up enough about wireless telegraphy to take down a few standard signals; and came ashore in Shanghai on 21 April 1927, just nine days after Chiang Kai-shek had torn up the Kuomintang–Communist alliance and started massacring every communist or trade-union activist in Shanghai on whom his agents could lay their hands – a bewildering experience, to say the least, for a then non-political, conservative, faintly religious and totally Western newcomer, to see batches of young people being marched through the streets to the execution grounds, his in-quiries fobbed off by solid white citizens with: 'Bandits, old man, terrorists!'

With enough money for a few weeks at most, Rewi got a job with the fire department of the Shanghai Municipal Council. The International Settlement had powerful international in-surance companies at its back and fire prevention was in their interests. He decided also to learn Chinese.

He was to relate later: 'I hired a teacher soon after I got a job. A charming man with a long gown and fan, and very pro-Kuomintang, which meant nothing to me at the time. He would drone on and on, putting me to sleep in the long summer after-noons, as he tried to teach me the Shanghai tones. I never learned much from him. But I did learn a lot of Shanghai dia-lect from my driver at the fire station, who was a gangster and knew all about the Shanghai underworld. He would stop the car and point: "See that chap getting into the car. He runs the Chialing brothels – a multi-millionaire," or "Look at that fellow getting out of the Rolls Royce. He's the king of the Putung Road opium joints," or "If you've got enemies – there's the man to get rid of them. His gang quotes the lowest rates in town." He had so many fascinating bits of underworld gossip to tell me as he drove me around that I couldn't help learning the language.

'Later I got an old Manchu teacher for Mandarin – the Peking language. He said: "There's only one way to learn – start with the classics." So I started with the *pai chia hsing* (hundred names), rattling off the names – Chao, Chien, Sun, Li – like Chinese kids did in the old days, and learning to write them. Then I went on to the trimetrical classics ... "Man is by nature good, but dependent on his education. Otherwise he remains the stone that is uncut – just a piece of stone lying at the bottom of the waste is not a gem ... The mother of Mencius, because her son would not work, cut the warp of her looms ..." and so on until I had mastered the trimetrical classics.

'Next was the *chien tze wen* – the thousand-character classic about worthies like engineer Yu the Great, who passed his gate three times and heard his baby crying, but went on with his job of building dykes ... Then on to other classics – the father who advised his son never to become a small man (worker) ... "intellectuals must always remain intellectuals" – and so forth.'

He learned spoken and written Chinese well enough to become eventually a translator of classical and contemporary Chinese poetry. Seven volumes of these translations have been published in Peking, including one devoted to the works of the eighth-century poet Tu Fu, usually considered the greatest of Chinese classical poets. (In May 1972, New Zealand's Victoria University conferred a Doctorate of Literature on Rewi Alley as an 'extra-ordinary, ordinary New Zealander', not only for his own voluminous writings, but for his translations of Chinese literary works.)

One thing that impresses most people at first contact with Rewi Alley is a rock-like quality in physique, as in character.

Edgar Snow described him, after their first meeting in 1929, as having 'tremendous rugged arms and legs' and said that 'when he stood with those giant's legs spread apart in a characteristic attitude, he seemed somehow rooted to the earth . . .'

Barbara Spencer, a New Zealand medical worker who served with her doctor husband for a couple of years at the hospital of a technical training school run by Rewi Alley at Sandan, in China's remote north-western province of Kansu, wrote of her first meeting with him at the Kansu capital of Lanchow, in 1947:

'Past fifty, but still with the build of a Rugby footballer, Rewi had fair hair, greying slightly, piercing blue eyes, a strong, determined chin and slow engaging smile. A man with a dynamic and forceful personality, it was largely due to his untiring energy and sincere love for the Chinese people that the co-operative movement has been such an outstanding success.'[3]

What started him off in his subsequent deep involvement in the Chinese revolution? It certainly was not any theoretical prejudices in favour of revolutions.

'One day in Wusih, about forty miles north-west of Shanghai, I saw five lads being carried, naked and hanging from poles. Right in front of me, they were dumped on the ground and an officer got down from a horse and pumped a bullet into the head of each of them. Next day I read in the papers that they were young "agitators" trying to organize a trade union among the silk filature workers.

'That did it. Conditions for the silk filature workers – most of them young kids – were atrocious; they were forced to stand for twelve and more hours in super-heated workshops over boiling vats, plunging their hands into almost boiling water to retrieve the cocoons. I had been trying to get the Shanghai Municipality to enforce mill-owners to install central boiling

3. *Desert Hospital in China*, Jarrolds, London, 1954, p. 21. The Gung Ho (Work Together) industrial co-operative movement (Indusco), set up by Rewi Alley, Edgar Snow and a few others in 1938, was primarily aimed at organizing industrial production from among the millions of refugees from Japanese invasion, in order to keep a resistance war against Japan from collapsing through economic chaos.

systems – without much result. That young chaps should be shot for wanting to do in their way what I had been trying to do in mine was the limit. I had already been sickened by seeing working conditions in Shanghai for over two years and by Chiang Kai-shek's continuing massacre of workers.'

An earlier incident – the execution of some labour leaders at Wusih in 1928 – had already left its mark. He described his mounting feelings of revolt in *Yo Banfa*, written a quarter of a century later:

'One day, the coldest of the winter, with a light fall of snow on the ground and a bitter wind blowing down the streets, I stood in my greatcoat watching a procession advancing. In the centre of the road the "convicted", with their hands tied behind their backs; flanking them on each side of the road, heavily armed guards.

'. . . The convicted were all politicals, men and women, school kids, peasants and workers. At the rear of the group came a man whose face and eyes are as clear to me today, some twenty years after, as they were then. He was tall, clothed in a single thickness of faded army uniform, too big for him, that the wind pressed against his thin body. His body was erect, his eyes calm, and he was smiling.

'The look and the smile struck me with the impact of a bullet. The moment his eyes met mine, and then looked on over the crowd – the fat shopkeepers, the curious street people, the guards, the whole sordid scene – in that moment I felt like doing one thing, throwing off my warm coat and joining him in his march to the bank of the great sullen Yangtze, where his life would be torn from him. But I only fell back against the shop front, retreated inside my great warm coat, stayed in a daze; once the pageant was over, curious onlookers in the street turned to stare at me, and I escaped up a side street and fled.'

After the shooting of the silk filature workers, Rewi Alley went to see a progressive English school-teacher – Henry Baring – whom he had come to know and like. 'I told him what I had seen and that things had become intolerable. What should and could a man like me do? He said: "You'd better start studying this whole thing deeply if you feel like that." A few days later he brought me some Marxist books – including *Capital*. "Read some of this and we'll have a discussion later," he said. I took them, read what I found bore on the problems surrounding me and talked about them to him. Finally I said: "Anything we can do to pull down this rotten society – you can count on me."

'There was not much I could do in those days. Sometimes Baring would bring a Chinese friend to the fire station where I had my quarters. I would look after him for a few days, then take him wherever he wanted to go in my red fire-station car, flashing through any controls to a point where he could continue on his own. Baring, it was said by those "in the know", was later murdered by the Ching Pang, who were still the power behind the Shanghai police and in cahoots with the Kuomintang. He was found in bed with a pistol in his hand to give the impression of suicide. But friends told us later of how this very fine man was shot by Ching Pang agents. Before he died, he introduced me to Agnes Smedley.[4] We set up a Marxist study circle with a small group of friends, including George Hatem,[5] Tabitha Gerlach[6] and others. By that time it was the early 1930s and I gradually found myself leading a double life, doing my official job in the daytime and something quite different at night.'

In the meantime, he had worked off some of his frustrations by devoting his summer leave in 1929 to famine relief work in China's north-west province of Suiyuan – appalled at the misery and suffering of the victims, the high-living, indifference and corruption of the official famine-relief bureaucrats which confirmed his growing belief that only radical revolution could

4. Agnes Smedley, an American writer who wrote several books on the early stages of the Chinese revolution, the best known of which are *Battle Hymn of China* (Gollancz, London, 1944) and *The Great Road* (published posthumously by Calder, London, 1958). She died in London in 1951.

5. George Hatem, an American doctor of Lebanese origin, who later adopted Chinese nationality and is known in China and abroad as Ma Hai-teh, an expert on epidemic diseases.

6. Tabitha Gerlach, an American, originally worked in the Y.W.C.A. in Shanghai but later became secretary to Madame Sun Yat Sen, working in the China Welfare Institute, headed by Madame Sun Yat Sen (Soong Ch'ing-ling).

provide the answer to China's problems. It was on his way to the north-west that he met Ed Snow for the first time – the beginning of a life-long friendship.

His work in famine relief was arranged by another American whom Rewi Alley greatly admired, Dr Joseph Bailie,[7] a missionary, who had come to identify himself with the miseries of the long-suffering Chinese masses. As a result of the famine relief work, Rewi adopted a baby boy orphan, Alan, as he was to do a couple of years later during another holiday stint of flood relief work at Hankow, naming the second boy Mike. He managed to bring them up to manhood despite the many changes in his situation – geographical and otherwise – during the years that followed. His experience in working on famine and flood relief gave him that deep understanding of the ills of Chinese society and of the talents, ingenuity and other qualities of the ordinary Chinese peasant and handicraft worker that were later to guide him in finding at least short-term solutions to China's problems.

As to what the 'something quite different at night' was, Rewi Alley still remains reticent, as he does when anything related to the revolution is concerned. Squeezing water out of a stone is simple in comparison. One of his biographers, a fellow-New Zealander, Willis Airey, who had access to family letters written before Rewi stopped sending letters back home about his activities, records that: 'He wrote under pseudonyms for journals, and he helped Agnes Smedley to produce her important books by translating Red Army documents and interpreting interviews with Red Army representatives secretly in Shanghai. He personally helped the communist underground by hiding members in his home and by harbouring radio stations for contact with the communist areas.'[8] Although these activities took place at a later period, he had already established inti-

---

7. Dr Bailie later shot himself, in the United States, after the failure of an operation for cancer of the prostate. His name was immortalized in the 'Dr Bailie' technical training schools later set up by the Gung Ho industrial co-operative movement.

8. *A Learner in China: A Life of Rewi Alley*, Caxton Press & The Monthly Review Society, Christchurch, New Zealand, 1970, p. 113.

mate contact with the revolutionary movement by the early 1930s.

In September 1932, thanks to his zealous inspecting activities at the fire department, Rewi Alley was appointed Chief Factory Inspector of the Industrial Section of the Shanghai Municipal Council, charged with checking safety conditions in all factories. Confronted with the almost total negligence of the most elementary safety precautions, coupled with a high incidence of employment of children too exhausted by long hours of work and starvation rations to observe even what safety rules existed, he was able to make some marginal improvements, while storing away information for the future. For the next few years he continued his double life, picking up a good deal on engineering techniques and factory management as a by-product of his inspection work. For a man of his inquiring, practical mind this was not difficult.

In 1935, two American Marxists, Grace and Manny Granich, arrived in Shanghai with plans to publish a weekly paper, the *Voice of China*, to focus attention inside China and abroad on the growing threat from Japan. The first number appeared on 1 January 1937; the fortieth and last, dated 15 November of that year, survived as a make-up 'dummy' only, the Japanese police having raided the premises a few days earlier, smashing up type and printing machinery. In the *Voice of China* Rewi Alley turned his hand to radical journalism for the first time, writing under a number of pseudonyms, the most frequent of which was Chao Ta-ch'i. His aim, like that of the paper, was to revive Chinese confidence and pride in their past, to stimulate resistance and to support the new United Front, forged at Sian, against the Japanese invaders. Thus in the 1 July 1937 issue – on the eve of the first Japanese attacks against North China, under the title 'Yo Fei – a Chinese Patriot', Chao Ta-ch'i writes of a twelfth-century hero who raised a peasant army to inflict severe defeats on the world-conquering 'Golden Hordes', but was executed by the reigning emperor for having refused to compromise with the enemy.

A couple of months later an article appeared under the same signature about Li Tze-ching, a seventeenth-century peasant hero who appropriately enough came from Yenan in North Shensi (where Mao had established his headquarters after capturing the city in December 1936) and led his people to many victories over the then decadent Ming Dynasty.

In the 17 October 1937 issue, under the title 'Some Other Incidents', Chao Ta-ch'i quotes an unidentified foreigner describing a visit 'to the headquarters of the honourable army on the Kiangwan racecourse', then on the outskirts of Shanghai:

'The entrances to my favourite stand are blocked with corpses newly made before my eyes. There are women and children among them; women shot through the back, their padded coats run through with military sabres; children whose bodies are riddled with bullets; men garbed as peasant farmers heaped grotesquely about, their wounds soaking into the ground ... The flames from the burning huts throw a curtain of red behind new captive groups of those who fled the fire. An officer turned one of the peasant group away to face the sun. His shining sabre flashes; the body falls; a second takes its place and once again the sabre finds its pulsing scabbard.' Chao Ta-ch'i comments: 'Shall we forget? No! A thousand times No! We must seek in the salvation of our own people, our own salvation. In collective action lies our strength and we must not fail.'

In the last issue, fated never to appear, alongside analyses of the military situation by Chu Teh, then C.-in-C. of the communist Eighth Route Army, is one headed: 'The Ground Is Ours' by Chao Ta-ch'i:

'From a building one could see the fires in Chapei (one of the northern districts of Shanghai) creep from house to house, school to temple, and temple to factory. Along the road on the bank of the opposite creek came a file of Japanese. A little group of refugees met them at a road intersection. The Japanese turned them back and ran them up an alleyway. Through the crackles of flame and the noise of falling timbers came a scream. A woman's scream. Through the haze of smoke, the green-clad morons turned back and continued down the shore. They thrust their bayonets through flimsy net covers in case there should be any live things beneath. Then in front of them stood two dogs, panting, their tongues hanging out and moving restlessly from one foot to the other. Not knowing which way to go they watched their old haunts burning out. One of the soldiers lifted his rifle and shot. The bullet passed through one dog and hit the other. Yelping, both ran, limping into the smoke. The Japanese moved sullenly on. Another victory! Sons of Great Nippon!

'The western area was burning. Through the barriers into the Settlement came a stream of refugees. The same people who each day had carried, through shot and shell, food for the city dwellers. A young wife in an advanced state of pregnancy staggered under the weight of her family possessions. Then she was knocked over. A basket was over-turned and a stream of dried beans slid out on to the hard shiny road to be trodden under by many feet. This was the last straw, for to her they were very precious beans. She had picked them, dried them and now they were her sole food store. She turned so that she lay across her bedding roll, and buried her face in it, sobbing. That side of the roll was sodden with blood. It dyed one side of her face an ugly red. A rickshaw puller nearby picked up some of her beans and replaced them in her basket. Then he took her by the arm and helped her up. He said in a North-river accent that he would pull her a little way although he knew she had no money. It was all he could give. It was a lot.'

It was his apprenticeship in the sweat-shop factories and the flood and famine relief projects that gave Rewi Alley the depth of compassion to know what the loss of a pound or two of beans meant and to bother recording the humanity of a poor, despised rickshaw puller. The account continues:

'Then came two little country boys, hand in hand. One held his free hand over an ugly wound in the face. Blood seeped down his fingers and ran down his clothes on to his bare legs. His younger brother tried to comfort him. Questioned, the smaller one looked up bravely and said that their parents were somewhere behind. The road over which they had come was littered with the bodies of blue-skirted peasants . . .

'A child of about seven, with beautiful features, but with the pallor of death already in his face, lay asleep. Over him an old woman bent to and fro, rocking on her hips. An unusually large explosion made the building vibrate. An old man in the corner came to life. "Is that one of our shells?" The woman stopped her movements and with a touch of pride said: "Yes."

'Flames licked up the front of tall factory buildings. A file of green-coated Japanese poked here and there like some unclean scavengers. A group of factory workers stood looking over the canal from the Settlement side. They did not talk but looked quietly at the destruction that went on in front of them. Finally one turned round and squaring his shoulders said: "Well, the ground is ours. They can't take that." "Yes," replied the others, turning back to their work, "the ground is ours." '

Any professional would be proud to have a piece of war-reporting like that in his scrapbook. But it could come only from someone who was totally identified with what he was describing. It was because of this deep knowledge of what was in the hearts of the ordinary Chinese, from the lowliest peasants to the students, even though the latter mainly came from the well-to-do, plus the impressions that Ed Snow brought back from his talks at Mao Tse-tung's headquarters, that Rewi Alley, Ed Snow, Agnes Smedley and a few other Westerners were convinced that the Chinese people wanted to, and could, defeat the Japanese invaders.

But there were very strong pressures within the top leadership of the Kuomintang to throw in their lot with the Japanese. What was known as the 'C.C.' or 'Political Science' group, headed by the brothers Chen Li-fu and Chen Kuo-fu, were for capitulation – and later on for siding with the Axis powers in the Second World War. As a component of the 'Four Families' who by then owned between them most of everything worthwhile in China, they were extremely powerful. (The other three families were in fact almost one – Chiang Kai-shek and his two brothers-in-law, H. H. 'Papa' Kung, married to the third sister of Chiang's wife, Soong Mei-ling, and the latter's brother, T. V. Soong.) A major argument of the capitulationists was that with most of the heavy industry already in Japanese hands, with the prospects of all the country's ports soon being occupied – as indeed they were – China could not possibly survive economically.

China depended on imports for all the sort of goods that the Kuomintang big-shots considered indispensable for daily life. They had not developed any manufacturing capacity for such goods. Hence China would 'starve' once the ports were lost. Rewi Alley, on the contrary, was convinced – and he persuaded others – that the energies and talents of the 'little people' could be organized to produce everything necessary to keep the country going. It was thus that 'Gung Ho' (Work Together), as he called it, or 'Indusco', as it was better known in the West, was born.

'The concept,' relates Rewi Alley, 'really originated in discussion between progressive people in Shanghai as to how best help after the Japanese had taken over all the ports. I took up this matter with Ed Snow and his wife, Nym Wales. "Put your stuff down on paper and we'll print it," was Ed's reaction.' ('We' being the *China Weekly Review*, for which Snow worked as a reporter and which was published in Shanghai by an American, J. B. Powell.) I wrote it, Ed added to it and Powell published it. Moreover, Powell knew a John Alexander at the British Embassy, who showed it to his ambassador, Sir Archibald Kerr Clerk Kerr, who turned out to be a change from the usual stuffed shirt. With Hitler on the rampage in Europe, some British, like Ambassador Kerr, saw the importance of keeping China on its feet. After much spadework by Ed Snow and hardnosed questions by the ambassador, the latter agreed to put the idea up to Chiang Kai-shek via Madame Chiang and his sister Madame Kung. The next thing I knew was that I was informed at 4 p.m. one afternoon that the Shanghai Municipal Council was releasing me from my work and that I was to travel with the British ambassador to Hong Kong at 6.30 p.m. as a start to taking up work with the Chinese government on industrial co-operatives.

'This was followed by a visit to Wuhan, to where Chiang Kai-shek had moved the government by that time. I found "Papa" Kung wanted to drop the whole idea. "We don't want co-operatives," he shrilled. "What we want is a million blankets immediately. Otherwise our troops can't keep fighting." I replied: "Give us the go-ahead and we'll make you the blankets."

He was still very suspicious, but Madame Chiang was all for the idea. She persuaded her sister, who persuaded husband, "Papa" Kung. With her Wellesley College education, Madame Chiang was certain that the U.S.A. would eventually have to back China in the confrontation with Japan and that it was essential to keep fighting to bring this about. She was on the "resistance" side against the capitulationists and, as far as our idea was concerned, her support – backed by Chiang's Australian adviser, W. H. Donald – was decisive. Madame Chiang also saw that the scheme would mobilize lots of international support – including financial support – a decisive factor in "Papa" Kung's view. So finally we got the green light to go ahead.'

CHAPTER FOUR

GUERRILLA INDUSTRY

Within two years, Rewi Alley was managing one of the then world's great industrial empires – certainly the most original and fast-expanding – of over 3,000 small co-operative factories in sixteen of China's twenty-four provinces, scattered over a front of 2,000 miles and employing upwards of 300,000 workers. In getting them organized, he had covered over 18,000 miles, many of them on bicycle, horseback and simply on those 'giant's legs'. In improvised factories near the front lines 40,000 textile workers were organized, turning out 'Papa' Kung's blankets, and they continued to supply the whole Chinese army with blankets throughout the anti-Japanese war. In addition, they produced tents, stretchers and uniforms, as well as military hardware – grenades, mines and all sorts of needed army materials. But primarily the plants were aimed at offsetting the Japanese blockade, which had been firmly clamped down by that time, by producing consumer goods that formerly came from abroad or the occupied coastal cities and traditional light-industry centres.

'Military resistance is only half the answer,' Alley had written in the *Chinese Weekly Review* article. 'The other half lies in economic resistance. It is not enough to mobilize at the front. The productive power of the nation must also be mobilized in the rear in second, third and fourth lines of economic defence.' He pointed out that by 1935, in seizing Shanghai alone, 'Japan immobilized nearly 70 per cent of all modern industry in China', and warned that China could be 'conquered by her own weight. Sixty million refugees have already swarmed into the interior, where they must eat, but where they can create nothing to take the place of what they consume, unless they are organized into new forms of production.' Among the refugees, he stressed, were many 'trained factory workers', and plenty of 'patriotic students, teachers, engineers, trained factory managers and others standing around idle . . . They only need to be given work to do.'

As an illustration of the dangerous lack of patriotism of the bigger Chinese capitalists, whom he knew better than any other outsider did, he pointed out that 'during the first four months of 1938, over 400 new Chinese factories were established in the western district of the International Settlement alone. During the same period less than fifty Shanghai industrialists moved their plants to the interior of China. This is a case for widespread alarm.' (The spectre of highly industrialized Japan doing what no Chinese government had been able to do – mobilize Chinese energy and inventiveness in modern industry to serve the Japanese war machine – was doubtless what had impressed the British ambassador most in the article.)

After putting the problem, Alley proposed an eleven-point solution, which included setting up 30,000 industrial co-operatives – 'small, mobile industrial units located in the hinterland towns and villages' which 'could function even after Japanese occupation of the communication centres'. He recommended that all movable machinery in areas threatened by invasion be requisitioned by the government 'in advance of Japanese penetration and transported to the interior, to be made the basis of the co-operatives'. This should be done compulsorily if the owners obstructed voluntary removal. He suggested three types of co-operatives: large ones located in the relatively secure areas in west, south-west and north-west China, furthest from the Japanese-occupied areas, 'performing primarily complementary functions in the government's big industry programme', smaller units between the front and rear areas, which if necessary could be transformed into the third category, the smallest units, operating in the front-line areas. 'The third or "guerrilla" type of co-operatives should use only light, easily portable tools' and their two-fold task was to provide essential items for the armed forces, as well as consumer goods – and farm tools – for the peasantry, thus 'preventing areas adjacent to the Japanese garrison zones from becoming economically colonized by Japanese goods'.

Millions of dollars spent maintaining refugee camps in the occupied areas, he pointed out, could be much better invested in the co-operatives instead of barely keeping destitute Chinese alive in the camps until the Japanese were ready to exploit their labour power. With precise data acquired through his position as Chief Factory Inspector, he was able to prove that of 8,000 Chinese factories operating in the Greater Shanghai area prior to the Japanese occupation, only 1,800 had resumed work nine months later and of 600,000 workers 'only 130,000 were back at work, 90 per cent of them in Japanese factories'.

Passages in this article read like a blue-print for many of the concepts on which decentralized industry are based in today's China. In the section 'Production Co-operatives and War', Alley wrote that 'the reason the present industrial disaster has been so complete lies in the abnormal development of Chinese industry in the past. Almost all the important factories and plants were built and concentrated in the principal coastal cities within a short range of the enemies' gunfire. Hence new plans call for radical change in the whole industrial structure and these are best expressed in the Industrial Co-operative idea.'

That the Gung Ho factories got off to a good start was partly due to the enthusiasm they immediately generated, partly because of Rewi Alley's drive, and partly because they had a small nucleus of Western-trained engineers to draw on, thanks to the visions of Joseph Bailie. At one point in his business of saving souls he arrived at the heretical conclusion that bodies counted also and that something ought to be done about modernizing China's miserably low productivity in all fields. He managed to interest Henry Ford, of all people, to put up money for a hundred boys selected yearly by Bailie from American-run colleges in China to be sent to the U.S.A. to get scientific, technical training. When they returned to China, many of them were without any outlets for their skills, frustrated and disillusioned, until Rewi Alley opened up before them the perspectives of the industrial co-operatives. From amongst them, he found some of the raw material for a sort of general planning staff, and managerial personnel for the seventy-odd main promotion offices and for many of the bigger factories.

From the beginning, the Kuomintang leadership regarded Gung Ho as a mixed blessing. Many of them had a similar reaction to the enthusiastic peasant support for the 'Northern Expedition' – fine if it establishes us in Shanghai, but aren't the peasants going to get uppish later! Granted that the Japanese economic blockade must be beaten – but workers and peasants running factories without any owners? Where would that lead? A few, like Madame Chiang Kai-shek and her American-educated banker-brother, T. V. Soong, approved. It had a tremendous propaganda value for the United States, especially among liberal opinion, where the reputation of the Kuomintang had become somewhat tarnished. It was a fool-proof magnet for tens of millions of good U.S. dollars, a few of which in fact did find their way into Gung Ho coffers. Madame Chiang and T. V. Soong supported it and tried to keep their brother-in-law, H. H. Kung – who continued to blow hot and cold – in line. They managed to sell the idea that Gung Ho represented some Chinese 'middle road' between capitalism and socialism, a concept that Rewi Alley totally rejected. He resisted having any ideological labels pinned to a project aimed essentially at keeping China on her feet and fighting.

Administratively the Gung Ho organization came under the Executive Yuan, the supreme executive organ of the Kuomintang government. Rewi Alley was officially designated the Chief Technical Executive Adviser, on a low salary which was never actually paid. The rare phenomenon of a white man accepting the same hardships as a Chinese counterpart won him great prestige among the Chinese staff and stimulated many engineers to give up better-paid jobs to work with Gung Ho. He lived and travelled on his retirement superannuation money, and when that ran out on the generosity of overseas friends.

'I used to go into the markets of South Kiangsi and start talking,' replied Rewi Alley, when I asked how a foreigner could have so much influence at street level. 'People would say, "Here's a foreigner going on about something. Let's go and listen." I would explain what we were after in a few sentences and then say: "If you want to get loans to start making something, there's an office down the street where you can get money for very low interest." The people who came could hardly believe it. Our interest rates were from 6 to 10 per cent per year, whereas normally they paid much more than that per month. The odd thing is that it was all paid back – we never had any bad debts. The simple things were the main things – like bringing six or seven blacksmiths together, helping to get them a few simple machines, an anvil or two, hammers, bellows. I've got them banging out things that people needed, repairing carts and farm implements, making soap or matches. Wherever you went there were refugees who had skills. All the women-folk could sew, for instance. People needed clothes, so sewing co-ops were organized. Once you started things going they went on by themselves. Sewing co-ops soon started making uniforms. Blacksmiths started turning out explosive mines and hand-grenades. One of our main slogans was "Get Things Moving". We hung up signs all over the place explaining what we were after. Once a small co-op was started, our technical people would make a call and see in what way it could be usefully developed – perhaps we had a bit of evacuated machinery that could help, or by teaching a bit of technical know-how it could branch out in all sorts of other lines.

'We could not have done anything if the people themselves had not wanted to move. If their enthusiasm had been matched on the top we would soon have had our 30,000 co-ops. The people grasped the point at once. We take part in the anti-Japanese war and gain our own livelihood! What could be better than that? Once they got moving, their natural spirit of inventiveness came out. In one area, where water-mills had been traditionally used for husking rice, they started adapting evacuated machinery, which we couldn't use for lack of electricity, to water-power. It was a revelation for our technicians. They spread the idea to other regions and we had people diverting streams all over the place to use direct water-power to turn machinery that had been designed for electricity. Later in our Shuangshihpu training school we drove a textile machinery plant with water-power. Such things were eye-openers for our schoolboys, who were all good peasant lads. They were also eye-openers for the Bailie-trained technicians from abroad, who did not know much about their own people.'

Once the Second World War started, the U.S.A. brought pressure to bear on Britain to reopen the Burma Road. This had been built at great sacrifice by the Chinese from the railroad at Lashio in northern Burma to Kunming, capital of China's southernmost mainland province of Yunnan, continuing on via Kweiyang to the last Kuomintang wartime capital of Chungking. Traversing series of great mountain ranges, it was designed to provide a back-door communications route after Japan had occupied all the coastal cities and imposed a total economic blockade. Shortly after it was finished, the British government, on the initiative of the Australian Prime Minister, Menzies, closed the road (Burma in those days was a British colony) on the grounds that its functioning was a 'dangerous offence to Japan'. With its reopening, the usefulness of Gung Ho in Kuomintang eyes began to wane. Coolness and underhand sabotage gave way to open hostility and harassment which fluctuated according to rising and falling hopes of American supplies.

When I arrived in Chungking in August 1941, travelling up the Burma Road with an early convoy after it had been reopened – astonished to find trucks stuffed with textiles and all sorts of luxury consumer goods instead of arms – I found the small press colony worried about a long overdue Rewi Alley, who had been expected for a conference. Eventually he turned up, bronzed, smiling, pumping everyone's hand – he was much admired by the journalists because of his energy and guts – but tight-lipped as to why he was late. Those who knew him best remarked at the unusually strained look around his eyes. Over thirty years later, I asked him what had happened:

'That was a bad time. It was rather like 1927 all over again. The Second United Front was beginning to crack up. The Kuomintang blockade against the communist headquarters area was in full force. The New Fourth Army had been lured into a trap by Chiang and practically wiped out in January 1941. In the winter of 1940–41, I visited Yenan for the second time.

They were doing plenty of their own Gung Ho type of organizing to survive.

'It was suggested that I should do my best to help the Eighth Route Army in the north-west Shansi area. I made some inquiries and found they didn't have much iron there for making hand-grenades, so I thought we could pay some of the iron-makers from south-east Shansi – where they've been making iron for 2,500 years – to go to the north-west. Also, I felt there should be some liaison with the South Shansi people on the technical side about smelting iron, at which they were also experienced. It was to South Shansi that the Japanese first went to buy iron-ore for starting their own industry. So I went from Yenan to Loyang, in North Honan, where we had a Gung Ho headquarters. People there were in touch with a traitor called Yuan, who was in charge of the local Eighth Route Army base. We didn't know he had secretly defected to the Kuomintang some months before and was responsible for many Eighth Route cadres being killed along the road. I fixed an appointment in a bathhouse with Yuan and then went with him to a restaurant. There, some Kuomintang types turned up and arrested me. The main charge was that I had come from Yenan.

'I explained that I was from Gung Ho, that we helped both sides within the United Front – we helped the Kuomintang side, we helped the communist side. Fortunately W. H. Donald[1] had obtained for me a very good passport, a good signature and

1. W. H. Donald, an Australian journalist, known as 'Donald of China' at one period, played an important if somewhat mysterious role on the Chinese scene for over two decades. In December 1928, he turned up as an adviser to the 'Young Marshal' Chang Hsueh-liang, whose father, the Manchurian warlord Chang Tso-lin, had been blown up with his train by Japanese militarists six months earlier. Donald encouraged the 'Young Marshal' to take a nationalist line and oppose Japanese encroachments. Six years later, Donald left the 'Young Marshal' to serve Chiang Kai-shek, turning up at Sian two years later with Madame Chiang for the negotiations which secured the release of her kidnapped husband. Strongly anti-Japanese, he was captured by the Japanese in the Philippines during the first days of their invasion in the Second World War, but it appears his captors did not know his identity. Released with other prisoners-of-war at the end of the war, Donald died later of lung cancer in Shanghai.

no expiry date. Very useful. They held me for a while till they checked that it was genuine and let me go. No use hanging around in Loyang, so I went back to Paochi in West Shansi, and it was there that I found out that Yuan was a traitor. On another occasion a year or so later I was arrested again and after being put through the same going over, the Donald passport did the trick again. But things were getting tougher all the time.'

Things got considerably worse for the Gung Ho movement after December 1941, when the Japanese bombed Pearl Harbor; China declared war on the Axis powers, including finally on Japan. Surely there would no longer be any shortage of supplies. Gung Ho could be ignored or liquidated, China was now part of the great anti-Axis Alliance, ports would be opened up and supplies would start pouring in. (There were some second thoughts when knowledge of the full extent of the damage at Pearl Harbor filtered through, as well as the British naval losses at Singapore and the speedy success of the Japanese thrust throughout South-East Asia.)

My second meeting with Rewi Alley was in the spring of 1942, in Chungking, and again he had been in minor trouble. 'At Imenchen, south of Paochi,' he related later, 'I was arrested at a control station. It was a freezingly cold day and they stripped off all my clothes, leaving me standing stark naked with an icy wind blowing up through a matting floor, while they went through my clothes and poked long needles through my sandals, looking for some secret documents they thought I must be carrying from Yenan. Eventually they hurled everything back at me – of course they found nothing. A passing truck picked me up and I remember we stopped a couple of miles down the road and ate hot mutton and drank a few ounces of *paigarrh* (a fierce brew with over 60 per cent alcohol content) which defroze my limbs.

'Things had got fairly impossible by then. It was about that time that I visited a unit at Hanchung in South Shansi to find that our depot-master, Li Hua-hsing, an excellent young chap, had just been buried alive. He had been a Y.M.C.A. worker in Mukden. Some Kuomintang special agents simply came, checked his name and took him out in the middle of the day, made him dig a hole, jump in, then they stamped the earth down over his body until there was no more movement. Things like that were happening everywhere. Reports came in from all our headquarters, Yunnan and Kweichow in the south-west, the Honan plains, the north-west, the old New Fourth Army area in the south-east – our people arrested, jailed, killed, equipment smashed.

'At the end of 1942, I was fired from my position in the Executive Yuan. Like the workers who handed Shanghai to Chiang Kai-shek without a battle in 1927, we had been too successful. So, like the Shanghai workers, we had to be liquidated. In Chungking, under new approval, we managed to retain a base, but under very weak leadership.

'Our time was running out. I was sacked ostensibly because of the Loyang affair, accused of having sent supplies and money to Yenan and other communist areas. It was all perfectly above-board as far as I was concerned – our job was to keep the anti-Japanese front going. But it was the principle of the whole thing that the Kuomintang reactionaries couldn't swallow. In Yunnan, for instance, when we set up units down there, the gentry started wringing their hands and crying: "The communists have come. The communists have come. They're setting up factories without owners or factory managers. This is terrible. It must be stopped." So I had to go down and talk with the assembled gentry and generals to keep them quiet for a while. But they soon came out of their holes again.

'Then there were all the Kuomintang generals who had been making a fat living from trading with Japanese goods in their military sectors. The last thing they thought about was fighting – their speciality was trading. And Gung Ho hurt them badly. For many of them Gúng Ho was the enemy – not the Japanese.

'On the other hand Mao Tse-tung saw the importance of what we were trying to do immediately. He sent us a letter full of encouragement a few months after we had started. He obviously wanted us to do as much as possible in the Liberated Areas. But it became increasingly difficult to send funds and supplies in. Our personnel were even scared to go into the Eighth Route Army liaison office in Sian.

'Although I was sacked from the Executive Yuan I stayed on as Field Officer of the International Committee of Gung Ho to continue doing what I could. But by then I had decided that Gung Ho had gone as far as it could go. The main job had been done: it had provided a slogan for going on with the war of resistance and some of the material means necessary for doing so. Chiang Kai-shek wanted to give up many times. Gung Ho was one of the things that stopped him. We had helped to hold Chiang in the war until that critical period was over at the end of 1941, when China became part of the anti-fascist alliance and there was less talk of pulling out, even though Tai Li[2] and a few more at the top still thought China should have joined the Axis side.

'One of Gung Ho's roles was to act as follow-up to the May the Fourth Movement in getting the idea of anti-imperialist struggle down to the peasants and workers. Through brutal practice they understood not only why they were bombed-out refugees, but also how it was possible to fight back and support their families at the same time. Then there was the substantial contribution it made by producing an enormous variety of articles to enable people to survive and the army to fight. Perhaps the most important long-term benefit of Gung Ho was that it laid the basis for co-operative economic enterprises which those of us who started it off were certain would play a role in the type of liberated China we visualized emerging from the war. Also we were able to help, though not as much as we would have liked, the revolutionary base areas to counter the effects of the double blockade – Japanese and Kuomintang – to which they were submitted throughout the anti-Japanese war, and make some contribution during the civil war.'

By 1941, with U.S. aid coming in and Kuomintang repression increasing, Gung Ho had done the job originally intended for it. Now for the future! Japan would inevitably be defeated, Chiang would concentrate on civil war again – and would be defeated. Rewi and George Hogg, an Oxford graduate who had come to China as a journalist and then volunteered to head

2. Tai Li was the feared and hated head of the Kuomintang Gestapo. He was killed in an air crash in 1947.

a training school for Gung Ho personnel, talked things over and agreed to draw up an eight-year training plan to turn out technical cadres for liberation.

'We'd agreed to take our kids at the Shuanshihpu school through an eight-year course, the elder ones helping to train the younger ones, so that we would have some worthwhile technical cadres for later. We started in 1941 and it worked out exactly, finishing in September 1949. Many were ready to go on out at the moment of the setting-up of the People's Republic, as engineers and trained technicians.

'By 1944, we had to move out of Shuanshihpu and move up to remote Sandan in West Kansu. It was there that George Hogg died from tetanus – he stubbed his toe playing basketball. We did not know at that time that there was a lot of tetanus in the pressed-earth floors and courtyards of those old Sandan houses. We could not get serum there in time to save him. This was in July 1945.'[3]

As could be expected, Rewi Alley had some original ideas on education, based partly on general principles, partly of necessity – he had to cope with 450 pupils, with a total staff of eighteen teachers and administrative personnel.

'I always felt that education should be a ladder,' he was to explain later. 'You've got to have the little ones and bigger ones together all the way up the steps – make a community of them together with the families, the workers, everyone concerned. We preferred to take in kids not older than twelve or thirteen. After that they don't change so easily. You get the elder ones driving trucks, doing repairs, taking this or that to pieces, and the younger ones crowding round. You don't tell them to get out of the way – they're nuisances. You encourage them to watch what's going on and they learn fast. They soon want to learn how a truck engine works. It's amazing how quickly they grasp explanations, even if they've never seen

3. When George Hogg died, Rewi Alley took over the Sandan school and a Dr Robert Spencer and his wife, Barbara, came from New Zealand to run a medical department. Rewi Alley wrote a book, *Fruition*, about George Hogg and his work in China. Dr Spencer is now one of New Zealand's leading surgeons.

anything more mechanical than a horse-drawn cart before. You don't need a whole lot of teachers lecturing on the theory of the internal-combustion engine, with algebra and diagrams. That can come later if they need it for higher studies.

'In that school, as distinct from Gung Ho production units, we were out to produce people, not things. We had to produce food, but that was a sideline. The motivation for the kids was quite clear – we're here to learn technique to serve our people. Of course the old intellectuals were against it. "These boys will be no good at all," they prophesied. "They're not learning enough higher algebra. No good can come of it." They provided the arguments for those who were determined to throw us out. They made many such efforts, but failed. We managed to hang on in some miraculous way, with much strong support from our older students and from the local Sandan people.'

The collapse of the war with Japan and the concentration of all Kuomintang forces against the People's Liberation Army – the name adopted for the communist forces once the civil war started – obviously stimulated new waves of repression against Gung Ho units and training centres. But in the rapidly growing areas liberated from Kuomintang control, those of them left provided useful support to the People's Liberation Army. Officially Rewi Alley adopted a 'neutral' position. 'We are training technical cadres to serve the needs of post-war reconstruction. We do not take sides,' was the standard reply to Kuomintang bullying. Barbara Spencer recalls a typical incident as the fighting closed in around Sandan in the hectic days of the civil war:

'It was a difficult time for everyone in the school, but particularly for Rewi, who had to keep things running smoothly. The Kuomintang army, which was expecting to make a big stand on the mountains near Sandan, did its utmost to force the Bailie school staff and pupils to leave so that it could destroy the school and its equipment. Indeed it was due to Rewi's great personal reputation that any of us survived, for he had deputations of army officers coming to see him every day, urging us to leave the school. But while they stormed and raved, and threateningly waved loaded revolvers at him, he simply remained as calm as he always was in those circumstances.'[4]

When I pointed out this passage to Rewi Alley years later, he smiled and said: 'Sometimes I had to behave differently. The Kuomintang kept arresting our boys when we sent them to one of the near-by cities on some job or another. They always tried to force them to admit they were communists, that the school was a communist school. Only two of them who had been beaten very badly said in the end: "We'll say whatever you want us to say if you'll only stop beating us." Another, our accountant Kuo Fang, was actually an underground Communist Party member and foolishly carried a notebook with his written quotes from Lenin and Marx in it. They arrested him and found the notebook. That looked serious, so I had to go down and put on my best imperialist air, banging the table and shouting about what a wonderful contribution these kids were making to economic reconstruction and what a serious international scandal there would be if it were known that such students were being arrested. They felt that anyone who dared make a row like that must have some very high-level backing, so they let him go. We quickly transferred him to another area.'

Another principle of Alley's was to train technicians to work willingly in the remoter places where they were needed. City-bred children, no matter how devoted to the revolution, would always have a hankering after the bright lights and city facilities. Thirty years after he had launched the training programme he remarked: 'Our greatest success was that all the boys we trained wanted to go into the deep country, they wanted to go to the oilfields, to Heilungkiang, to Sinkiang, to Chinghai. They used to laugh and say: "Country bumpkins are best in the country." They liked living in Sandan – they had a free and open life. They swam a lot in summer. If a boy wanted to come to class with his shirt off – that was all right. As long as he was clean, that was all we asked. We didn't like long hair – in those conditions it meant lice and nits. But clean skins in a pair of shorts – that was fine.

'Technical education in other parts of China was the oppo-

4. *Desert Hospital in China*, Jarrolds, London, 1954.

site. It attracted children towards the urban areas where all the higher schooling was situated. The trainees then wanted to stay in the cities. If they couldn't get the job they had been trained for in industry, they went into an office. Our kids were just dying to get out and do the things they had been trained for. They were brought up with the idea: "*pu yao chia chien*" ("don't talk money") – go where you're needed, do the job that's needed. Later I was to meet them all over the oilfields in county towns and other tough areas, running all sorts of engineering projects. They had got a feeling for co-operative living, of organizational life in a family sort of atmosphere, and took to the post-liberation organization of life and work like ducks to water.

'Any number of local lads from the Tibetan and Mongolian minorities, who came leaping over the sands like mountain goats, a bit of felt around their middles and lice in their hair, to join the school, turned out to be excellent students. I have run into them since in industry and training schools in the remotest places, always doing good jobs.

'The school was also good at mingling the many races who lived and worked together as one family. Apart from Hans, there were Tibetans, Mongols, Hashis up from Yunnan and many others – even some Japanese. Kansu is a place with many pink and white people, the heritage of being one of the main Old Silk Road gateways into China in ancient times.

'By mid-September 1949, the People's Liberation Army began closing in and the Ma generals fighting under the Kuomintang banner pretended to be readying for a tremendous battle to stop them. But after a decisive defeat at Lanchow, the capital of Kansu province, they panicked. However, they sent a thousand troops to wipe us out, and later two truckloads of explosives were parked at strategic points near the school. Our scouts soon informed us of their purpose.

'They were to kill all of us older people – obviously my name was first on the list – take the younger ones off as conscripts and blow the whole place up. But by that time the People's Liberation Army had cut the road to the west of the city. No sooner had the trucks arrived than the Kuomintang started a mad stampede out of the city, killing all the prisoners in the jail before they left. In the couple of weeks before this they had killed some two to three hundred people in the area as "suspected communists". With the road to the west cut, they had to abandon the two trucks, explosives and all, and started off on foot to the mountains in the north and into Mongol territory. There was a big lama temple there where our boys used to buy skins and furs. They went up a few days after the Kuomintang troops left and were staggered at what they found. All the monks had been killed. There were bodies everywhere, all disfigured as if an army of sex maniacs had stormed through. They seemed to have gone completely crazy when they realized the end had come. These were the troops of Ma Pu-fang, governor of Chinghai and Kansu provinces, a bandit and warlord who eventually fled to Cairo, taking vast amounts of treasure in gold bars with him.

'Early on the morning after the Kuomintang flight, I was rolled in my quilt in bed, with no clothes on in the good tradition of the north-west, when my dog started barking and I heard steps. A People's Liberation Army officer – General Huang – strode in. He was a brisk, smiling chap. I jumped out of bed, put on a pair of shorts and made coffee. He asked if I could get everything in the way of transport ready for his troops to go immediately to liberate the Yumen oilfields before the Kuomintang had time to blow it all up. He said: "We want you to take all the bits of trucks out of the pits where you've hidden them, assemble them, and get oil and petrol so we can get moving as soon as possible."

'We had hidden almost everything away from the Kuomintang, who were on a mad looting, killing and burning rampage. We mobilized the whole school, students, workers, teachers, technicians, kitchen hands – everyone. The blacksmiths' shop got to work repairing machine-guns and other weapons. The rest started assembling the trucks. We worked all that day and night and by early next morning we had them assembled – twenty-two, I think. Two that we had kept intact were loaded early with P.L.A. men and, with our boys as drivers, they set out to liberate the Da Ma Ying remount station at the foot of the Chilien Alps.[5] The trucks came back with holes in them – one of the lads had a bullet-hole in his overcoat – but they had liberated the whole station and captured 2,000 demoralized Kuomintang troops. That's the way things were going at that time. Then, the rest of the trucks ready, they started off for the oilfields, with two big five-tonners in the lead – every truck with big red flags – loaded with enthusiastic P.L.A. men, one of our farm technicians, Max Wilkinson, proudly at the wheel of one of the trucks. His father, "Red" Wilkinson, had been one of the founder-members of the New Zealand Communist Party. The P.L.A. men arrived in time and took over the Yumen oilfields without incident. Some of our Sandan technicians were soon on the spot checking over equipment and getting production started.'

About a week later, the People's Republic was proclaimed in Peking and another cycle of Rewi Alley's activities began to wind down. There were still a thousand or two Gung Ho co-operatives of various sizes all over the country, ready for expansion into bigger productive units, or to be revived where the Kuomintang had succeeded in closing them down. They fitted perfectly into the new order of things. At Sandan there were 450 enthusiastic young engineers and technicians ready to go anywhere and do anything wherever they were most needed. They included a dozen young English-speaking surgeons, trained by the Spencers, lacking academic qualifications but rich in experience, acquired especially in the last months of the war when they had handled quite a few wounded army men.

Under the People's Government, the Sandan school was gradually expanded until later it became a major Oil Technical School with 1,600 students and a staff of over 400. Rewi Alley remained as titular headmaster, but found himself more and more in Peking, drawn into activities on the international scene. In 1953 his status was changed to honorary headmaster until

5. From the time of the T'ang Dynasty (618 to 907 B.C.) there was always a *chun ma ch'ang* – army horse station – in the Sandan area for reserves of horses for military purposes, with up to 50,000 animals available in ancient times.

the Cultural Revolution transferred such activities to a revolutionary committee.

Something which Rewi Alley has always shared with the leadership of the Chinese Communist Party is his limitless faith in the qualities of the Chinese people. In discussions before the Great Leap Forward, I had found him somewhat gloomy about the exclusive emphasis on big modern industry and the tendency to organize the whole of China's productive forces under central ministries. 'With everything run from the top,' he said during one memorable discussion, 'they are going to lose that wonderful inventiveness and ingenuity which is inborn in every Chinese worker and peasant. The richness of initiative that comes from the compost heaps and factory benches can never be dreamed up by bureaucrats, no matter what their technical and academic qualifications, working at some central planning centre. It's just not something that computers can handle.'

PART THREE

'GET ORGANIZED! DEVELOP PRODUCTION!'

CHAPTER FIVE

SUPPORTING HALF OF HEAVEN

Our guide, a small energetic woman with bobbed hair and pro-truding teeth, steered us through a line of glowing furnaces and clanging anvils, dangerously close to the sledgehammers which were banging down in split-second rotation to beat steel bars into crank-handles. The hands that clasped the tongs, moving the red hot bars from furnace to anvil, deftly twitching them into position so there should not be a misdirected blow, were women's hands. So were those that wielded the sledgehammers. The owners of the hands were neatly dressed young to middle-aged women in white coats or coloured blouses and traditional loose black trousers. One bespectacled young woman in a floral blouse, part of a team of five hammering away with full-muscled blows, would not have been out of place as a receptionist at a beauty-parlour.

On an upper floor, separated only by space from the man-agerial table where tea and fruit had been laid out for the visitors, were more groups of women, beating out metal hemi-spheres for a variety of headlamps, tail-lights, cabin lamps and 'specials' with tiny slits to allow light through. These, one could imagine, would light the way for trucks on the night convoys along the Ho Chi Minh Trail.

We were at the Chungking Motor Vehicle Lights Workshops and our guide, Mrs Teng Ssu-chu, was head of the revolutionary committee, the organization that runs every administration, in-stitution, enterprise, farm and factory in China today. (The term 'manager' one soon discovers is a dirty word, tainted by old class relationships, and in fact no longer correctly describes the functions of leadership.) Mrs Teng demonstrated an awesome mastery of works of Chairman Mao Tse-tung, from whom she quoted liberally as she described what was going on.

'Basing ourselves on Chairman Mao's line of "self-reliance and hard work and keeping the initiative in our own hands", we have achieved some results,' she said and rattled off production statistics. We asked again how the plant had come into being, expressing admiration at women handling such work – there was an exhibition of shining finished products on a near-by table.

'As Chairman Mao said,' she continued, 'we women have been "supporting half of heaven on our shoulders" and the day is long past when we could be regarded as inferiors. Chairman Mao was right when he said: "What men can do women can also do." So we built this factory and fulfilled the production plan every year.' When we pressed for details, Mrs Teng referred to some notes and continued: 'We took as our guide-lines Chairman Mao's call to "Aim high! Go all-out to produce better and more economically." ' At this point, a placid-faced, grey-haired little woman, introduced later as vice-chairwoman P'eng Chun-liang, whispered a few words with a gentle smile and Mrs Teng, after a momentary stare of amazement, put away her notebook and made a fresh start. We were the first foreign visitors and she had obviously been used to handling the standard middle-school excursionists.

'We responded to Chairman Mao's call during the Great Proletarian Cultural Revolution to go into production in a big way,' she continued. 'In 1966, twelve of us housewives from this neighbourhood talked over what we could do. We decided to make motor vehicle lamps. But we had no money, no tools, no premises, no technical know-how. After carefully studying Chairman Mao's work on self-reliance we started off in a small room of 9 square metres with a few hammers and some scrap metal. We took an old truck lamp to pieces and then chiselled a mould out of a piece of rock and beat the bits of scrap metal into the right shape. That's how we got started.'

But why motor vehicle lights? Somewhat reluctantly – the resentment of millennia of male supremacy obviously still rankled – Teng Ssu-chu conceded that her husband was an electrician and Mrs P'eng's husband worked in a truck-assembly plant. As the lamps were imported from another province, the husbands had suggested they try their hand. The local authorities would support such an initiative. The husbands of the first twelve helped to set up the equipment and chisel out the first moulds. Gradually they picked up bits of discarded equipment from their workplaces and helped their wives to rearrange them nearer to their own needs.

'In the first year we made fifty headlamps of one type,' continued Mrs Teng, 'for which we received 500 yuan. For the first six months – May to November 1966 – we put all our earnings into buying more equipment. After that we started taking out wages or 13 to 17 yuan per month. The following year we made tail-lights as well, increasing output to 12,400 yuan ...' She soared off into the realm of statistics again – a saga of dramatic yearly increase in types and value of products up to the estimate for 1973, based on the first six months' output, of 160,000 units of fifteen types of products for a total value of 600,000 yuan. The workshop had soon acted as a magnet for other housewives. The labour force grew. They added other products – engine covers and cowlings, dashboards, oil canisters and – the latest line – crank-handles. Wages were gradually increased to the present 28 to 36 yuan a month, decided by themselves according to profits. Much went into expanding the premises and buying new equipment. The original 9 square metres was now 700. Everything from digging the foundations to laying the bricks and tiling the roof they did themselves. The dozen housewives had expanded to a workforce of nearly 200, including a few men.

'Our city badly needs lots of small plants like this,' explained Teng Ssu-chu, 'to supplement the output of the big factories. We are almost all housewives, used to looking after babies, cooking meals and keeping the house clean, and nothing more. But by the end of this year we will have contributed 1,570,000 yuan's worth of products to the state without it having to invest a cent.'

Visiting the workshops we noticed a few rather embarrassed elderly men, spanners and oil rags in hand, keeping away from our camera lenses. 'Our plant is 95 per cent staffed by housewives,' explained Teng Ssu-chu, 'but we have also taken on a few retired factory workers from our neighbourhood.' She conceded also that her husband did 'not have too many Sundays off these days', and that he had installed the electric lighting and power points in the new premises free of charge. The thought crossed our mind that it would be a bold husband who would stand up to the barrage of quotes from Chairman Mao that Mrs Teng was capable of unleashing at any sign of Sunday slacking!

When we inquired about working hours, the reply was: 'We just worked any old hours at first until we got production properly organized. Then we started working an eight-hour day and a six-day week.'

No wages for six months, working 'any old hours' – it sounds a bit shocking to trade-union-educated Western ears. Sweatshop conditions? Partly they were, but the contribution was a voluntary one, not aimed at undercutting a competitor or at forcing down general working conditions, but at contributing to the national well-being, not to mention the emancipation of the housewives. The workshop was their own co-operative property and they could make their own rules – rough and ready, as we could see. While the machine-gun rhythm of the sledgehammers below went on unabated, the metal-beaters left their moulds and gathered around the managerial table, hammers in hand, roaring with laughter at the mention of some of the more hilarious misadventures of the early days. No one with a stopwatch was there to time such a diversion. Nor, as Mrs Teng remarked with some asperity when we mentioned trade-union controls on hours and wages, had there ever been anyone around to check on their wages and hours of work when they were engaged in household drudgery!

The Chungking Motor Vehicle Lights Factory is known as a 'neighbourhood unit'. The fact that only a few years previously such units were known as 'street' or, more familiarly, as 'backyard' factories is an index of the quick growth of this original form of economic development.

Chiang Hai-t'ing, general secretary of the Chungking city revolutionary committee, a tall, greying man with deep wrinkles around his eyes, summed up the role of such units as follows:

'They were started as a result of Chairman Mao's call to "Get organized! Develop production!" They are almost exclusively staffed and run by housewives who have husbands and sons in factories and who decided that they could do a bit of industry themselves, while continuing to look after family affairs. The essential thing was that such industry must be located right where they live. They started developing something from nothing, from small to big. There are 840 such units in Chungking, with a total workforce of 35,000 which is being added to every month. This is not counting some which started as street factories and developed on such a scale, or produced items of such high quality, that they have been transformed into state factories.

'Altogether some 800 different types of products are turned out by the neighbourhood units,' continued Chiang Hai-t'ing, 'including many that local factories don't produce but that others need. They make a major contribution to our goal of maximum self-reliance for the Chungking area. You will find very humble-looking units making elements for sophisticated techniques – jewels for watches and precision instruments, industrial diamonds for drills, even rubies for laser beams. They can be considered as supplementary to the big industrial plants. They make excellent use of machinery discarded during plant modernization. Their raw materials are often metal scrap and what we call the "three wastes" – the solid, gaseous and liquid waste elements of what you call pollution. Quite a few of these workshops run by the housewives are better than many industrial units of the pre-liberation days as far as efficiency, labour productivity and quality are concerned.'

We asked if they would continue to gallop ahead and all end up as state plants, losing their housewifely flavour. Chiang Hai-t'ing thought not, a view later echoed by responsible cadres in other areas.

'There will be a continuous process of moving out of overcrowded premises into more modern buildings, but the main point,' he stressed, 'is that these are small factories run by women who live in that particular street or group of streets. They have aged parents to look after, husbands and sons who come home from work, babes and infants in the neighbourhood crèches and kindergartens, children at school. They don't want to move far away from all that. The essential thing is that the neighbourhood welfare facilities keep pace with what has become almost a craving of the housewives to move into activities which are infinitely more exciting than household chores and which provide substantial contributions to the family budget and to the country's economy. They will multiply and expand, but will retain the flavour of local industry and depend on the housewives of the neighbourhood in which they are located. Our job at the municipal level is to provide every possible facility to lighten the burden of household tasks.'

Further west from Chungking in Chengtu, capital of China's biggest province, Szechuan, which has a population of around 80 million, we came across a neighbourhood unit started in December 1965 by a handful of housewives and two sixteen-year-old lads – the latter turned down for jobs elsewhere because they were too small. This tiny group persuaded a retired black-smith to join forces with them in making the lowliest product they could think of which would still qualify as 'industrial production' – general purpose screws. They had no money, no skills, but the blacksmith helped them to get hold of an old bench with a vice and a set of antiquated dies. Using steel wire salvaged from scrap heaps and lubricating the dies with cooking oil from their kitchens, the housewives started to turn out screws. They could sell as many as they could make. For three months each member took 8 yuan from the proceeds for food, reinvesting the rest in equipment. From screws they moved up to nuts and bolts. With China's fast-developing industrialization programme there was an insatiable appetite for such things. More housewives joined in – most of them with husbands able to contribute ideas and practical help for new products.

By the time of our visit, the fifty-five-year-old chairwoman, Tseng Cheng-fang, one of the founder members, could well afford to laugh at the old days as she escorted us past lines of machine-tools at which fellow-housewives were honing and polishing castings for the 160-pound punch-presses the plant was by then turning out. The two 'small boys', Tai Yuin-seng and

Tin Chuin-seng – each twenty-four years old at the time of our 1973 visit – recalled with grins how they had to stand on boxes to tend the first machine-tools the plant acquired. Now they are members of the plant's revolutionary committee, part of a work-force of 197, including an enthusiastic old woman of seventy.

Chengtu was famous in the past for the arrangement of its streets according to craft activities, the goldsmiths, silversmiths, copper-beaters, leather-workers, coffin-makers and so on each having their own street. Now the streets are becoming famous for the factories they have spawned. Thus, Wang Chia Kwei Street is now famous not only for the Lan Ho punch-press workshop, but also the Nan Ho machine-shop, which had a somewhat similar history. Stimulated by what was going on almost next door, a slip of a girl, Tung Fu-wei, talked eight of her housewife neighbours into doing the same sort of thing. 'Serve the revolution by making screws,' was her line. The best she could find for premises were some abandoned pig-sties in a pool which had long been an offence to the eyes and noses of those living near by. These days, all over China, city walls – no longer needed to keep out official or unofficial bandits – are crumbling. Traditionalists may wring their hands at the disappearance of the picturesque walls but cannot stop practical young people like Teng Fu-wei and her eight housewives from wheeling away hundreds of barrow-loads of rubble, as they did from the Chengtu city wall to fill in the pond, and hundreds more barrow-loads of bricks to enlarge the pig-sties into premises for making screws. That was in March 1966, three months after Mrs Teng's group set up shop. The nine founder-members emptied their pockets, and presumably those of their husbands also, for a total of 15 yuan – their first working capital. They worked over factory scrap heaps for steel wire and other metal scrap. Later on they scrounged around inside the factories for discarded machinery that could be had dirt cheap or for the effort of wheeling it away. Obviously with an eye on the developments next door, they badgered their husbands for ideas and technical know-how in a Chengtu version of the Chens keeping up with the Wangs. Screw-making was regarded only as the nursery school to enable them to climb out of the kitchen windows. If the Wangs could move up from screws to punch-presses, the Chens could move up to ... they settled for truck parts. Front axles, back axles, engine housings, gear-boxes. By 1973, the premises had been enlarged several times to become a real factory, with 184 workers, 121 of whom were housewives, averaging thirty-five years, all from Wang Chia Kwei Street or its tributaries.

Annual output value was running at 500,000 yuan but was expected to make another big leap forward in 1974, as 1973 was regarded as a mark-time year during which higher-productivity machine-tools were installed. Incredible as it seemed, their first machine-tools – a shaper, planer and milling-machine – had been made by themselves with the help of a few retired workers. (All male industrial workers in China retire at sixty or sixty-five according to their work – women five years earlier – at 70 per cent of their wages at the time of retirement. They are not averse to coming back to active life and keeping their 'hands in' by working under housewives' management.) When the 1973 re-equipping period is over, the Nan Ho plant will have thirty-three machine-tools spaced out in a plant built entirely by the workers from bricks hauled in hand-carts from a kiln over a mile distant. Teng Fu-wei still heads the managing committee, aided by Chou Ching-yung, forty-nine at the time of our visit, one of the original nine founder-members, whose knowledge of machinery at that time was limited to the hand-cart to which she and her husband were yoked as transport workers. Production will obviously be hitting the million yuan mark by 1974.

What is astonishing is the speed with which the often almost illiterate housewives master (perhaps mistress will become the appropriate word in China) extremely complex techniques. Energies and talents bottled up for thousands of years by feudal concepts bubble forth like champagne once the restraining wire is removed from the corks. If it was the victory of Mao's revolution that removed the wire caps, it was the Cultural Revolution that sent the corks popping and old taboos flying in all directions. Whatever the future holds, no one will ever be able to put those old taboos back into the bottles.

The mysteries of the machine represented a challenge –

'heights to be scaled' is the way the housewives put it, a previously exclusive male domain which even inhibited family conversations when sons and husbands returned from their factories.

When you walk through the neighbourhood units, you see those same faces that used to belong to lines of glum-looking women sitting on stone steps at entrances to courtyards, breast-feeding their babies in the late morning or evenings, gossiping and quarrelling with each other. The same faces, but changed. There seems to be some special luminous quality in the Chinese skin which gives it an extra glow when people are happy and an extra lack-lustre effect when they are not. In the workshops today the housewives radiate that inner glow – you can almost hear them purring even when they are belting away with sledge-hammers, the toughest physical work we saw any women doing. Even the older women who used to hobble down the streets with their sticks and tiny bound feet can be found grouped together and glowing away, making paper flowers, wooden toys and a hundred and one other things, integrated into the ever-expanding social and economic life of their street communities.

With the younger women it is not quite the same. They were born into a new society, or formed by it from nursery school onwards; they expect more or less equal status in all fields of activity open to them. A machine-tool or high-frequency diffusion furnace is no mystery to them. They came to grips with such things at middle school and are very much aware of what goes on in the world around them. But the only implements with which the middle-aged women ever came in contact were knitting needles, meat choppers, cooking bowls and chop-sticks – not even egg-beaters! The neighbourhood units opened up an entirely new world to them. It was because they had been so far behind that they made superhuman efforts to catch up.

At the Nanking Radio Elements Factory we were met by two typical 'glowers', youngish middle-aged women, Chu Li and Feng Tze-niu, chairwoman and deputy chairwoman respectively of the revolutionary committee and two of the seven women who had founded the original workshop. It was the usual success story that would have inspired Horatio Alger, except that his newspaper-boy-to-millionaire stories were always based on individual success, whereas the heroines of the neighbourhood units remained materially poor but morally enriched by having served the community. The radio-elements factory was one of the rare cases we encountered in which it was the Great Leap Forward of 1958 that had uncorked the bottle of housewifely initiative.

'When the central committee issued the call for "the whole nation to go into industry in a big way",' said Chu Li, a robust woman with a strong, intelligent face, 'a few of us got together to see what we could do. The husband of one of us worked in a radio-assembly plant, the parts for which were made elsewhere. She asked him to bring home the simplest element and he brought back a bit of button-shaped ceramic with three holes in it. The edges had to be highly polished and the holes drilled at the plant. We received permission to take on that polishing and drilling work. The local street committee let us set up a couple of treadle-operated machines in an unused temple. The husband from the assembly plant acted as a spare-time consultant. We had no great difficulty in mastering the polishing and drilling techniques and we had more orders than we could fulfil. The word spread and other housewives joined us – twenty for a start and that soon doubled. We started soldering wires on to the ceramic buttons.

'A year after we started, our street committee sent us some middle-school graduates. They brought education and technical skills with them, so we started making complete parts. The middle-school graduates ran classes on literacy and technical skills, explaining about radio circuits and the basis of electronics. As our skills grew and the variety of products expanded, the street committee helped us get a state loan of 50,000 yuan for equipment and made some vacant housing available for new workshops. Within two years we had paid back the loan and we put enough aside to finance further expansion.'

By mid-1973 the plant was housed in three double-storeyed brick buildings with generous window space for lighting, built on waste land close to the old temple. Of the 332 workers 75 per cent were women, the rest being made up of a handful of pensioned-off technicians and some husky young fellows who were engaged in lifting, carrying and charging the furnaces in which kaolin and other essentials were baked into ceramic. All the fine work, including micro-welding and other mysteries of electronic micro-miniaturization, was done by the housewives, as intent over their micro-welders as they had ever been over their embroidery needles a few years earlier. The vital control work was being done by middle-school graduates. The plant by then was turning out twenty-one types of products, each in several variants – diodes, triodes, relays and pin-head-sized gadgets with a few wires dangling like mosquito legs but which under the microscope came to life as complicated electronic circuits.

'Yes,' admitted Mrs Chu with a rosy blush, to one of our first questions. 'Elements from our plant went into China's first man-made earth satellite.' Their products went not only to every province in China, but were also exported, stapled into small plastic bags inscribed in the international jargon of electronics.

Watching the lines of white-coated middle-aged and elderly housewives, tweezers in hand, manipulating almost microscopic bits of gold leaf or hair-like wires into the right spot for welding, poring over blue-prints of electronic circuits – work so remote from their lives of yesterday and centuries of yesterdays – one could only marvel at the human capacity for change.

'By 1962 we thought we were doing well when we turned out 140,000 units,' remarked Mrs Chu Li. 'But in 1972 we turned out seven million. Our weakness is still lack of mechanization, too much waste and an inferior quality in certain of our products as compared to those of the bigger factories. We shall overcome such problems, however. Since the Cultural Revolution, we have invited university graduates to lecture to the middle-school graduates on higher level techniques. We must at least grasp the correct terminology for the chemical-electrical industry.'

As she escorted us through the machining-shop, she pointed to machines, including fifteen lathes that they had made themselves.

'What about the designing?' we asked.

'Some of the simpler models we designed ourselves. For some of the others, we bought one model that suited us and made as many copies as we needed.' Patent rights lose their meaning once private industry no longer exists!

At Harbin, we came across a rare case of a neighbourhood unit headed by males – at least at the very top. The average age of the workers was twenty-seven. Yang Tze-p'ing and Yu Tze-ssu, chairman and vice-chairman respectively, were in their early thirties. Together with three young women members of the revolutionary committee, each of whom headed a work-shop, they described the evolution of the Tung Chiang (the name of the street where it was located) Transistor Factory.

'Before the Cultural Revolution,' explained Yang Tze-p'ing, 'a few of us, who later formed the nucleus of this plant, ran a tiny co-op on the other side of the river[1] for repairing nylon raincoats. The press and radio were talking a lot about the need for a new upsurge, modernization of the economy and so on. Why should we not do something more ambitious? Modern in-dustry depended on electronics and Harbin was very backward in this field. Why not see if we could help? One view in the co-op was: "We're already doing a useful job with something we know about. We are serving the people because they need to keep their raincoats in good shape. To talk about making transistors and that sort of stuff is just not reasonable!" But the majority view – we were only seven – was that we should sound out the prospects through some contacts we had in the radio industry. When we started talking about it, another ten young people said they would join in if we got started. We put the idea up to the Municipal Committee and they gave us two week-end summer cottages on the northern bank of the river for premises.

'We started by collecting some old equipment from other plants, picking up a few bits and pieces in the second-hand mar-kets. We managed to get a couple of our lads into one of the bigger factories to get the hang of things in the electronics field. They persuaded some radio-technicians to come over on their

1. The Sungari river. Harbin lies along its southern bank.

days off and advise us how to start off on the right foot. The important thing was that we had decided to adopt Chairman Mao's line of "self-reliance, hard work and learn from Taching".[2] It took us three months to set up the equipment and to grasp the essentials of what we were out to do. Then we went into production. We got off to a good start, thanks to our contacts in the radio industry. We gradually improved our technique and added to our equipment, until today we turn out over a hundred types of transistors and other elements for automation of industry, as well as for radio and T.V. sets. Within a couple of years we were supplying everything the local market could absorb and now we supply to some twenty provinces and municipalities.' He pointed out the building work going on as they prepared for further expansion.

'In the seven years since we started,' continued Yang Tzep'ing, 'we have trained a number of skilled workers and technicians, through practice in the workshops – not universities.'

Yu Tze-ssu, bristling with energy to the tips of his close-cropped hair, chipped in to say: 'Although we are not skilled workers or university graduates, it was because we knew we were on the right track, breaking new ground for the country's progress, that we succeeded. As our workforce built up and production was diversified, quite a few middle-school graduates came to work here. Of course we heartily welcome them and the theoretical and practical skills they bring with them. Thanks to them the quality and diversification of production was stepped up.'

This plant, like the one at Nanking, worked on the basis of state contracts with standard payments graduated according to quality. In return the factory was supplied with raw materials and equipment by the state at prices which were standard throughout the country. On the basis of each year's output, the elected plant leadership at a general meeting with the workers

2. The development of the Taching oilfield, also in Heilungkiang province and mainly responsible for boosting China's oil production to over 50 million tons in 1973, was praised by Mao Tse-tung during the Cultural Revolution as an ideal example for industry in overcoming seemingly insuperable obstacles by 'self-reliance and hard work'. See Chapter 6.

submitted a production plan for the following year. Once this was approved it was submitted to the provincial authorities for co-ordinating with the plans of similar plants within the province and the results forwarded to the state planning commission in Peking. Any modifications due to a shift in emphasis or development of new varieties of product would come back down the line and be discussed. Once agreement was reached, the plan became the blue-print for the following year. We were assured that the passage back and forth was fast and smooth and did not cause hold-ups in production. The factory, like the others described, was collectively owned, but its production was integrated into state planning. As it was not, however, owned by the state, expansion was financed from its own profits. The leadership could also apply for very low-interest state loans – a rare thing in any factory because of pride in 'self-reliance'.

In the workshops there was the usual evidence of Chinese frugality and spirit of ingenuity. A big vacuum tube had been bought second-hand for 30 yuan, instead of the new price of 700, because it had a hole – which was promptly patched up by the glass-welding department. In the upper compartment of an old refrigerator a vacuum-sintering furnace had been installed, a big rock from the Sungari river in the lower compartment giving perfect stability. The first heat-diffusion furnace they had built generated such outside heat that no one could work near it, so they placed it in a small room of its own, installing the control mechanism outside with an insulated screen in between. Such improvised gadgets are more or less museum pieces now, but they financed the sophisticated equipment and today remind young recruits of what it takes to be 'self-reliant'.

In well-lit rooms overlooking the broad Sungari, where Mississippi-type paddle boats, including stern-wheelers, were puffing up and down, there were pig-tailed girls bent over microscopes or tiny welding lamps, engaged in scores of delicate operations which it seemed only the sensitive fingers of women or ultra-sophisticated equipment could tackle.

'Far too much still depends on our hands and eyes,' sighed Mei, the apple-cheeked young woman in charge of No. 1 Workshop. This became almost painfully obvious as we watched a row of white-gowned girls, tweezers in hand, individually testing tiny elements at electronic metering devices.

'Our next big investment will be in mechanizing much of the control work,' said Yang Tze-p'ing, reading our thoughts.

A neighbourhood unit frequently shown to visitors is Peking's Western District No. 1 Transistor Equipment Plant. We have had our eyes on it almost from its birth in 1965. It was transformed into a full-fledged state plant in March 1970.

Another of those which started its gestation period during the 1958 Great Leap Forward, it was then a fifty-member co-op, operated mainly by housewives making and repairing those simple rod-and-cord balancing scales that one sees in street markets all over Asia. It continued on this line until the Cultural Revolution, when two of the members startled the rest by suggesting a 'leap forward' into scientific instruments, starting with diffusion furnaces for making transistor elements. Diffusion furnaces! Nobody had ever heard of them. But a few of the boldest joined the first two in exploratory forays into factories where some of their neighbours worked. The others loyally redoubled their efforts to accumulate funds for whatever came out of this hare-brained scheme. As their scales sold at 6 mao a set, capital accumulation was obviously difficult!

The local Communist Party branch encouraged the setting-up of an experimental group and arranged for some of the co-op members to take a short course at Peking's famous Tsinghua University of Science and Technology. Li Hua, now a buxom, bespectacled, jolly woman of forty-eight, one of the experimental group, today blushes like a schoolgirl when she relates how the Tsinghua students and teachers roared with laughter as she inevitably got her blue-prints upside down. 'I could make nothing of them,' she recalls. 'To make it worse all the signs and symbols were in foreign letters.' But she soon learned to memorize circuits by sight and at the time of our 1973 visit she was in the skilled-worker category, welding transistor elements into the automatic control device of a high-frequency diffusion furnace.

'It was terrible at Tsinghua at first,' she said. 'We were used to practical work but not to studying. We all got severe headaches, but we swallowed some pain-killer and studied very hard. After the first shock of seeing clod-hoppers like us, students and professors were very patient and helpful. Within two months we had grasped the techniques we were after. So we came back to the factory and helped get things ready for production.'

At the time of our 1971 visit, Li Jung-hsieh, the forty-one-year-old chairwoman of the revolutionary committee, had told us: 'If we are going to modernize industry, then we are going to need lots of transistors, and transistors need silicon crystals, which is where our diffusion furnaces come in.' The first pilot model was turned out early in 1966 and since then the plant has never looked back. The original fifty members were gradually absorbed into the restructured works and the labour force had been expanded to 350 by the time it became a state enterprise. Soon Peking 'Yuetan' (after the street where the plant is situated) diffusion furnaces were in use all over China – and had replaced the home-made model at the Harbin transistor plant.

'We've saved the state a lot of money,' said Li Jung-hsieh with justified pride, as she showed off some of the production models. 'Furnaces like this,' and she pointed to a white-enamelled object about the size of a sewing-machine, 'were formerly imported from abroad at £3,500 sterling. We turn them out at 2,000 to 3,500 yuan, according to the model. This high-frequency job,' pointing to another the size of a small refrigerator, 'cost £50,000 to import. We made a pilot model for a sixth of the cost – about 50,000 yuan – and now it is in serial production for 19,000 yuan. And no foreign currency is involved.'

The plant was expecting its first university graduate in 1974 – a middle-school graduate who, together with a fellow-graduate, had developed miniaturization of the control element for diffusion furnaces. Her reward was to be sent on a full science course at Tsinghua University.

By 1973, the plant had branched out into serial production of a very compact, battery-operated, portable electro-cardiograph machine, experimental production of a photo-copying apparatus, serial production of an instrument expressing temperature in terms of light beams and serial production also of super-clean, dust-free cabinets for handling materials sensitive to dust. In addition, a steady expansion of constantly improved models of diffusion furnaces.

Since the Cultural Revolution, everyone in China from kindergarten onwards has studied Marxist theory at some level or another, including the workers and leadership at the Western District No. 1 Transistor Equipment Plant. When, during our 1973 visit, we asked how things were going after three years' state ownership, we got the following reply from Lin Hsin-chuan, the cheerful vice-chairman of the revolutionary committee:

'By March 1970, a contradiction emerged between the productive forces and production relations. We had reached a point at which a change in production relations was imperative. The making and repair of scales, for instance, was handicraft – a small-scale production which we continued as a sideline long after we started making diffusion furnaces. It was easy to get raw materials locally – mainly wood – for making scales and the output could be disposed of in local shops. But as the new production began to dominate, buildings had to be enlarged and we needed new types of raw materials which could only come out of state plan allotments. Obviously the goods we were making could no longer be distributed by local shops. Our products were of national importance and could only be absorbed by the state. We got to the point where we could no longer advance, so we applied to be integrated entirely within the national plan, as a state enterprise. This was accepted and our means of production now coincide exactly with our production relations.

'This is a general tendency,' continued Lin Hsin-chuan. 'Collective ownership, that is ownership by groups of individuals, is gradually being transformed into ownership by the whole people – that is, state ownership. It is a gradual process, however. In our locality there are nine neighbourhood units, of which three, including ours, have become state plants. The others, like the hemp-rope makers and the sewing, knitting and book-binding co-ops, have local markets available and rely on local raw materials. They will remain as they are.'

Could a state-owned plant retain its neighbourhood flavour? Lin Hsin-chuan replied as had Chiang Hai-t'ing in Chungking. 'Yes, it can and will, because the major workforce will remain the housewives who live in the area and have their parents and children here. Local women make up 72 per cent of the labour force in this plant,' he pointed out. 'Of nine members of the revolutionary committee, six are women. We may continue to expand, but the principle of keeping the factory right in the locality where the housewives live will be retained, and this is true of the other neighbourhood units.'

We visited many more such units all over China, but those described represent a fair cross-section of their origin, organization and functions. By releasing the potential energies and talents of that half of the adult population which had previously been 'supporting half of heaven' by household drudgery, the housewives' factories play a major role in women's real liberation. As far as their role in industry is concerned, they correspond to the deconcentration that Mao Tse-tung has constantly advocated, bringing it down to street level in a guerrilla-like approach to economic affairs, with maximum opportunity for local initiative, typical of Mao's style. They encourage that initiative from below, with planning streaming upwards from the base and not downwards from the top. They rely on the concept of building 'something from nothing', which is central to Mao's economic philosophy and has involved him in head-on clashes with advocates of more orthodox economic developments. A dramatic illustration of this latter aspect and other original contributions to women's liberation are revealed in the development of the Taching oilfield, the results of which have transformed China's position as an oil-producer.

CHAPTER SIX

OIL FOR THE COGS OF CHINA

On 26 September 1959 a drilling team in the middle of the vast grasslands of the Sang Liao basin, in Heilungkiang, struck oil. It was just five days before the tenth anniversary of the founding of the People's Republic. The event was considered so propitious in timing and importance that the drillers dubbed the test well 'Ta Ching' ('Great Celebration'). The name was later officially adopted for the whole field. A driller's bit thus precisely marked the point at which a new name, Taching, was to have its place in the atlases of the world in years to come. It was clearly a rich strike and, in more ways than one, could hardly have come at a better moment as far as China was concerned. A few days later premier Khrushchev arrived in Peking, brimming over with the 'Camp David Spirit' and Mao discovered that he had gone back on a Soviet pledge to help China to develop its nuclear potential. Mao realistically interpreted this as the beginning of the end of co-operation in such strategic fields as oilfield development, oil supplies, and many others.

Mao was right. Within eight months, all Soviet specialists had been withdrawn, including those from the Sinkiang and Yumen oilfields – China's biggest at that time – taking their blue-prints with them, leaving hundreds of plants in a semi-finished condition. At that time, China was almost entirely dependent on the Soviet Union for oil supplies. Four years later however, at the end of 1963, Chou En-lai was able to announce to a meeting of the National People's Congress that the country had become basically self-sufficient in petroleum products. Fourteen years later, in the first days of 1974, Chou En-lai could tell the visiting Japanese Foreign Minister, Ohira, that China had produced 50 million tons of oil in 1973, thus entering the ranks of major oil-producers, thanks mainly to the spectacular developments at Taching.

Chinese specialists had long suspected that underneath the Sung Liao basin lay a great natural oil reservoir. They were not the only ones. Some Western experts even suggested that the field was an extension and drainage area of the Soviet oilfields in Siberia. At the end of last century, when Tsarist Russia occupied Harbin and other parts of Heilungkiang province, Russian oil prospectors explored the area and found nothing. Almost half a century later, the Japanese, having occupied all of Manchuria – now China's north-east – also prospected the area, but without results. Their conclusion, backed by some other foreign experts, was that there was no oil and China should reconcile itself to the fact that it was an oil-poor country.

'We ignored their conclusions,' explained Liu Wen-chiang, the quiet-spoken chief engineer of the oilfields, when we visited them in the summer of 1973. 'We went ahead on the basis of Chairman Mao's teaching that "practice comes first". We summed up our own experiences at Yumen and elsewhere and studied some advanced prospecting techniques from abroad. After much study and research we came to a tentative conclusion that there were indeed vast quantities of crude oil and natural gas in the area.'

It was one thing confirming that oil was there and quite another to get it above ground. The year 1960 was a most unpropitious one for getting anything new moving in China. A serious attack against Mao Tse-tung's leadership had started within the upper echelons of the Communist Party hierarchy, based on what the critics, spearheaded from the rear by the then President Liu Shao-ch'i and from the front line by the then Defence Minister and Politburo member Peng Teh-huai, claimed to have been excesses and failures of the 'Great Leap Forward'. It was also the first of three years of a cycle of floods, droughts and the insect pests which accompany them – years of glacial winds howling across the plains. Making living quarters without building materials was the first problem. Although Chairman Mao had a majority at the decisive Central Committee meeting, Liu Shao-ch'i managed to get the fund allotment greatly reduced and to switch materials that had already been earmarked for Taching to other areas. One thing which kept up morale from the beginning was that everyone realized they were going to take part in a monster project – not some 'flash in the pan' affair.

'The People's Liberation Army lads had brought tents with them and shared them as best they could, but they were only a drop in the ocean. We used our bare hands and any bits of scrap iron we could find to make hoes and shovels to dig big holes in the ground, covering them with poles and dried grass. These were our first living quarters. Fortunately the various units had brought a bit of grain with them and this was shared around. We boiled water, salted it and called it "*bouillon*"; collected herbs and roots and called them "vegetable side-dishes".'

(We found at Taching, as at many other places we visited, that the Cultural Revolution and the 'struggle between two lines' were not discussed in abstract, ideological terms, as was often the case in Peking, but in bitter, practical terms by the workers and cadres who were on the receiving end of Liu Shao-ch'i's policies.)

The nationally honoured hero of Taching was Wang Chin-hsi, an oil-driller from the Yumen fields, known at Taching as the 'Iron Man'. His photos – he had died by the time of our visit – reveal a man with as stubborn a face as one is ever likely to find. Nothing – short of death – could stop him. No cranes to unload his rig? No trucks to move it? But the show must go on! He persuaded his team to dismantle the monster and haul it bit by bit – including six-ton bits – by human muscle-power, the 10 kilometres from railway siding to drilling site. Once they had dragged the first piece over, there were volunteers from other teams for the rest. Then they helped each other, the People's Liberation Army units lending an efficient hand, until all the rigs had been dragged into position. Drilling started and after each test well was sunk the rigs had to be dragged by hand, often through knee-deep mud, to the next site.

Wang Chin-hsi was in the thick of every battle that raged against ideological, bureaucratic or physical obstacles. He yoked himself and some other stalwarts to an improvised wooden plough and ploughed up patches of grassland to sow grain and vegetables. Most of all he led the fight against directives from Liu Shao-ch'i's headquarters to close the field down, leading groups in the study of some of Mao's work, such as *On Contradiction* and *Practice*, to persuade cadres and workers that they were solidly based ideologically in pushing ahead with the work.

Little was known publicly about the 'two-line' struggle within the top leadership at that time, or the fact that Mao had virtually lost control, but Wang Chin-hsi, probably without knowing it, had come down solidly on one side. It was a bit of poetic justice that it was drilling team 1205, which he headed, that first struck oil in exploitable quantities on 1 June 1960. The well they opened up that day has been producing a steady 40 tons per day ever since.

Later, when Mao triumphed in that particular phase of the 'two-line' struggle and the victory was consecrated at the Ninth Party Congress in April 1969, Wang Chin-hsi was elected to membership of the Central Committee. He typified the new, vigorous blood that Mao wanted injected into the party leadership.[1]

In those early months at Taching, there was no ditch-digging equipment for the pipes which would conduct the oil to collection centres – everything was dug by hand, with the indefatigable 'Iron Man' always in the lead. He epitomized the 'fearing neither hardship nor death' quality which Mao held up as the model for good party members. After he was elected to the Central Committee, he continued to give the lead wherever heavy or dangerous work was involved – something which doubtless hastened his death from a stomach cancer.

We had visited such big fields as those at Baku in the Soviet Union, Ploesti in Romania, Hassi Messaoud in Algeria and others, so Taching was a surprise. There was no forest of derricks pumping the oil to the surface. As far as the eye could see, as we drove for a good 60 kilometres through the heart of the

1. This policy was dramatized at the Tenth Party Congress in August 1973, when a young Shanghai textile worker, Wang Hung-wen, who had waged a similar stubborn struggle against the Liu Shao-ch'i line, was promoted to third position in the Communist Party leadership.

oilfields, were small brick shelters like white daisies amidst the lush green of the grasslands. Spaced between 300 and 2,000 metres apart, each shelter contained U-shaped pipes, through which gauges showed that the oil was pulsing regularly on its way to the collection centres. The only derricks were at what was described as the advanced front, where new drilling was going on.

Chief engineer Liu Wen-chiang explained the absence of derricks: 'When relations with the Soviet Union were good,' he said, 'some of us went to their oilfields, not just to copy Soviet methods, but to extend our knowledge. Oil production is comparatively new for us. The Yumen field was built up with the help of Soviet experts, but the results were not very good. So we had to learn from negative example. We studied lots of useful technical data from other foreign countries, but during the Great Leap Forward we broke away from old methods and old thinking, including that of advanced foreign techniques. The Karamai field in Sinkiang province was also designed and developed by Soviet experts, but it did not yield anything like what had been expected. The flow was uneven and production soon began to drop.

'We sent specialists to Moscow to discuss this, but got nowhere. We knew something was wrong but could not put our fingers on it, that is not until we had opened up the Taching field by our own methods. Later we visited the Soviet field at Rumaskin in the Urals – considered their best field in technical quality. We studied the data of that field over and over again and we were determined to do even better. After studying everything we could lay hands on in the technical field, and also Chairman Mao's works *On Contradictions* and *On Practice* in the theoretical field, we came to the conclusion that the main contradiction in oil production – that is the presence of oil deep underground when we want it out on top – can only be satisfactorily solved by achieving stable pressure from below to make the oil come out on its own. The field must be treated as a whole so that the oil flows upwards evenly through stable pressure from below. To do that, we were convinced that the essential thing was to have an exact picture of what lay underground, not only of the various levels of oil-bearing strata, but of all other phenomena.

'After careful study, our experts listed twenty kinds of materials and seventy-two categories of data from every test bore as the necessary criteria for getting that picture. For every metre drilled, we took up to ten samples of the core to be submitted to laboratory analysis. Altogether we took out a total of 34 kilometres of core; 560,000 samples of core material were analysed and 3,800,000 comparisons of data were made, based on the different characteristics of the various drillings. In this way we were able to draw up exact charts of the situation underground, based on scientific reality – a principle on which Chairman Mao lays the greatest stress. We rejected any guesswork based on random sampling. This is crucially important because, if you drill in the wrong spot and there are gushers or blowouts, you lose pressure and have to install expensive pumping systems.

'The work was not done only by technicians like us' – Liu Wen-chiang was surrounded by about a dozen other specialists – 'but by workers, cadres and specialists living and working together on the drilling sites as a three-in-one combination, a single team. As a result, you will notice that apart from the fact that there is not a single *k'e t'ou* (bowing) pump on the whole field, the wells are irregularly spaced. That is because there is no hit-and-miss boring. Every time we sink a well, it is because we know it will be a strike and exactly at what level the oil will be found. We can open up new areas with great rapidity – up to one well in a single day's drilling by the most experienced teams.'

The chief engineer agreed when we raised the point that the geological data charts could be compared to the acupuncture charts one sees in every Chinese medical clinic.

'Learning from our results here,' continued engineer Liu, 'we sent specialists back to the Sinkiang field in late 1960. They soon found out what was wrong. The Soviet engineers had done some surveying and prospecting and had prepared geological data charts, but they were incomplete – based on drilling only about a dozen test wells. This was not due to ill-will,' he stressed.

'Our relations were good at the time the field was opened up. They do the same thing on their own fields. Their engineers had established an "average figure" based on the few test drills and drew up plans on that basis. But the "average figure" was wrong because it was not based on reality and everything else in the designing work went wrong from there. We found that the bottom of the Sinkiang field was not fine sand as their charts showed. There were only a few patches of sand – the rest of the floor was made up of large pebbles, making it porous. This was why a stable pressure could not be maintained and the flow was uneven. Soviet standards call for maintaining stability of flow for ten years, but even this was far from being achieved at Sinkiang. Here, at Taching, oil has been flowing at a stable rate for thirteen years and all the signs are that this will continue for many years to come.'

A closer look at the little white houses, each covering a well, illustrated much of what engineer Liu had been saying. Their innards were somewhat more complex than could be imagined from outside. In each there was a coloured chart showing the strata structure through which the bore passed, right down to the bottom of the lowest of three oil-bearing strata. A series of gauges showed not only the rate of flow, but the pressure of oil and the state of water in the nether regions. There were regulators by which pressures could be adjusted; and a chamber where natural gas was separated from the oil. Enough of the oil was diverted into an automatically controlled furnace which heated it to a temperature suitable for a smooth flow to the collection centre, the rest being piped off to serve local industry, including an oil refinery. We visited one of a series which are known as the 'Women's Wells' because they are supervised by teams of young women.

Chiang Fu-hsiang, a tall, blushing young woman of twenty-eight – who could have passed for eighteen – from No. 6 Women's Squad of well-watchers, very trim in blue overalls, explained how things worked. She was in charge of a team of ten, including herself, which kept a twenty-four-hour watch over six wells, making their regular rounds like nurses taking the temperature and feeling the pulses of their patients. The well at which we found her had come into production on 1 October 1960 and, for over twelve years since, oil had been flowing at the regular, daily rate of 70 tons – a little over 320,000 tons up to the time of our visit. When necessary, team members adjusted pressures and once a month they tested the volume, pressure and other data in each of the oil-bearing strata. Pointing to the chart, she explained that it showed the thickness of the oil-bearing strata to the centimetre and that a series of plugs in the well-tubing, adjustable through gadgets in the little house, made it possible to tap each strata in turn and prevent oil in any unruly strata from producing out of turn. This was possible because they had exact knowledge of the depth of each strata. With due modesty, she also explained that, although she and her team-mates were not trained technicians, they were doing what was previously considered as specialized work.

'We learned through practice,' she added, and went on to say that every single leak of oil or gas would be detected by the well-watchers and immediately dealt with. This accounted for the absence of any smell of oil or gas on the field. When Miss Chiang showed us the gadgets for controlling the water-injection system, we had to turn to engineer Liu for enlightenment.

'It is a system used on Soviet oilfields,' he explained, 'but they use it only as a last resort. When a field is almost exhausted they pump in water to push the remaining oil to a level where the pumps can get at it. We call that running away from a main contradiction. We inject water from the very beginning – the water-injection system goes in with the well-drilling. In this way we can establish an even pressure and this also enables us to work the field, strata by strata, without any loss of pressure, exploiting the various underground water supplies.'

After a visit to the first well drilled by Wang Chin-hsi and a museum illustrating some of his prodigious achievements, we drove 60 kilometres over a good asphalted highway to the Advanced Front Headquarters. First stop was at Wang Chin-hsi's old drilling rig – Team 1205. The 'Iron Man's' successor was a younger chap who had come with him from the Yumen field.

Shy, brown-faced, smiling thirty-seven-year-old Chiao Sen-yuan clambered down from a platform from which he was supervising the drilling operation. In 1966, under the 'Iron Man', the team had scored what was claimed as a world record by drilling just over 100,000 metres. Chiao had managed to keep his team just a nose ahead of the nearest friendly rival – Team 1202. To our question whether any more records were being broken, Chiao Sen-yuan said:

'We topped 127,000 metres in 1971, but we don't count in metres any more. From 1971 we just take one day to move and set up the rig, one day to drill down to the oil, another day to dismantle and fix things up for the unit which does the capping and controlling. One well every three days has become routine. For instance, we arrived here yesterday, started drilling this morning. We are down to 1,100 metres' – it was about 4 p.m. – 'and will soon be down to oil level.'

The cadre in charge of the Advanced Front Headquarters, Chang Hung-fei, a jolly man with massive shoulders and shaven head, like a laughing Buddha, added that between 1960 and 1971 Team 1205 had sunk 460 wells – 7·8 times the total sunk during all the years that the Kuomintang had 'played around' with oil development.

When we asked what was the secret of such rapid drilling, Chang Hung-fei said that Chinese engineers had developed a number of super-hardened drilling bits which enabled drilling at a speed unimagined a few years earlier. One of the champion drillers, from Team 1202, Chu Ching-hua, who had come to the Yumen oilfield straight from the People's Liberation Army, later told us that his first great difficulty in drilling was to get the rig in a perfectly vertical position. During the Great Leap Forward his team had jumped from around 700 to 3,000 metres drilling per month.

'The main thing was that we dared to go our own way,' he said. 'We had long been influenced by Soviet experts who warned us that the higher the drilling speed the greater the possibility of accidents. In fact we speeded up and used higher pressures and it turned out we had less accidents – an example of Chairman Mao's saying, "reality is born of practice". Then our industry developed the specially tungsten-hardened bits for real high-speed drilling and we never looked back.'

Drilling went on day and night, teams of forty-five to fifty men working shifts of four hours on and four off in an eight-hour working day. The drillers lived in comfortable, movable caravans alongside the drills, returning to their families for rest days, which were rotated to maintain the work tempo.

Work on the new field had started in April 1973, two months before our visit, and with twenty-nine drilling teams at work 'well over one hundred' wells had been sunk, which meant that, at a conservative estimate of an average of 50 tons daily per well, production at Taching was being increased at the rate of at least a million tons per month – and perhaps twice that amount, depending on the exact number of wells. Our experience is that Chinese cadres these days are masters of understatement in discussing such matters. At the rate Team 1205 and its closest runner-up, Team 1202, were drilling, they had sunk forty wells between them in the two months. And what about the other twenty-seven teams? No absolute figures on production were available, but we were told it had been increasing at a steady 30 per cent a year for the past several years and that the figure for 1972 was three times that of 1965. To our question how Taching measured up to the world's great oilfields, the smiling reply was:

'It is a vast field of which we have only scratched the fringe, so we have no basis yet to compare it with the world's great fields.'

The basin stretched many hundreds of kilometres ahead in the direction in which the advanced front was moving and for many more hundreds of kilometres in the opposite direction from the 'Iron Man's' original well. When we asked whether there was oil under the whole of the basin, we were told that prospecting teams fanning out ahead of the advanced front were still striking oil at the same rate as around Taching itself, and that Taching was almost in the exact centre of the lowest part of the basin, which covered many tens of thousands of square kilometres.

At the Taching Petro-Chemical Works it was clear that the

scope and tempo of production had caught the oil-refinery designers by surprise.

Wang K'o-chü, vice-chairman of the revolutionary committee, a quiet-spoken, efficient-looking executive, explained that the works were built 'in accordance with Chairman Mao's line of self-reliance, preserving independence and retaining the initiative in our own hands', a slogan much in vogue after the Soviet Union withdrew its specialists. Building had started in April 1962 and part of the plant started refining oil in August of the following year. At that time the annual refining capacity was 1,000,000 tons. 'It was designed and assembled entirely by ourselves,' explained Wang K'o-chü, 'and virtually all the equipment was made in China. By the end of 1966 we had to increase the capacity to 2,500,000 tons and later we had to double this again to its present capacity of 5 million tons.' In an earlier visit to the Peking General Petro-Chemical Works, which had an annual capacity of 2,500,000 tons, we found that 80 per cent of the crude oil came from Taching. Another million tons was being exported from Taching in its crude state to Japan in 1973,[2] and an undisclosed amount was being piped straight from the wells to huge underground concrete reservoirs scattered over the grasslands. For a 'scratching at the fringes' Taching was doing fairly well! And with China in the world market for the latest types of drilling equipment in large quantities, it was a fair assumption that the tempo of extraction at Taching was going to be stepped up still further.

In the beginning, the builders of the refinery ran into the same sort of difficulties as the well-drillers. In 1962–3 the ideological tug-of-war was intense and Liu Shao-ch'i and his supporters were riding high in Peking. As Li Huei-hsin, the deputy head of the Taching revolutionary committee's secretariat, expressed it, 'Mao was saying "Forward! Advance!", and Liu was shouting "Halt! Dismount!" A lot of people were confused as to which was correct.'

'There were still no cranes when the equipment started arriv-

2. This was increased to 5 million tons in 1974, with forecasts of further big increases. By 1974 China was also supplying Thailand and Hong Kong with small quantities of crude and refined oil products.

ing,' said Wang K'o-chü, 'and there was a great shortage of trucks. Much had to be removed from the railway siding by hand. A veteran worker, Li Ching-ling, in charge of transport, performed miracles – moving equipment up to 30 metres long and weighing up to 40 tons, by teams of workers with ropes and skids, himself always in the lead. Later we got all the cranes and trucks we needed, but the assembly work was never halted for lack of them.' (Fortunately the petro-chemical works is right alongside a railway siding.) Wang K'o-chü spoke of the unleashing by the Cultural Revolution of 'new creative energies', expressed in many technical innovations which had improved working conditions and provided short cuts in increasing the oil-refining capacity. 'Our chemists,' he continued, 'substituted a series of seven different types of catalysts in the ammonia-nitrate fertilizer plant, eliminating a whole series of complicated processes in the designing stages. This enabled us to miniaturize that plant to about one tenth of the normal size, resulting in a great saving of steel.'[3]

Another of the chemists' technical innovations resulted in the annual production of 100,000 tons of high-quality coke direct from crude oil, 'highly appreciated by the Japanese for their steel industry because of its small, even size and low sulphur content', said Wang K'o-chü. 200,000 tons of crude oil were diverted annually to produce 50,000 tons of benzene for polyester fibres, insecticides, T.N.T., various types of catalysts and other products. The next step would be to produce synthetic rubber. But despite some forty different types of specialized items turned out by the seventeen production units of the petro-chemical works, Wang K'o-chü was not satisfied. 'We have hardly got off the ground as far as chemical products are concerned,' he said, but mentioned that a branch factory was being

3. In visits to other industrial plants, it became obvious that Chinese designers – like their Japanese counterparts but even more so – pay great attention to miniaturization. In plant after plant – except in the heavyweights of hydro-power engineering, where Soviet equipment is still appreciated – we were shown cumbersome Soviet, Czech and other foreign machines, some of them still working, others discarded, and the much smaller, lighter, more productive models that the Chinese had designed and made themselves.

built about 10 kilometres distant for the multi-utilization of other chemical by-products.

After looking over a good cross-section of what was going on, it was difficult not to agree with Li Huei-hsin when he spoke of the high speed with which everything had been done.

'Once the presence of oil was confirmed, it took only fifteen months to get a complete picture of the geological data. Even before we had that information, production was in full swing and within another six months we were getting our first refined products. From an economic viewpoint, in the thirteen years of operations the profits to the state represent just ten times the amount it invested. And we have trained many hundreds of technicians who have gone off to other fields. The oilfield is itself a higher technical training establishment of a quality impossible to achieve in university conditions.'[4]

Having come – as the first writers to visit the area – to find out why 'Learn from Taching' had become such an important national slogan, a thing that intrigued us in driving through some of the residential units was to see 'Learn from Tachai' banners across the streets. We knew that the common denominator between rural Tachai and industrial Taching was that each symbolized the concept of 'self-reliance and hard work' and of overcoming all obstacles to push on with socialist construction. But why Taching oil-workers should learn agriculture from the Tachai production brigade was something worth looking into.

As so often is the case in today's China, in picking up this simple thread of inquiry we unravelled a whole skein of unexpected developments.

4. In most enterprises we visited, the merit of having trained technicians on the spot was listed as second only to the achievements in production. Thus Chiao Sen-yuan, in charge of Drilling Team No. 1205, considered that 'even more important than our team's pace-making in drilling is the fact that we trained fifty-four cadres and 124 technicians'.

CHAPTER SEVEN

'SOMETHING FROM NOTHING' TOWNSHIP

That there was no 'oil boom town' atmosphere at Taching, no bars, brothels or night clubs doing a roaring trade as technicians and oil drillers with fat pay cheques swaggered in from lonely drilling sites for a long week-end, obviously did not surprise us. That concept of 'Great Celebration' left for Taiwan with the Kuomintang. It was difficult at first to locate Taching city – an oilfield capital. We found there were three big urban centres, spaced 5 or 6 kilometres apart, in each of which a lot of planned building was going on, and forty more townships, each surrounded by two or three satellite villages, the whole connected with a network of good roads and provided with free bus services. All this came under the general heading of the Taching Municipality.

'When premier Chou En-lai came here in 1962,' explained Li Huei-hsin, of the oilfield's secretariat, who turned out to be an indefatigable and wonderfully well-informed guide, 'he advised us to make this a new type of model enterprise. Industry should be integrated with agriculture, with production and local administrative power. There should be an all-round development of industry, agriculture, stock-raising, fish-breeding, etc. We should become an autonomous community, with production, distribution, education all under "one roof". Living quarters should not be concentrated in one spot – they should be scattered according to where the oil is found. Workers' families should go into agricultural production – become producers instead of consumers. This is what we have done. People say that the city looks like the countryside and the countryside looks like the city.'

This explanation, backed up by our further investigations, threw an entirely new light on the 'Learn from Taching' slogan.

Taching was to be the vision of an unpolluted future for new industrial development. Green industrial centres! A thing which had struck us before was that huge patches of the grassland had been transformed into fields of ripening wheat and early maize, growing not only right up to the little white well housings but also in the fields where actual drilling was taking place. We had our photographs taken with the shift-workers of Team 1205, up to our knees in a heavy-yield wheat crop, with the drilling rig towering above us 20 metres away. Some of the wheat was knocked down when the rigs were dragged by stubby little tractors to the next site, but this was infinitesimal compared to the rippling ocean of wheat lapping right to the base of the rigs. Obviously the usual forest of derricks and oil-wells could not have co-existed with the grain fields. Only the complete automation of scientifically spaced wells made it possible.

We were invited to visit any of the townships we liked and could not resist Chuan Yeh ('Something from Nothing') township, not only because the name itself was one of the key themes of our investigations, but also because one of the township's satellites was the home village of Hsueh Kuei-feng, the nationally famous female counterpart of the 'Iron Man'. We found her a diminutive, grey-haired woman, modest and gentle. We were the first foreigners she had ever seen and she had to be prompted by her fellow-members of the Chuan Yeh revolutionary committee to relate one of those epic stories so typical of the development of Chuan Yeh. She had come with some members of her family to join others who had left Yumen for the new oil centre.

'We arrived here in April 1962,' she said, 'and the conditions were really tough. We were given some tents but the men drilling some 15 kilometres away were living in improvised huts or holes in the ground, lacking food supplies. We decided we had to do something – grow them some food. So we set out, five of us, with babes on our backs and lanterns in hand – and each with a shovel.' (This episode has entered into the folklore of Taching as that of the 'five-shovel brigade'.) 'We went to the first drilling site – the men had already moved on, but had left some improvised huts. We moved into one of them. It was very cold and terrible; gale-force winds roared over the plains. At night wolves came howling around and some of us were frightened for the babies. The first time they came, we just blocked the door with our five shovels, ready to fight them off in case they got in. Afterwards we got used to them – they are cowardly beasts. One afternoon a couple of them came circling round, getting closer all the time. I took my shovel and beat it on the rocks, howling twice as loud as the wolves, and they soon went slinking off. We had no more trouble with them after that.

'We started digging up the grasslands with our shovels, but the soil was half-frozen and it was heavy going. Later, we were joined by thirteen more wives and we found an abandoned plough. So we formed a team of ten to pull the plough, nine yoked in front and one behind to steer. We were not used to marching in step, so the first rows wandered all over the place. We stopped and discussed the problem and decided: "If men can do it, women can also do it." (By that time the 'Iron Man' team had also been at work.) We decided to shout in unison at every step, and in that way got the rows straight, breaking up the big clods later with wooden clubs.' (We suspected that it must have been the traumatic experience of seeing and hearing a twenty-legged creature, roaring at every step, that scared the wolves out of that part of the grasslands for ever.)

In that first, bitter season Hsueh Kuei-feng and her group managed to cultivate 5 acres and sow it with wheat. The next year new reinforcements brought the group to seventy – and they cultivated 18 acres. In 1964, all the wives from the township's 300 households joined in and they put almost 100 acres under crops.

'Things are very different now,' she said, in conclusion, 'we have tractors and harvesters and get more grain every year, and plenty of fruit and vegetables as well.'

If anyone wants to get down to the real essence of Women's Lib. in China, it is difficult to imagine a more appropriate spot than 'Something from Nothing' township. For several hours we sat around talking with the organized housewives and visiting their creations. With glowing cheeks and flashing eyes, they prompted each other to relate how they had tamed the grasslands – and by inference their husbands. The most eloquent of all was Li Chang-yung, a classic peasant beauty who could have stepped straight out of the title role of a film, ruddy-tinged bronzed cheeks, perfect teeth, coal-black, glowing eyes and a husky vibrant voice. As vice-chairwoman of the revolutionary committee she was the most explicit about women's emancipation.

'We can prove our progress in farming with statistics,' she said. 'What we can't demonstrate with statistics is the changed social consciousness of everyone here. Before, we women had only our menfolk, kids and household chores to think about. Now we think about the whole country – the whole world – starting with the oilfield and ending with Tien An Men.[1] There has been a revolution in family relations. A husband may be an advanced oil-worker – but his wife is an advanced farm-worker. What's the difference? Now there is real respect for each other. We discuss each other's problems – the oilfield or the wheatfield – and encourage each other. We've acquired really equal status. When our husbands come home they help with the cooking and washing-up. They help look after the kids. We're really emancipated, socially, politically, economically. There are no longer any sharp divisions between husband and wife because we have proved by deeds that Chairman Mao was right when he said: "What men can do, women can do." '

Cho T'a-ching, another vice-chairwoman, provided some of the factual background to Li Chang-yung's enthusiasm.

'When we arrived,' she said, 'we were faced straight away with a choice: everyone for herself, or the collective road. At Yumen we had hardly stirred out of our houses. But here it was a different situation. We have gradually increased to 713 households, 2,760 people altogether, and by this year we have 500 acres of cultivable land, 391 pigs, 133 cows, 57 horses and 590 sheep. We also have eight tractors and two combine harvesters. Last year we produced 225 tons of wheat, 550 tons of vegetables and 7 tons of meat. By several years of hard

1. Peking's famous Gate of Heavenly Peace, where national celebrations are held.

work we have brought Chuan Yeh up to the standards suggested by premier Chou En-lai, that Taching should become an integrated industrial–agricultural area. We have maintained the good old tradition of hard work and plain living, but our living standards have improved year by year.' 'Something from Nothing' was a self-contained community, with a nursery, kindergarten and schools, a thirty-bed clinic, hair-dressing saloon, bank, post-office, public baths and well-stocked shops which between them kept open from 6.30 a.m. to 9.30 p.m. There were workshops for producing noodles, soya sauce and vinegar, a bakery, a sewing centre for repairs and tailor-made clothes, and repair shops for bicycles, radios and watches.

Housing and shops had been built by the housewives – the typical single-storeyed adobe buildings of the north-east, the almost flat, asphalted roofs having enough of a hump for the snow to be pushed off easily.

'We have tried to do everything to free ourselves from useless labour,' continued Cho T'a-ching. 'In the old days we used to waste a lot of time making noodles, for instance. Now, we take one pound of flour to the noodle mill and within a few minutes get back one pound and two ounces of noodles (presumably the water gave the added weight) and pay a fee of one cent.' Two housewives ran the noodle mill, and two more the tiny plant which produced soya sauce and vinegar, both of these extracted in the same process from soya sauce, after which the residue was fed to the pigs.

We asked Hsueh Kuei-feng whether she preferred Yumen or Taching. 'No comparison,' she said. 'Taching. In Yumen we had no chance of working in the fields. There are only sand and rocks there. We didn't know then about the experience at Tachai[2] or perhaps we would have done something. We came here to support the battle for oil, to support our men-folk, and we see that we did make a contribution. We feel we have done something new.'

The irrepressible Li Chang-yung broke in to say: 'Of course it's new. This is a rural area, but it's like a small town. We have electricity, telephones in the offices, central heating – everything

2. Described in Chapter 8.

that a small town has. But we grow grain and vegetables right up to the walls of the houses and raise cattle, pigs and sheep, so although it looks like a small town it isn't. You can say we're small-town dwellers, but in fact we're farmers. Per acre yields may be low but they're rising all the time.'

We visited Hsueh Kuei-feng's village, one of three satellites of Chuan Yeh. The waist-high wheat promised an excellent crop, and there was a great variety of vegetables, tomatoes, red and green peppers, garlic, apple and peach orchards, and even young grape-vines. Everything was neat and geometric, the fields bordered by trees for windbreaks, the ground levelled off to facilitate mechanized ploughing and harvesting. It looked like a well-tended market garden, with only the grasslands around the perimeter to recall what had been. From a little knoll overlooking the village, as the sun etched a golden line around the clouds, as far as one could see in every direction in the sea of green were the little white houses over the disciplined wells passing on their quotas of oil to the collection centres twenty-four hours per day.

As the Chuan Yeh people – and this applied to those from the other thirty-nine townships and the satellite villages – had built everything themselves from nothing, it was hardly surprising that all the main facilities were free. Free rent, free lighting, free natural gas – piped into each house for kitchen fuel and heating – free cinema, free bath-house, free bus-rides, free medical care for the oil-workers and at half-cost for the dependants. The combined earnings of husband and wife averaged between 110–120 yuan per month, whereas living costs for a family of four – mainly food – averaged around 15 yuan per head, so that half the earnings could be banked away or spent on such things as sewing machines, radios, watches and bicycles – the four most popular hardware items in rural China today, with cameras and portable T.V. sets looming over the horizon.

We were invited, as usual, to criticize the imperfections but, surrounded by the 'Something from Nothing' women, glowing with the pride of achievement, it was difficult to find anything to criticize. Thinking over things on the way back to our lodgings, we had some overall critical reflections. The emphasis on the collective, as far as amenities were concerned, was overwhelming, but perhaps a corrective was needed from somewhere higher up. Trees planted in abundance as windbreaks round cultivation patches and along the roads were lacking along the township and village streets or around houses. Asphalt was used generously on the excellent roads linking residential areas with each other and the oilfields, but not on the rutty streets and footpaths which became mud bogs when it rained – as it had done most fiercely just before our arrival. There is no lack of space – the grasslands are state property and the new townships and villages can help themselves to as much as they like for building and for developing agriculture – but township and village streets are relatively narrow and the space between houses leaves little room for gardens which would blend in with the surrounding area. But the current mood in the Taching area, as elsewhere in China, is so much that of 'the family should hold back' that it would need a Chou En-lai to visit the place again and say: 'Well done, but don't forget your own homes, streets and villages! There's plenty of space for all. Make it beautiful as well as functional.'

Such advice, at this stage of China's development, has to come from a topmost level. For anyone to suggest it at Chuan Yeh would be to risk a thorough ideological dressing-down by Cho T'a-ching, Li Chang-yung and their fellow committee-women!

Another outlet where the women could 'do their bit' was the Taching Sewing and Mending Centre. It had been set up in the first bitter winter that the field had been opened up – December 1960 – by a People's Liberation Army veteran, referred to simply as 'Old Yen' by Wang Feng-ying, the energetic, middle-aged woman who directed the Centre.

'Old Yen and a friend of his persuaded six of us how much better it would be if, instead of each of us wives just looking after our own husband's clothes, we pooled our efforts and looked after those of everybody. The country was in great economic difficulty. There was plenty of high-level sabotage too. It was clear there was not going to be enough decent clothing to go round. Keep what was available clean and repaired – that was Old Yen's idea. We scrounged around and found some abandoned cow-stalls and two big iron pots that had been used for preparing cow-fodder. We set them up in the open, and collected the dirty overalls at the drilling sites. They were usually stiff with oil and mud. We boiled them in water hauled from a pool a mile away, rinsed them in the old feeding troughs and spread them all over the cows' old stalls to dry, patching them up before returning them. We were eight when we started, but we were soon joined by eighty other wives. We got to the point where we could send mobile teams to make the rounds of the drilling rigs, sewing on patches and buttons on the spot and bringing back what had to be cleaned.

'Next spring, the men started throwing away their cotton-padded jackets and fur caps because they had become impossibly ragged. We cleaned the cotton padding, trimmed the fur, saved what cloth could be saved and made new fur-lined jackets and quilted caps for the next winter. The local authorities saw we were doing a good job, and when things looked up a bit they bought a few sewing machines to help things along. Gradually we expanded our activities until we had built up to this present little factory.'

The factory now covered 2,000 square metres of floor space and employed 404 women workers – 80 per cent of them wives of the oil-workers – with rotating boilers and centrifugal dryers, made by themselves, doubtless with a helping hand from their husbands. There were five workshops, including a first-class tailoring atelier where electric cutters sliced through a hundred thicknesses of new cloth, according to the chalked outlines for standard-sized coats and pants. With hillocks of discarded clothes in front of them, groups of women were cutting out geometric pieces of cloth for linings of padded coats, setting aside the cotton padding for sterilizers and teasing machines which would make them like new again. With the meticulous attention to detail that is now taken for granted, Mrs Wang produced a much-thumbed notebook to inform us that, in the almost thirteen years since the sewing and mending centre was formed, they had recuperated 500,000 metres of cloth, and 25 tons of cotton wool from old padding – a saving to the state of some 2·4 million yuan.

Although they now had a generous allotment of new cloth and padding, nothing of the old was wasted. Even tiny scraps of cloth that could not be used for patches were teased back into cotton wool. If they were a bit bigger, they were turned into tiny purses which would be presented to the oil-workers with needle, thread and a few buttons, together with their repaired clothes. From bits of old waterproofs, they made working aprons, or sewed the remnants of fur from abandoned caps and turned them into fur-lined capes with head-hoods attached. From still smaller bits of waterproofs they made boot covers for the welders to prevent sparks falling on their feet.

It was another version of the 'something from nothing, small to big' theme which we were to encounter in a thousand variations wherever we went in China.

In a last talk with him before we left, Li Huei-hsin again stressed the original pattern of development of the oilfield. 'We have completely broken away from the old idea of first building up a city with housing and all sorts of facilities, the family dependants inside the city and the workers away on the distant drilling sites. In our concept, small communities with all urban facilities go parallel with the development of the field.'

Taching had gradually built up to a population of over 300,000, dispersed in three big urban centres, forty townships and over a hundred township-satellites – the latter purely residential but within easy walking distance of the townships and their urban facilities. Serving this community was one higher educational establishment of university level, three specialized technical institutions giving higher secondary education and 269 primary and middle schools. All children of school age, as elsewhere in China, received their schooling free. 'There is no "boom town" atmosphere, because workers receive the same wages as elsewhere and prices in the remotest oil-drilling site are exactly the same as those in Peking or anywhere else in China,' explained Li Huei-hsin – something we had checked for ourselves.

Although the negative aspects of urban conglomeration had been avoided, there were over 160 public health centres and clinics, including hospitals with up to 300 beds in the Taching area.

Whether this impressive de-concentration of population – like the underground oil-storage and distribution centres – was also part of the 'be prepared against war' strategy was not mentioned, but Li Huei-hsin did point out that the oilfields 'have the equivalent of a full division of people's militia, the members of which also take part in productive labour. If an enemy ever attacks, everyone will take to arms to defend the oilfields.' Referring to the early sabotage, Li commented: 'The grave miscalculation of Liu Shao-ch'i was that he under-estimated the determination of the workers to press on and develop the field. Without that grass-roots determination, sym-bolized by such comrades as Wang Chin-hsi and Hsueh Kuei-feng, nothing could have been done.' As is customary when the time came for us to leave, Li touched on the shortcomings as the oilfield leadership saw them:

'Our drilling equipment – apart from the high-speed bits – is basically what was used in the early 1950s. The level of mechan-ization and automation in many processes is not high. Per-hectare yield in agriculture is comparatively low; we are lagging behind in re-afforestation. We will have to work hard to over-come these weaknesses, but we are determined to do this.'

At the Taching siding as our train pulled out, the parallel tracks were filled with long lines of cistern-cars being readied for a long haul south and freight trains discharging mysteriously shaped equipment which we assumed was for the new chemical plant. From the train window during a fast non-stop run to Harbin, interspersed with fields of rice, wheat and market gar-dens close to the urban centres, we saw vast plains in which herds of beef and dairy cattle and droves of horses grazed up to their middles in the lush grasslands and flocks of sheep nibbled at herbage on the fringes of bald patches where wind erosion had lifted off the top soil. It was an extension of the Sung Liao basin, of which Taching was the heart, and one envisaged it in years to come dotted with the same white oil-well housings.

Alongside every railway siding were scores of squat grain

silos covered with woven matting, and more were being prepared. At Harbin we were informed that Heilungkiang province,
of which it was the capital, had reaped excellent harvests for
thirteen years in succession – unaffected even by the natural disasters which smote most of the rest of the country in 1960–62 –
and that 1973 promised to beat all records in wheat and soya
bean production. The state of the crops along our route from
Harbin southwards and the scope of the construction of new
grain-storage space at almost every railway siding seemed to
confirm the estimates.

What a contrast the Yumen field presented as compared to
Taching. From a control tower we felt as if we were on the
bridge of the flagship of a fleet, supervising the performance of
the smaller fry. Below for as far as one could see were the kow-
towing pumps obediently nodding their heads, while a com-
puterized tape on the 'bridge' registered their performance.

The Yumen field is at an altitude of over 7,000 feet (2,300
metres) on the Old Silk Road, along which camel caravans used
to pass between Ancient Cathay and the Arab world. The
presence of 'black water' – oil seepages – in the surrounding
Gobi desert was noted by early travellers like Marco Polo, and
by still earlier Chinese travellers in the eighth century. The
American Texas Oil Company was promised by the Kuomintang a majority lifetime interest in any oil found. It prospected
in the Yumen (West Kansu) area in the early 1930s but reported
there was no oil in exploitable proportions. A Chinese geologist
disputed this view in 1938 and small-scale production started
shortly after. American specialists predicted then that it would
be worked out within ten years. After the People's Republic
was set up the field was developed with Soviet help and peak
production of 1,200,000 tons was reached in 1959, falling off
gradually to 620,000 tons in 1972. Two new fields were being
opened up at the time of our visit, with new Chinese-made
drilling equipment which must be the envy of the Taching
drillers. The more cumbersome and slower Soviet and Ro-
manian equipment is no longer used.

The new fields are to be developed along the lines of Taching, using the water-injection system to maintain stable pressures. Yumen seemed a big field during our early visits to the area. It will produce for about fifty years to come, according to the Chinese engineers on the spot, at a level sufficient to fuel the rapidly growing industry and transport needs in the area. But it is completely dwarfed by Taching.

One of the most valuable functions of this pioneer field is that it trained, and sent out to other fields, some 63,000 technicians and specialized workers and provided over 2,000 pieces of oil-exploiting equipment made in the factories built to serve the field.

At the wells where pumps are being used, average production is 6 tons daily. The newer ones, based on stable pressures, average 30 tons daily for an expected five years, after which pumps will have to be used because of the pressure lost during the exploitation of the older parts of the field.

As a measure of China's progress, it was interesting to look in at the old oil refinery and, in one section alone, count machinery from fourteen different countries, none of it made in China. At the new Yumen refinery, as at Taching, apart from some ultra-modern measuring instruments, everything in the petro-chemical plant was Chinese-made.

One of the epic achievements, a parallel to Chuen Yeh village, was the transformation at Gobi Chuang – Gobi Desert Village. Inspired by the 'Learn from Tachai' slogan, families of the oil-workers had transformed wastes of sand and stone, in the shadow of towering Mt Yao Mo (13,000 feet), into flourishing fields of wheat, vegetables and oil-bearing plants, the farms even running up the slopes of the Chi Lien mountain ranges, where there are only ninety frost-free days a year. As at Tachai, they had used the rocks for terrace walls, hauling earth in buckets and baskets and tamping it down to depths of 3 and 4 feet. They made small reservoirs free of the mountain shadows, where the water would be warmed before snaking its way down through irrigation channels to slake the thirst of the crops. Added to year by year, at the time of our visit almost 1,200 acres of land had thus been brought under cultivation in a group of farms, one for each department of the oilfield complex. Except for spare-time help by the men-folk on holidays and their weekly rest-days, the farms are run by the dependants of the oil-workers.

On every hand the same ingenuity! We watched the laying of irrigation channels made of big stones and wondered why the joints were not filled with cement as the stones were laid. But another team followed behind the stone-layers, stuffing straw rope into the cracks. It was explained that when the water flowed, the straw rope swelled and gradually became impregnated with mud which gave a permanent waterproofing which never cracked – as did the cement in the intense cold. What central planning organization would ever have included straw rope and mud in its material allocations for an irrigation project?

CHAPTER EIGHT

LEARNING FROM TACHAI

It was in November 1964 that Mao Tse-tung launched the slogan 'In Agriculture Learn from Tachai', and we and some 700 million Chinese learned that the Tachai brigade of the Tachai commune, in an old revolutionary area of Shansi province, had transformed a barren, drought-ridden area of stony hills into one of China's most flourishing commune brigades. This was essentially due to the dogged perseverance of Chen Yung-kuei, the local Communist Party secretary, a counterpart in agriculture to Wang Chen-hsi, of the Taching oilfields, in industry. (Chen Yung-kuei, like Wang Chen-hsi, was elected to the Communist Party's Central Committee at the Ninth Party Congress and to the Political Bureau, as Wang Chen-hsi undoubtedly would have been at the Tenth Party Congress, had he lived.)

Close examination of the situation at Tachai revealed that more than a fight against nature was involved and that launching the 'Learn from Tachai' slogan was an important element in Mao's counter-attack against the ideas of Liu Shao-ch'i. He chose Tachai as his model in the 'two-line struggle' on agricultural policy. The vital issue was whether there should be a highly centralized system, with the communes under the strict control of the state, financed by a central banking system and integrated in planning from the top down to individual households, or whether it should be on a 'do it yourself' basis, with planning initiated from below and state interference at a minimum.

Within the Tachai commune, we discovered there was a brigade which not only had not 'learned from Tachai' but had very much opposed it. We were also surprised to find that the brigade which had caused so much noise throughout China, Tachai itself, was tiny – only eighty-three households with a population of 446. The Wu Chia P'ong brigade, which had been reluctant to follow the Tachai example, was much bigger – 270 households and a population of 1,100. The fields of the two brigades adjoined and their two headquarters were about a kilometre apart. Why on earth did they not pull together? It was the question we put to Kuo Lai-liang, a former head of the brigade militia who emerged as chairman of the revolutionary committee of Wu Chia P'ong once mistakes were corrected.

'Our party leadership was not united,' he said, replying to our first question. 'There were historical reasons for this. Our village consists of three hamlets and the people in each of the three have the same names. The Kuo family, from which I come, of about 100 households in Miao P'ing hamlet; the Li family of about ninety households in Nan K'ou hamlet; and the Wangs in Pei hamlet with eighty households. Each hamlet made up one team of our three-team brigade.

'The Communist Party branch committee had nine members, three from each hamlet, in effect three from each of the clans. It was not a united committee but a coalition of the clans. At party meetings the comrades were not thinking of the interests of the brigade but were fighting for the interests of their respective clans. Even within the clans, cadres did not further the interests of the whole clan but mainly those of the leading members who were often the most backward, reactionary elements. Each clan said: "We must have our cadres in the leading body, otherwise we'll be discriminated against." When a member of one spoke up to criticize some bad tendency in the brigade, the other clan representatives shouted "Discrimination", and if he criticized one of his own clan the others shouted "Running dog". The masses had no confidence in themselves because of this clan-based sectarianism.

'Leadership of the brigade rotated every year to "give every clan its chance". So between 1958, when the commune was set up, until 1965, when we changed things, brigade leadership had rotated eight times, the leaders of the three teams twenty-four times. There was no stability at all. Production went up and down, as methods were changed each year according to what the new leaders thought would be in the best interests of their clan. The idea of all pulling together as they did in the Tachai brigade was quite contrary to our ideas.

'We simply papered over the realities of class differences within the teams and approved Liu Shao-ch'i's fallacious line about the dying away of class distinctions. Many things happened between 1957 and 1964 which demoralized the ordinary brigade members. Landlords and rich peasants, using the old authority of their position in the clan hierarchy, started taking back things that had been distributed to the poor and lower-middle peasants. There were cases where they threatened to kill cadres who resisted this.

'Normally such class enemies would have been dealt with by the party branch committee, but they were able to get away with it because of the absence of unity within the committee.

'Another reason why we were against Tachai was that we had really started taking the capitalist road and continued along that road although many of us could see it was against our interests.' Although Liu Shao-ch'i was continually referred to as a 'capitalist-roader', to have concrete examples of this at commune level was rare at the time of our first visit to Tachai, so we pressed for details.

'In 1956,' continued Kuo Lai-liang, 'we had joined with what is now the Tachai brigade, to form a socialist-type co-operative under the leadership of Chen Yung-kuei. Grain production rose immediately to about three quarters of a ton per acre, the highest we had ever harvested. Members earned 80 fen per work-day that year and the grain allotment was 400 pounds per head. But although we had done so well, we pulled out of the co-op the following year, basically because Liu Shao-ch'i wanted to reduce the number of socialist-type co-ops and complained that things were going too fast. The former landlords, rich peasants and other elements were in the forefront of wanting to pull out. They argued that we would only lose by continuing with Tachai. Their fields were on ridges and in gullies while ours were on the plains. Why pool good and bad fields? Also, they pointed out that, although Tachai had a good harvest in 1957, they insisted on selling too much to the state – we could get by with selling much less to the state if we were on our own.

So we pulled out and formed our own so-called "advanced co-op". From that time on, Tachai and our co-op took different roads.

'Tachai forged ahead on the revolutionary road of "self-reliance and hard struggle" while we went ahead on the road of material incentives and individual interests. This was the time when Liu Shao-ch'i started introducing the idea of household quotas of contributions to the state, to encourage the development of private plots and return to individual household farming by the back door. He also promoted side occupations outside the farm to bring in extra money. We went further and set household quotas for the side occupations, sending forty of the most able-bodied men into the county town to work, on the understanding that they contributed from 400 to 600 yuan per head yearly to brigade funds. Under the cover of "side occupations" they went in for all sorts of black-marketing ventures that brought them in from 1,500 to 1,600 yuan per year. They came back for week-ends with bikes and wrist-watches, but production on our "advanced co-op" went down and the masses got more and more demoralized.

'We lost not only their man-power, but their manure as well, so the quality of the soil deteriorated.[1] Even the plots of land got smaller as headlands were not ploughed owing to lack of man-power; nothing was done to check erosion, washed-out soil was not replaced. By 1964 the per-acre yield had gone down to slightly over half a ton of grain and members were paid only 49 fen per work-day. Those who had gone to the county town got richer, those at home poorer. The 1964 rice allocation was only 200 pounds per head and for the previous few years we

1. The question of human manure in China is of crucial importance to agriculture. One of China's greatest experts on agriculture, Chi Chao-t'ing, in what is considered a classic book on the subject, *The Five Economic Areas of China*, maintained that there is no limit to the productivity of the land if you put back into the soil all the waste from all the people who live from it. These days China is aiming for this to be supplemented by one pig – as a walking fertilizer factory – for every person on the land. A good pig gives 5 tons of compost manure a year. Human and animal excreta are modified by chemical products into a compost considered far more effective than chemical fertilizers.

had been borrowing 40,000 yuan a year to buy foodstuffs.

'On the other side of our fields in Tachai the yields got bigger as ours declined. Where there had been stony hillsides there were now terraced fields. Instead of wasting their man-power in black-marketeering with the products of the private plots, they had invested it and their manure in transforming their land into high-productivity fields. By 1964 the rank-and-file members of our co-op were getting very restive, but we were also confused because we were convinced that we were the ones who were applying party and government policy and that it was Chen Yung-kuei who was on the wrong road. Then came Chairman Mao's call to "Learn from Tachai" and everything was clear. The former poor and lower-middle peasants were most enthusiastic. For them, they only had to look across at the Tachai fields to know who was right. It was they who insisted that we follow the Tachai road immediately.'

We asked them when it was that they had started to correct the muddle. It appeared that some of the more politically minded now insisted on starting study and discussion groups and they invited Chen Yung-kuei over to give a hand. Study was soon concentrated on the question of class-differentiation.

'We had a lucky break on this,' said Kuo Lai-liang. 'One of the early decisions taken was to move an old cemetery and consolidate the graves so that they would not take up as much land. We opened one, where a landlord and poor peasant had been buried side by side. They were both Wangs, but the landlord had been draped in silken clothes, with gold and silver ornaments, laid out in a very solid coffin. All that was left of peasant Wang were his white bones on the remains of a bit of woven matting. All brigade members were asked to come and have a look and were treated to a talk on the spot about class questions. The fact that people have the same name does not mean they are of the same class or even the same family. No matter what your family name, you are a class enemy of the exploited if you belong to the exploiting class. But if you are exploited, even if you have different names, you are class friends. The poor and lower-middle peasants grasped the point immediately. When we had elections to the leading bodies after that, it was no longer on a clan basis but a class basis. We have never looked back since.' And he started rattling off production figures to prove the point. (We were to return in 1973 and see startling changes at the Wu Chia P'ong brigade.) As to what had happened to the forty workers who had gone off to the county town: 'They all came back – they had their families here. They had to have some re-education and came to realize that they had been on the wrong track; that working for the collective good was better than just lining their own pockets. Not that it was their fault – they had been encouraged by the party leadership at the time they first left.'

What about Tachai was so special that it had caused Mao to launch his famous slogan in 1964, and led him to invite Chen Yung-kuei to Peking? Developments there started in the winter of 1953, at the time of the formation of the co-operatives. Chen Yung-kuei led a group of fifty able-bodied members in building twenty stone terraces across a valley, packing them with 3 or 4 feet of fertile soil carried in baskets from a mile or so away. Year after year, this work was continued by almost superhuman exertion of muscle-power. The only equipment was hammers and chisels for trimming the stones, shoulder poles and carrying baskets. The terraced fields produced bumper crops, and were added to year by year. On average, 1,800 work-days went into every acre of terracing, surely an expenditure of effort that no cost-accounting system could justify.

The farm of about 140 acres was split up into seven sharp ridges and eight steep gullies, down which roaring torrents used to pour in the rainy season, carrying huge chunks of the embankment with them. In pre-liberation days, the area was split up into 4,600 pocket-handkerchief fields from which rocks had been cleared, and the annual grain yield averaged 600 pounds per acre. The greatest trial of the terrace-builders was at what was known as Wolf-Track Valley, a mile-long ravine with half a dozen offshoots leading up into the hills. In the dry season there was never a blade of grass; the rainy season always brought flood disasters. In one winter, the co-op members built thirty-eight stone embankments across the valley, backing them up with soil. In 1956, just as they were due to reap a good harvest, flood waters washed everything away, crops, embankments and all. They rebuilt more solidly the following winter, but in 1957 it was all carried away again in a great rush of water, provoked by the enormous rain-storms which generate in the Taihang mountains, of which Tachai forms part of the foothills. In the winter of 1957 they tried again, going much deeper with the foundations, cementing the foundation rocks together and curving the embankments inwards towards where flood waters would come, so that the stress and pressures would only consolidate the massive walls of rock. In twenty-seven days and nights, with Chen Yung-kuei always in the lead, but reinforced by volunteers from other areas, the Tachai brigade members rebuilt the embankments and for the next few years all was well. Rainy season flood waters were diverted into wells and irrigation channels built at the same time as the solid embankments. Grain yields showed a steady increase.

Then in 1963, when most of China was enjoying the first normal year after the three years of what are described as 'natural disasters', Tachai was hit in early August, after seven days and nights of torrential rain, by a super-flood which carried everything away, including 97 per cent of the houses and farm buildings, in the greatest catastrophe ever to hit the area. Attending a county meeting when news of the disaster reached him, Chen Yung-kuei rushed back, wading through waist-high waters, and after being reassured that there were no lives lost is reported to have said: 'As long as our people are there, we can do anything. The terracing was done by man, the houses were built by man. We shall rebuild the terraces more solidly, the houses more beautifully than before.' The government in Peking offered to send money, grain, medicine, clothing and other relief supplies. Brigade members held a meeting and adopted a 'Three Don't Wants' resolution: 'No state money! No state grain! No state relief materials!' A plan was drawn up to reconstruct the terraced fields within five years and rebuild a modern Tachai township within ten years. Meanwhile production would continue.

The flood water had swept over 90 per cent of the fields, but members went out into them and propped up the grain stalks one by one, tying them to sticks thrust into the ground. In the end they reaped a good maize harvest, with an average of 2·25 tons per acre, and incomes did not suffer much. They even managed to deliver 120 tons of grain to the state.

So much for the official saga of the first part of the Tachai story. Perhaps it was the rejection of state aid which first attracted Mao's attention. Self-reliance in such circumstances was a perfect example of what he was fighting for.

After Mao had launched the 'Learn from Tachai' slogan, Chen Yung-kuei announced that the 1964 harvest was a record 2·4 tons of grain per acre.

'Liu Shao-ch'i did not want to accept the implications of such a success,' said Chia Lai-heng, a slight, bullet-headed former People's Liberation Army man, vice-chairman of the brigade and deputizing for Chen Yung-kuei on one of our visits. 'So he sent in a so-called "work-team" of seventy people to try to pull us down. They stayed for fifty days. First of all they wanted to prove that we had cheated on acreage – that the grain we had produced came from more land than we had claimed. They spent a lot of time tramping all over the farm with their surveying instruments and tapes and found that we had erred, but on the right side. The brigade had 796 mou of cultivable land, whereas we had taken an old figure of 802·6 mou as our basis. Our per-acre yield was higher than claimed.

'In 1964, we had sold 300,000 jin of grain to the state,[2] having averaged 240,000 jin from 1959 onwards,' continued Chia Lai-heng. Liu's people said this must be incorrect, so they wasted more time checking figures at commune and county level. They found we had delivered what we had claimed. Then they decided that we must have faked the figures for grain stored in reserve. They weighed and measured and wasted much more time, but found our reserves were as we had said. They then called a meeting of brigade members and tried to get someone to denounce Chen Yung-kuei for having "wasted too much labour power".

2. The Chinese calculate grain yields in jin (half a kilogram) per mou, the latter equalling one sixth of an acre or one sixteenth of a hectare. For convenience sake, we have usually transformed yields into ton per acre.

The former poor and lower-middle peasants were furious and marched out of the meeting. Finally, Chen Yung-kuei told them: "It's because we are correctly carrying out Chairman Mao's line that you want to prove that Tachai is no good. Get out!" So we threw the "work-team" out. All they wanted to do was to take the Red Banner away from us and plant it in Tao-yuan.[3] Later, within the framework of the Socialist Education Movement in the countryside, the Central Committee sent a real work-team here which very quickly decided that our brigade was good politically, economically and organizationally, and that we were firmly applying party policy.'

In 1963, during the battle to repair the flood damage, it was decided to abandon the time-wasting practice of calculating the daily work-points. The old People's Liberation Army man, Chia Lai-heng, had been waging a campaign against the system even before the commune was formed in 1958 with the argument that if they had gone on like that in the P.L.A. they would never have beaten Chiang Kai-shek! Chen Yung-kuei had proposed abandoning the system several times through the administrative hierarchy, but the word had come back from Liu Shao-ch'i's headquarters categorically forbidding any changes. Now they abandoned it in favour of payment according to working days contributed, with some rough adjustments, suggested by brigade members themselves, according to how they evaluated their own work. It was another pioneer step by Tachai which many other communes were to learn from.

In our visit to Tachai in mid-summer 1973 we were struck with how beautiful it had become: the terraced hills and valleys softening the otherwise harsh contours of the dividing ridges; the stretches of green maize and golden wheat curving behind the solid embankments; the water glistening in stone-faced irrigation canals in every direction. Much of the surround-

3. Taoyuan brigade of Luwangchuang commune in Funing county of northern Hopei province had been selected by Liu Shao-ch'i as the model for his concept in agriculture. His wife, Wang Kuang-mei, took personal charge of affairs there for a certain time under an assumed name. After Mao's praise for Tachai, the latter was referred to as a 'Red Banner' brigade.

ing countryside as we drove in from the Hsiyang county seat had terraces climbing like broad staircases up the hillsides; rivers were contained between solid, stone-faced embankments. Tachai's ten-year rebuilding plan had been completed, with long single- and double-storeyed grey stone apartment buildings set out among willows and other trees on high ground, well away from future rampaging waters. Less than a kilometre distant there was furious building activity going on at Wu Chia P'ong. Donkey carts were hauling chunks of rock, stone-masons were chiselling them into shape and smoke was pouring from brick kilns behind rows of stone and brick houses in various stages of completion.

Tachai had come through its severest test the previous year, when the whole of Shansi and several neighbouring provinces were hit with the worst drought for over a century. At Tachai not a single drop of rain fell for 300 days and the year's total rainfall was one fifth of normal. But, at the same time as providing terracing, in the ten years since 1963 the Tachai brigade had ensured an adequate water supply, partly because the People's Liberation Army had helped them to build a 7-kilometre canal from a reservoir built some years earlier, partly because they had dug a network of wells to contain the flood waters. In 1971 they had topped 3·3 tons of grain per acre, and although this fell about 10 per cent in 1972 they were still able to sell 200 tons of grain to the state and the total income of commune members was up by 10 per cent owing to an increase in vegetable and fruit production. Chia Lai-heng showed us around again. He escorted us through lush fields of wheat and maize to hillside orchards aglow with ripening apples, through vineyards heavy with bunches of grapes.

'We have cut down the working days for new terracing from 1,800 per acre to 600 with the cable cars we put in last year,' explained Chia Lai-heng, 'and since you were last here, we have redone a lot of the terracing to make the fields big enough to work with walking tractors. The biggest before were about three quarters of an acre. Now they run to 3 or 4 acres. We have planted 40,000 fruit trees,' he said, polishing a couple of apples on his sleeve for us to taste, 'and by 1980 our income from fruit alone will be greater than our present income from all sources.' Turning from a vantage point to look back over the new village, Chia Lai-heng commented: 'All this was built without a cent or ear of grain from the state.' When we remarked on the excellence of the grain stores and stables, he laughed and said: 'It is a fact that our animals are housed better than the rich peasants were in the old days.'

It became clear as we continued up the slopes to the topmost ridge that the secret of survival in the 1972 drought had been that almost as much work had gone into irrigation and water control in the previous few years as into the original terracing work. 'If the whole country should learn from Tachai,' Chia Lai-heng commented, 'Tachai should also learn from the whole country. Chen Yung-kuei visited other advanced brigades who had done good work in water control. He brought back new ideas for trapping water and we now have it trapped at every level in underground storage wells, everything linked up so that we can beat any drought. This is why we can say that Tachai has definitely become a stable, high-yield agricultural area.' It was the 'stable, high-yield' aspect of Tachai which by 1973 was being publicized all over China as an additional reason for continuing 'to learn from Tachai'.

It was a big surprise to see how Wolf-Track Valley had changed its shape. The previous winter, the whole brigade had turned out – this time with bulldozers and cable cars to help – and in three months of round-the-clock work they had removed several small hills and turned the whole area into a series of big fields, each retained by walls so massive that they looked like fortress battlements. There was now a total of 8 acres of land, which could be worked by tractors, where there had been 3 acres of small patches which could only be hoed before.

Chia Lai-heng advised us to visit the Ssu P'ang brigade of the Li Chin Jong commune next door. This we did, being taken in hand by Chen Yu-t'ang, head of the brigade and secretary of the party committee, a robust, middle-aged man with tobacco-stained teeth. He started by escorting us to see the results of two winters' hard work in 1970–71 and 71–2. From time immemorial Ssu P'ang village had been troubled by a stream that was a dry, stone-filled river bed most of the year, but a raging torrent in the rainy season. It was the usual cycle of drought and flood. 'We are in the drought belt,' explained Chen Yu-t'ang, 'traditionally short of grain and even drinking water. In the rainy season, masses of churning, chocolate-coloured flood water, impossible to drink, stormed down. There is very little artesian water at any levels that we could reach. After having seen what they had done at Tachai, we decided at least to tame the river. Chen Yung-kuei came and looked things over, giving us some good advice. The river bed was simply waste land. Why not put the river into a tunnel, then fill in the river bed over the tunnel with soil and turn the whole thing into grain fields? The idea made some of us gasp.'

In these two winters of very hard work, the brigade members built a series of three tunnels, 3·5 kilometres, 1·1 kilometres and 600 metres long respectively, each of them 10 feet high and 12 feet wide, faced with solid blocks of stone; 36,000 cubic metres of stone went into the tunnel facings. They then dumped 500,000 cubic metres of fertile soil over the top of the tunnels and into what had been the sterile river bed for most of the year, giving the brigade an extra 50 acres of fields, under which the river flowed in a disciplined manner in the few weeks of the flood season. 'The tunnels can also serve as excellent air-raid shelters,' said Chen Yu-t'ang as we admired the usual excellence of the stonework.

On top of the kilometre-long tunnel, they had rebuilt Ssu P'ang village, with two- and three-storey apartment buildings. The three-storey brigade headquarters was located on what had formerly been a hillock at the junction of two streams. 'One of the things that had first impressed us at Tachai,' continued Chen Yu-t'ang, 'was the re-housing programme and we thought we would start by doing the same thing. Fortunately Chen Yung-kuei advised us to tame the river first and build houses later.' He went on to relate a story somewhat similar to that of the Wu Chia P'ong brigade, in so far as they had neglected agricultural work until Chairman Mao's call to 'Learn from Tachai'.

'We thought that as the village had little cultivable land and a rather large population (460 households and 1,900 people) we should divert man-power to work at the county centre. Deprived of their labour and fertilizer, our grain output dropped from 360 tons in 1960 to 250 tons in 1966. In that year, we understood our mistakes, pulled the man-power back from the towns and really settled down to work. We doubled our output to 500 tons in 1967 and in 1971 we produced 1,230 tons, dropping back to just half that figure in 1972 because we had not carried out irrigation work on the scale at Tachai and were really hit by the drought. We harvested 2·4 tons of grain per acre in 1971 and will exceed that if all goes well this year. We had built small reservoirs at the head of three gullies in April 1972, but they remained dry throughout the year. We are building a bigger one now and have also got enough water to irrigate 150 acres from a deep well. We discovered a spring and now pump water up to a tower to supply the village with decent drinking water for the first time ever. But we still have a lot to do to catch up with Tachai.' We asked about those who had gone off to the county town. How had they readjusted?

'They didn't go off – we sent them,' he said. 'It was because of the wrong political line carried out by us cadres, especially myself. Of course we were influenced by Liu Shao-ch'i's erroneous policy, but the main thing was our own low political level, our inability to distinguish between a correct and an incorrect line. I have been the secretary of the party branch here for twenty years, and have headed the brigade since it was formed. Before that I was in the People's Liberation Army. I thought I was always for the revolution. I fought hard in the P.L.A., I worked hard here. It took the Cultural Revolution for me to realize that I had been mechanically following a wrong line because I didn't use my own head and I had been leading everybody else into making mistakes. We did some thorough study after we realized our mistakes and talked everything over. If we are now on the right track and have achieved something this is because we have followed Chairman Mao and learned from Tachai how to push on with the socialist revolution.'

On the way back to the Tachai brigade headquarters, we

called in on Wu Chia P'ong again, to find brigade-leader Kuo Lai-liang in fine form. He immediately produced his notebook and quoted production figures running from 1·5 tons per acre in 1967 to 3 tons in 1971, dropping back to 2·2 tons in the 1972 drought year. 'We are in the middle of a five-year plan to be completed by 1975,' he said. 'There are six main aims. All fields to be irrigated; more acreage of rice and wheat; two crops yearly instead of one; hills to be planted with orchards and vineyards; increased mechanization; the old clan villages to be totally replaced by a new central village. As you can see,' he said, with a sweep of his hand towards the building activity, 'we are well advanced with that. Within two months all the Wang, Li and Kou families will be living intermingled in the one village, with electricity and piped water to every house.' They were good-looking houses of grey bricks and cream-tiled roofs. Twenty middle-school girls – it was the summer-holiday period – were turning out 20,000 bricks per day at a site just above the village, from hillside soil, softened up with water, shaped by a home-made mechanical contrivance, then baked for a week in the glowing, smoking kilns.

'Whether we attain all our aims,' continued brigade-leader Kou, 'depends on whether we continue to apply Chairman Mao's revolutionary line and learn from Tachai. Thanks to irrigation projects already started, half of our farm may now be considered stable, high-yield land, which is why we did not suffer as much as some brigades in last year's drought.' One of the Li houses, he explained, was to be kept as a museum piece to remind future generations of the bad old clan days. All the others would be demolished and the land they stood on put under cultivation. The new village was on high ground overlooking the old.

Chen Yung-kuei's activities had not been limited to Tachai. As vice-chairman of the Hsiyang county revolutionary committee from the time it was set up in 1967, he had initiated a project to tame the river which was the main cause of all the havoc wreaked in the flood season. This involved damming the upper reaches and confining the rampaging waters to a stone-lined channel about one third or less the width of the original meandering river bed. The land on each side of the channel had been reclaimed by the usual method of dumping soil into it from other areas. A good 200 acres of fertile fields had thus been brought into production. The work of re-arranging the topography of Hsiyang county, of forcing rivers to obey man's will and not that of nature, never stops. And more and more villages are adopting the Tachai type of communal re-housing, with a basement living quarters backed into the loess hillsides serving as supports for one or two more storeys above them, making the most economic use of steep hillside land unsuitable for cultivation and providing living space of a quality that the landlords would have envied in the old days.

The self-critical remarks of Chen Yu-t'ang about his inability to distinguish between a correct and incorrect political line, although he was a veteran Communist Party cadre, was something we were to hear very often. The point was that, until the Cultural Revolution brought out into the open ideological differences which had existed at the top for many years past, cadres at Chen Yu-t'ang's level had no idea that there were 'two lines' and 'two headquarters' – for them there was only one. If instructions came from Peking they must invariably be in accordance with that one 'party line', to be unquestionably obeyed, as far as orthodox party leadership was concerned. It was a handful of stubborn people like Chen Yung-kuei and Wang Chen-hsi, applying the Mao principle of 'dare to think, dare to act', who stood out against instructions when they felt these violated the fundamental building of socialism as they understood it. Old soldiers like Chen Yu-t'ang tended to obey automatically any instructions from above.

It was certainly because of the lack of basic theoretical knowledge, revealed at almost all party and organizational levels during the Cultural Revolution, that a drive was launched to encourage the study of Marx, Engels, Lenin and Stalin – in addition to Mao Tse-tung. From housewives in the neighbourhood units to higher cadres in the May the Seventh schools, everyone was studying basic Marxism from the *Communist Manifesto*, to Engels' *Anti-Dühring*, Marx's *Critique of the Gotha Programme* and Lenin's *Empirio-Criticism*. The idea was that everyone should have his own ideological weights and measures, so as to be able to decide whether whatever line was being proposed upheld basic Marxist doctrine.

CHAPTER NINE

EXPERIENCES IN TAOYUAN

Peitaiho is a pleasant, drowsy seaside resort some 230 miles north-east of Peking, on Pohai Bay, enclosed on three sides by the Yellow Sea. Another dozen miles further east is Shan-haikwan and the beautiful massive 'First Gate under Heaven' which marks the beginning of the Great Wall. A big sign stating just that and painted 500 years ago reposes inside the tower, which rises above the 30-feet-high wall, along which five horse-men could gallop abreast in the old days. On the 'other side' lie the north-east provinces and the relics of battlefields and old encampments where successive invaders from the north tried their luck at pushing into mid-China in ancient times. A few weeks earlier we had also visited 'The Most Magnificent Gate under Heaven', 3,000 miles distant at Chiayukwan, the last gate at the western end of the Great Wall, and pondered over all the history that lay between, since Ch'in Shih Huang, the first Emperor of the Ch'in Dynasty, who unified China and gave it its name, linked up the various fortresses some 2,200 years ago, to create the Great Wall, one of the greatest building achievements in world history.

Generations of Western residents of Peking have sunned themselves on the white sand beaches of Peitaiho and bathed in its usually placid waters. Six hours by train from Peking, today's diplomats, journalists and foreign specialists spend week-ends and summer holidays there, sometimes taking a ritual cup of afternoon tea with cakes or ice cream at the municipal restaurant, which for most customers retains its old name of 'Chi-Ss-Ling' – a survival of pre-liberation days when it was the local branch of the then foreign-owned Kisserling Restaurant in Tientsin. These days, in the wide stretches between the few beaches still reserved for 'foreign friends', Chinese holiday-makers and workers from rest sanatoria also splash around very much as friendly equals and tan their lithe bodies in the sun. To the west the beaches are bounded by a fishing co-operative and in the east by the Chingwangtao port, now being deepened to handle ocean-going ships of up to 40,000 tons.

Peitaiho is not famous only for its sunny, fine-sanded beaches. It was from there on the night of 12 September 1971 that the former Defence Minister and heir-apparent to the leadership in China, Lin Piao, took off on his precipitate flight to the Soviet Union, crashing to his death in Outer Mongolia. It was in Peitaiho also that on 29 August 1958, after a brief session of a Working Committee of the Communist Party's Central Committee, the decision was announced to support the setting-up of People's Communes. The session was led by Mao Tse-tung, fresh from on-the-spot investigations into the latest trends in the countryside. By what followed, it seems clear that Liu Shao-ch'i, having failed to prevent this new 'leap', adopted the old British diplomatic strategy of 'If you can't stop it – join it'. If there were going to be communes, he was determined that they should conform to a certain pattern.

In that same month of August 1958, Liu Shao-ch'i and his wife Wang Kwang-mei inspected some farm co-operatives in the vicinity of Peitaiho, including one situated at the village of Taoyuan, about one hour's car drive from the resort. They were understandably impressed and fooled by an agro-technician, Kwan Ching-tung, when he unblushingly lied to them that on experimental plots he was getting the equivalent of 30 tons per acre of *kaoliang*.[1] When Liu Shao-ch'i asked if he could boost this to 45 tons, Kwan thought there would be no problem in performing this and a number of other agricultural miracles. A former upper-middle peasant, Kwan Ching-tung seems to have been a persuasive, smooth-tongued operator who had talked his way into various important posts during the

1. *Kaoliang*, sorghum or giant millet, resembles maize except that the seeds are not wrapped in neat cobs but hang in festoons. It is mainly used for food but sometimes transformed into, among other things, fiery and popular spirits with an alcoholic content of over 60 per cent, of which *mao t'ai*, usually served at official banquets, is the best known.

formation of the co-operatives. During the organization of the co-operatives that preceded the commune, he formulated a rule for the low-level co-operative he led. It was called the principle of 'three haves'. Members had to bring in capital or good land, or carts and horses, otherwise they were not permitted to join. His was a co-operative of middle peasants, alongside which was another set up by former landless and poor peasants under Wu Chen, a farmer from one of the poorest families in the area. Later, as the higher-stage co-operative came in, these two co-ops had to merge, despite opposition from Kwan Ching-tung. It is part of the folk-lore which visitors to Taoyuan heard later on that Kwan Ching-tung had the bull from his rich co-operative killed rather than let it serve the cows of the poor peasant one.

What is certain is that he made a good impression on Liu Shao-ch'i and apparently an especially good one on Madame Liu. Within a few weeks of his pledge on *kaoliang*, Kwan was invited to Peking, where at a dinner with the President and his wife he assured them that the just-completed harvest had confirmed his 30 tons per acre, and with suitable material support he would get 45 tons by next harvest. As a token of such support, Liu Shao-ch'i presented him with five Angora rabbits and two Ukrainian pigs for farm experimental work.

By the end of December 1958, Taoyuan had been incorporated into the Luwangchuang commune, one of the last to be formed in China, except for those in the national minority regions. And also, by the end of the year, Kwan Ching-tung had visited Peking on two more occasions, while Liu Shao-ch'i had visited what was now the Taoyuan brigade once more, he and his wife being admitted as 'honorary members'. Taoyuan had thus become Liu's chosen model for the future of Chinese agriculture and Kwan Ching-tung a sort of low-key miracle Luther Burbank!

With such high-level patronage, it was not surprising that Kwan became the effective head of the Taoyuan brigade. His word was law and he managed to infiltrate numerous old cronies of doubtful background into leading positions.

It is interesting to compare Liu Shao-ch'i's choice of a model brigade with flat, rich land and a good concentration of equipment and draft animals, led by an upper-middle peasant, with Mao Tse-tung's choice – Tachai – the most unpromising farm brigade in the drought-ridden mountains of Shansi, and with a former landless peasant, Chen Yung-kuei, leading it.

The Taoyuan brigade was encouraged – not that they needed much encouragement – to request special allocations of fertilizers, high-yield seeds and heavy financial aid from the state to ensure that the brigade became the perfect model. In the years that followed, 644,000 yuan of state aid was invested in building roads, laying on electricity, buying machinery and so on, and the commune sold off the electrical equipment which it had bought out of its own funds and which had never been properly accounted for.

It appears that the question of 45 tons per acre of *kaoliang* was discreetly dropped. The highest yield ever reached was in fact 12 tons, according to those who now run the Taoyuan brigade, but grain production in general gradually increased from an average of 1·2 tons per acre to 1·3 tons per acre for the first three years after the commune was formed, and there were even slight increases during the three years of natural disasters. This was due to a heroic effort by commune membres of Changli and Funing counties, where Taoyuan is located, in a Great Leap Forward project of building the Yang Ho Reservoir. With a dam a mile long, a three-mile-long lake was formed which from 1959 onwards supplied water to all communes in the area. In view of this, and the special aid Taoyuan was getting, the increases were marginal and Tachai was overhauling Taoyuan hand over fist. In 1963, when despite a disastrous flood Tachai harvested 2·25 tons per acre, Taoyuan reaped only 1·7 tons. This was because of a general malaise about the quality of the leadership, the personal lives of Kwan and his cronies, and the thefts of communal property, all of which lowered working spirit.

Matters came to a head in the spring of 1963 when one of those house-cleaning campaigns which are periodically launched in People's China was started as a Socialist Education Movement. Ostensibly this was aimed at strengthening the leadership of the communes by weeding out the incompetents – and especially the corrupt. Objectively, it became part of the continuing 'struggle between two lines' and was used by each side to strengthen their concept of the correct way forward. Mao sensed what was coming and issued a directive that this should be a very discriminatory process because '95 per cent of the cadres and masses are good or relatively good', and he aimed it at those in authority in the Communist Party who were taking the capitalist road.

Kwan Ching-tung was an immediate target of criticism at Taoyuan, one of his chief attackers being the former head of the 'Poor Men's Co-op', Wu Chen, once in charge of the brigade which had played a leading role during the land reform movement. For obvious reasons it was the poor and landless peasants who were not only the most ardent enthusiasts of land reform but also the most vigilant afterwards in seeing that everyone got a square deal. The real 'cleaning-up' process got under way after the autumn harvest was in and things started to look very bad for brigade leader Kwan. There were deficits in the grain reserves. Some 2,000 yuan was missing from the brigade till, which could only have passed through Kwan's fingers. One of his chief protégés had siphoned off half a ton of grain in black-market operations during the three bad years. There were many other peccadillos for which Kwan was clearly the chief culprit and some of which he admitted to.

In November 1963, an unusually large 'work-team' arrived at Taoyuan to direct the 'four clean-ups'. It included a woman cadre, whose name was given as Tung Pu, with the title of 'security secretary for Hopei province' (in which Funing county is located). The heat of investigation was immediately diverted from Kwan Ching-tung to Wu Chen, denounced variously by the energetic Tung Pu as a 'vagabond', 'trouble-maker' and 'bad element', with especially prepared dossiers from the security bureau to back up her charges. Wu was demoted and expelled from the Communist Party on the spot, in violation of party statutes, but the 'work-team' was able to prove that it had unlimited powers, which it promptly proceeded to exercise. Within a very short time, forty of the forty-seven elected office-holders of the brigade were dismissed, and of twenty-two Communist Party members four were expelled, including Wu Chen's deputy, three more were placed under 'surveillance', two were given 'serious reprimands' and most of the rest were given 'bad marks'.

Third-degree methods were used to interrogate Wu Chen for forty-five days on end to try to get him to admit that he had been a Kuomintang agent and an opium-dealer, and had committed all sorts of crimes as stated in Madame Tung's dossier. He stoutly refused to confess. After another six weeks of interrogation by a six-man team, he was attached to a work-gang for 'reform through labour'.

The 'work-team' remained in Taoyuan until April 1964, when Tung Pu and most of the rest withdrew, leaving a 'consolidation group' and a badly-shaken and demoralized brigade membership behind. Kwan Ching-tung was whitewashed and took over the brigade leadership. Just as she was about to leave, it was revealed that 'Tung Pu' was in fact Wang Kwang-mei, wife of the then President Liu Shao-ch'i, and that the 'consolidation group' would remain in permanent telephone contact with her Peking bureau. Brigade members then understood why 'Tung Pu' had not practised the 'three withs' (to live, eat and work with the peasants) but had her own special food and living quarters, and a photographer to record her occasional activities as she pretended to work out on the fields. Wang Kwang-mei busied herself in Peking preparing a report, 'Experiences in Taoyuan' – later to be widely circulated (except in Taoyuan itself) – extolling the virtues of tight state control over the communes. Taoyuan production took a 20 per cent nose-dive because of widespread demoralization and disorganization in the absence of Wu Chen and other leading activists. At the time when Madame Liu Shao-ch'i was politely sneering at Mao's 'self-reliance and hard work' formula, grain production in Taoyuan dropped to 1·4 tons per acre, while in Tachai it moved up to 2·4 tons. Tachai supplied 120 tons of grain to the state, whereas Taoyuan had to buy 9 tons for members' own consumption.

The seemingly incredible fact that the wife of the President would personally take charge of such an operation is explicable only by the crucial importance which Liu Shao-ch'i attached to a decisive victory for his line in agriculture. It was not just the Taoyuan brigade. It was his future.

The struggle had been going on at various levels and on various fronts from the time the movement to form the co-operatives started, and the higher the form of economic organization envisaged, the tougher the struggle. Liu Shao-ch'i later became branded as a 'capitalist-roader' because he was obsessed with the idea that China needed an overdose of capitalism before passing from semi-feudalism to socialism. We observed this right at the beginning of land reform. The climax came with the formation of the communes which represented a point of no return as far as socialist, and later communist, organization of agriculture was concerned. If Mao's line on the communes succeeded, then control of the countryside in the Liu Shao-ch'i concept of bureaucratic control would be irrevocably lost.

At a Central Committee plenary session in January 1961, which Mao Tse-tung did not attend, a report was approved recording economic setbacks and advocating a considerable scaling-down of projects started during the Great Leap Forward. To quote *China Reconstructs* of November 1967: 'He [Liu Shao-ch'i] advocated the extension of plots for private use and of free markets, the increase of small enterprises with sole responsibility for their own profits or losses and the fixing of output quotas on the basis of households and actively encouraged "going it alone". He said: "Sufficient retreat should be made in industry and also in agriculture, even to the extent of fixing output quotas on the basis of households and of going it alone!", "there is nothing to be frightened of if some bourgeois elements should emerge in society. There is no need to fear the flooding in of capitalism." ' Liu Shao-ch'i also advocated 'four freedoms': freedom of buying, selling or renting out land, freedom to employ hired hands, freedom to practise usury, and freedom for private trade.

At another stormy Central Committee Plenum in September 1962 which Mao *did* attend but in which he and his supporters were still in a minority, he uttered a warning that the class struggle in the countryside should never be overlooked, a direct slap at Liu Shao-ch'i's thesis that the main contradiction by that time was between 'the advanced socialist system and the backward social productive forces', another way of saying you cannot run big units like communes unless you first have all the mechanization and specialization necessary for large-scale farming. You cannot learn to fight by fighting, you must wait until you have enough tanks and planes!

By 1963 it had become a question of whether the Tachai or the Taoyuan way would prevail. Though the politically aware Chen Yung-kuei would grasp the objective importance of what he was doing, Kwan Ching-tung had no clear idea of the stakes involved or the role he was playing. Kwan had the feelings of his class – he was from upper-middle peasant stock. Chen Yung-kuei also had his class outlook – that of the poor peasant.

Following the 1964 harvest, Wang Kwang-mei returned to Taoyuan, this time setting up her headquarters in the Peitaiho police station, avoiding any pretence of practising the 'three withs'. The strange goings-on at Taoyuan had been reported back to the Hopei provincial party committee but the party secretary there preferred not to stick out his neck in an affair of such dimensions.

Despite declining production, Kwan Ching-tung continued to ride high, Wu Chen remaining in disgrace and the affairs of Taoyuan, run by Wang Kwang-mei through the 'consolidation group' under her personal control, ran on for a second period. Any member of the group who expressed reservations about what was happening was speedily replaced.

The situation remained the same for a couple more years, until students of Peking's Tsinghua University posted up their *ta tze pao* (big letter poster) denouncing Wang Kwang-mei. In the early days of the Cultural Revolution she had headed another 'work-team' sent into the university to stamp out the first sputtering fuses that were to detonate the explosion of revolt, using similar methods to those used at Taoyuan. She and her 'work-team' were thrown out by the students in August 1966, after Mao Tse-tung had put on a 'Red Guard' armband and reviewed 'Red Guard' contingents from Peking's Tien An Men Square, thus giving the highest sanction, as far as the masses were concerned, to the flames of revolt. The Cultural Revolution brought the fight out into the open. There came the sixteen-point document from the Communist Party Plenum setting out the guide-lines for action. This was sent to Taoyuan, as well as to factories and communes all over the country. Kwan Ching-tung refused to circulate it, putting himself at the head of his own 'Red Guard' unit instead. An opposition rebel group was formed to expose Kwan and his backers. Their activities came to a climax on 11 October 1966, when thousands of *ta tze pao* denouncing Wang Kwang-mei, Kwan Ching-tung and a few others as 'swindlers' and 'capitalist-roaders' were plastered up all over Taoyuan villages. They included some 300 drawings in which peasant artists portrayed with graphic realism some of the enormities that had gone on, showing how a veritable reign of terror had taken place at one period.

Three months later, a big meeting was held, with peasants and cadres from communes in surrounding counties assembled to hear, at first hand, the special form which the 'struggle between two lines' had assumed at Taoyuan. The charges against Wu Chen were swiftly dismissed as nonsense, and later he was unanimously elected chairman and vice-chairman of the revolutionary committee of Funing county. It was Kwan Ching-tung's turn to be sent to reform himself through labour.

When we first visited Taoyuan in 1968 we found that the revolutionary committee had been formed a few months earlier (on 1 March 1968). Wu Chen was very much in charge of the situation. A husky northerner, too lean for his size at that time, with a frank, open face, he was philosophical about his personal ordeal, but bitter in his denunciation of the Wang Kuang-mei line. He described good or bad times in the usual Chinese way, not in terms of his own misfortunes but through the level of grain yields and of deliveries to the state. In the first year after the real 'clean-up', production had increased to a little over 1·8 tons per acre and prospects for 1968 were for about 2 tons. Morale was high, unity had been restored, brigade members had worked as never before. Lu Chuo-yi, another vice-chairman of the county revolutionary committee, with Wu Chen and other participants in the struggle at his side, related what had gone on, at one point jerking his thumbs to the rafters over-head in the brigade meeting-room, where Wu Chen had been strung up on Wang Kwang-mei's orders.

'That's all over now,' said Wu Chen. 'Things are really moving again. The reservoir, which was started in 1958 and finished the following year, has proved decisive. Before 1959, the land was often flooded several times each rainy season. Right here where we are sitting at brigade headquarters, the water would come up into the houses. We alternated between flood and drought. The reservoir solved both by regulating the flow of water. But no state money went into that. If we got a bumper crop last year and are due for another this year, it's because 78 per cent of the fields are now irrigated and because our member-ship now put all of their spirit into their work.'

In the summer of 1973, we re-visited Peitaiho, its sunlit beaches and placid waters, and our friends at Taoyuan again.

Wu Chen, balding slightly but otherwise in better physical shape than five years earlier, was in radiant form. Despite drought and typhoon in the previous disaster year, they had harvested just over 2 tons of grain per acre, slightly down from the previous year but sure to be topped by a record crop for 1973. Fields were now 90 per cent irrigated, mainly from the Yang Ho reservoir, but also from thirty deep wells which the brigade members had sunk themselves.

'We have recently learned from Tachai,' he said. 'We now have stable, high-yield fields. No matter what sort of flood or drought, we can keep the land in good condition and raise good crops. Last year we had the worst drought anyone can remember. For the first time in my life even the old wells for drinking water dried up completely, but thanks to irrigation we got a fair harvest and no one went short of drinking water.

'Wang Kwang-mei had insisted that we follow Liu Shao-ch'i's line of "specialization" – we should stick to raising sorghum. But now we diversify. Wheat and rice account for 60 per cent of our grain production, maize, millet, soya beans and sorghum for the rest. In the old days most peasant families were lucky if they could get five pounds of rice a year and a bit of wheat flour for the New Year. Otherwise we ate millet and *kaoliang*. But even last year, we were able to distribute 130 pounds of rice and 50 pounds of wheat flour per head. And sell to the state 30 tons of grain above our quota of 190 tons.'

We asked what it all meant in terms of people's everyday life, apart from eating more rice and wheat and less *kaoliang* and millet. He rubbed his hand over his balding, dome-shaped pate and said: 'Nobody has any more worries about the sort of things that weighed on almost everyone in the past. They see the clear relation between what they are doing and improvement in living conditions. No worries about food, about clothing. No worries if someone gets sick – a thing that could ruin a family in the past. At that time those of us who used to work for the landlords lived in their old sheds and pigsties, in disused brick kilns or rough shelters made from any bits of scrap we could find. Now, 40 per cent of our members live in new houses built in the last few years, and the rest in decent housing built since liberation. Before, even if parents could scrape up money to pay the fees to send their kids to school, they had no money to buy them clothes and the schools simply would not admit them barefoot and in rags. Now, of course, all children are at school. Infant mortality in this area was 70 per cent before liberation. There was just one bicycle in Taoyuan – it belonged to a landlord's son. Now there are eighty bicycles, fifty-seven sewing-machines, thirty-eight radio sets and a communal T.V.' (The latter was fixed on a swivel so it could be turned from its corner in the brigade meeting hall into a window overlooking a big courtyard.)

We dropped into the commune school – it happened to be a playtime break. A healthier bunch of children you could never wish to see – the elder ones playing basket ball, volley ball and quoits, the younger ones shrieking away at ring-a-ring-a-roses or lined up for their turn at the twirling skipping-ropes. A whistle was blown and in the twinkling of an eye they had left their games and were lined up in rows and moving into their classrooms. 'When I think of my childhood ...,' said Wu Chen, who had accompanied us to the school, and left it at that. He showed us a square-shaped monument just opposite the school, with the characters 'Never Forget' carved into it. It had been erected by Kwan Ching-tung, out of the brigade's borrowed funds, to commemorate the 'honour' paid by Wang Kwang-mei in patronizing the Taoyuan brigade, just as a couple of hundred photos of her working in the fields had been distributed among her Peking admirers! We asked Wu Chen whether there were any who regretted her departure and the defeat of the Liu Shao-ch'i's line:

'A few who later were the loudest in criticizing the Liu line,' he replied, 'in fact still have a hankering after the privileges that smart operators used to get. People's ideas don't change all that quickly. Once they get used to the kick-backs, it's hard to get unused to them. But these represent a tiny handful who managed to wangle privileges even in the old days. The over-whelming majority saw that the Liu line was leading us back to capitalism. They rejected this and now keep their eyes open.'

As regards such questions as tractor maintenance, electric pumping stations, machinery for processing food and fodder crops, grain threshing and other purposes, Wu Chen was cate-goric:

'There's no problem at all. We had a few difficulties in the very early days – horse-drawn carts were about the only "machines" we knew about. But we soon learned, especially the young people. They learned from each other and from more experienced farm technicians elsewhere in the county. Our level of mechanization is still low. Sowing and harvesting is still done by hand. But we use tractors for ploughing and electricity for the irrigation pumps, threshing, winnowing and food-processing. We shall invest in seed-drills and mowers soon. Our members are much more machine-minded now and have no worries about taking on new types. We remain in close touch with county industry where the leadership keeps in mind the special kinds of machinery that our area needs.'

CHAPTER TEN

IN CASE OF WAR

In the shadows of the towering, grimly beautiful Taihangshan mountains, where the borders of Shansi, Hopei and Honan provinces meet, lies Linhsien county in Honan, the other side of the range from Hsiyang county in Shansi. As far as the drought-ridden, famine-plagued country was concerned, there used to be little to choose between the two counties. Today, if Hsiyang is famous for Tachai, Linhsien is no less so for the Red Flag Canal, hacked out of the sheer sides of those mountains, where both the Japanese and Kuomintang had come to grief. Water from the Chiang river, trapped in the canal, not only serves a whole county in Shansi, where it rises, but reaches every commune field in Linhsien county, converting it to another of those stable, high-yield areas which produce rich crops regardless of drought or flood. But water for Linhsien means more than abundant food.

At the Linhsien Cotton Textile Mill, the housewifely chairwoman of the revolutionary committee, Mrs Hsun Hei-hsi, explained: 'Water for us means not only rice, but cotton and cheap electric power. This used to be a tiny workshop, set up as a weaving co-operative by twelve peasant women in 1950 with three hand-operated looms and cotton yarn brought in from other counties. Now that we've got our own home-grown cotton, we have over 200 workers using ninety electrically driven spinning machines and looms. As in all other county industry,' she continued, 'our products go to serve agriculture directly.' At that time, the little plant was turning out 20,000 dozen small towels a year – the sort that the farming population in that area wear around their heads or necks and use to cover their pillows – as well as 90,000 dozen handkerchiefs and 50 tons of cotton yarn.

'It's all because of the canal. Who could have thought of growing cotton here before? Our little plant can only absorb a small part of the crop. But' – and she pointed out of the window where lines of donkey-drawn carts were queueing up to unload bricks on to fast-growing neat stacks – 'we are getting ready to expand.'

'Long before the building of the canal,' said Li Feng-chih, vice-chairman of the revolutionary committee of the Linhsien Chemical Fertilizer Plant, 'our peasants wanted chemical fertilizers, but what could we do without water or electricity? As the canal neared completion, we started work on this plant with local labour. Some People's Liberation Army men and a few miners came to give us a hand. The water and the cheap electricity started to flow and with these two combined with coal, which is plentiful around here, and air, we could produce sulphate of ammonia. We produce 12,000 tons of chemical fertilizer a year now and' – he also pointed to new buildings going up – 'we'll increase that to 20,000 tons next year.' This was the smaller of two chemical fertilizer plants at the county centre.

Another plant which owed its rapid growth to the canal was the Tung Feng (East Wind) Agricultural Implements Factory. It had been formed in 1943, as a tiny co-op with five blacksmiths, an anvil and bellows and two hammers between them, one of many thousands set up within the framework of the 'Industrial Co-operatives' movement.[1] Vice-chairman Kuo Lin-yung, a stocky, veteran worker, explained that: 'The chain reaction of water, followed by electric power, has transformed the requirements of the farmers and forced us to make equipment that we never dreamed of before. Even more than other county industry our task is exclusively to serve agriculture. Setting up the communes gave us our first big push forward – from a blacksmiths' co-op to a county-run farm implements factory. Now the communes and brigades have much better machine shops than our old co-op. We have designed a whole range of power presses for them which supersede the old

1. See Chapter 4.

hammer-and-anvil technique. When canal-building started, we sent our technicians to see what part we could play. By the time the builders were ready to put in sluice gates, we had the frames ready, with water regulators of a dozen different calibres.'

From five blacksmiths the labour force had grown to over 200 workers. Set out in well-lit workshops, 60 per cent of the machine-tools had been made in the plant, including the castings for special-purpose lathes and other tools. They had also made their overhead crane, with a hoist capacity of 510 tons, and a power press of 150 tons. Smaller ones of 75 tons were banging away at 210 strokes per minute as we passed through the workshops.

In a big courtyard, several hundred peasants, many of them in the traditional white smock-type tunics, with towels around their heads in the style of the North China peasants, were eyeing a machine-driven mowing-machine which was being tested. Kuo Lin-yung explained that they were part of 1,500 delegates to a conference of poor and middle peasants then being held at Linhsien. It was rather moving to see the gleam in their eyes, the smiles lighting up the wrinkled faces of the older people, as they turned from the mower to inspect chaff-cutters, threshing and winnowing machines, set out in the courtyard.

'We have no lack of customers,' continued Kuo Lin-yung. 'Our problem lies in the gap between the growing appetites of the communes and our capacity to produce. Apart from giving the communes everything they need to make many types of implements themselves and maintain them, we have to turn out a whole variety of machines to ease the burden on the women-folk and free them for productive labour. It is not fair on them that they lose work-points by having to spend a lot of time on housework. At brigade and even team level, they need electrically powered machines to make noodles and flour, for pressing soya beans and peanuts for cooking oil and making soya sauce and vinegar. Everything must be done to make even the smallest units as self-reliant as possible.'

A surprise find at county level, but something which illustrated the last point made by Kuo Lin-yung, was the Linhsien Electric Light Bulb Factory, expanded from a carpenters' workshop that had previously turned out wooden plough frames and some other wooden farm tools. Lin Tung-p'ai, the self-effacing plant chairman, explained that the initiative had come from the carpenters when they realized that with water would come electric power, so light bulbs would be needed. The party line was to encourage people to be bold, develop initiative, discard conventions, 'dare to storm heights', and so the carpenters had put up a project to send some of the members of their families to an electric light bulb factory in Nanking for a training of one to five months to find out how they were made. The water would also mean good crops, the farmers would have more money to spend, all the communes would want electricity for lighting. The county officials agreed. While their families studied the art of bulb-making, the carpenters went ahead with building the factory, according to dimensions relayed back from Nanking. As an awesome example of how fast things move these days, the building started in February 1970 and the plant produced its first bulbs in July of the same year.

'Of course making light bulbs for commune homes was serving agriculture indirectly,' continued Lin Tung-p'ai, 'but we wanted to serve it more directly. With the water, insects also came. How to maintain high productivity with so many insects feeding off the crops? We studied how to kill them by using the attraction light has for all insects. We discovered that one low-powered neon tube attracts every insect within an area of 10 acres. We developed two methods, a tube set against a one-metre panel of glass, with a vat of chemically treated water underneath into which the insects fall after knocking their heads against the glass, and a tube set within a very slightly electrically charged frame which electrocutes them. We produce 250,000 of these tubes annually and they are very popular among commune members.' (As far as you can see over Linhsien county on a summer night, the fields are lit up like some vast flat city.)

The county had invested in the equipment suggested by the Nanking factory – a furnace for making the tubing was made locally – and in three workshops 170 workers and staff were turning out 200,000 bulbs of from 25 to 300 watts annually, apart from the neon light insect-killers.

Altogether thirty factories had sprung up in Linhsien county in the wake of the waters and electric power from the Red Flag Canal, including small steel and cement works, employing altogether 7,000 workers. In the neighbouring county of Anyuan, over 150 factories had been set up since 1958. They included an iron and steel works, plant for ball-bearings, machine-tools, diesel engines, cement, chemical fertilizers and bicycles, and a great number of others producing over 500 types of consumer goods, from cigarettes and matches to soap and textiles. Anyuan had grown from a city of 60,000 at the time of liberation, when it was without electricity, roads or paved streets, to a modern centre of 400,000 people, including those in the outskirts, 100,000 of whom belonged to industrial worker families.

An unusual example of the sort of initiative that has come from county industry is the tremendous development of re-inforced-concrete boats, the manufacture of which started at Wusih county in Kiangsu province – a province with around 50 million population, where practically everything is moved by boat. The county is very poor in timber resources, and the problem of replacing old boats and catering to the ever-increasing demands for lighter and barge transport seemed insoluble until some bold spirits during the Great Leap Forward put forward the idea of concrete boats. There was no lack of boat-builders to fashion frames out of steel mesh made from wire produced by the Wusih steel plant – itself a product of the Great Leap Forward. The boats are built upside down, the cement being sprayed over the steel mesh frames. When they have dried, the boats are righted and float as well as any other craft. After a couple of experimental shells had been made, in 1958, a full-scale tug-boat was turned out. It was still chugging away pulling strings of barges in the Wusih area in the summer of 1973.

Now these boats are produced by the hundreds of thousands, in all shapes and sizes. At one of the Wusih factories we watched the finished boats being lowered by lifts to the river. Following the Wusih county example, they are also being turned out in counties and communes all over the eastern coastal areas. Girls who used to sit around their front doors doing embroidery are now weaving steel mesh or spraying cement on to steel frames at the commune boat-building works. They require no more horse-power than ordinary boats of the same size and have proved to be more stable in stormy waters than wooden boats. They are easily and cheaply repaired and last much longer. Their only drawback is that they need more careful handling when approaching other boats or jetties because of the impetus the extra weight gives them. One sees them everywhere, laden to the gunwales, bringing into the communes the precious silt-manure dredged from the bottoms of canals or fishing on Lake Taihu and the myriad rivers and canals. They range from small two-tonners to sixty-ton lighters. The success of the very big industrialization projects along the Yangtze valley also depends on cheap transport, a problem well on the way to being solved by the cheap and efficient tugs and lighters which the substituting of concrete for wood or steel has made possible.

It is by no means only in the more sophisticated centres that such things are being manufactured locally to give people the essentials for their work and living. It goes on in the remotest areas. On the Old Silk Road in West Kansu in the far north-west, at a town which Marco Polo refers to as Camptieu and which was also known as Kanchow but has now reverted to its original name of Changyeh ('Knockout Blow under the Armpit'), we found that some local wood-working co-operatives had joined together and were making everything necessary for the timber industry. They had their own foundry, made their own castings and had built machine-tools, with a smooth, stream-lined finish just as good as those from Shanghai or Peking. It had developed from a modest machine-shop in 1956, with fifty-eight workers, to a big plant with just over 500 workers, 85 per cent of them young people. When we asked why there was such a high proportion of youth, the reply was that as they trained workers up to a certain standard, they let many of them go back to their communes to develop machine-shops there. With their locally made machine-tools, they turned out buzz-planers, electric band-saws, portable electric tree-felling saws –

everything imaginable for the wood-working industry. They provided machine-tools to the communes so that they could repair their tractors, diesel engines and processing machinery without coming into the regional centre.

Steel is likewise being made all over the country, in medium-sized plants in virtually every province and in many counties. In Chungking, the old iron and steel works, which the Kuomintang used to show correspondents as proof of their determination to carry on the war against Japan and which produced just 5,700 tons of steel in the last year of Kuomintang rule, turned out over 400,000 tons in 1972, and with two new Bessemer converters, which were being added when we visited the plant in the summer of 1973, production will soon be increased to 700,000 tons. New rolling mills were also being built, to bring rolled steel capacity up to 800,000 tons by 1974.

We asked Liu Cheh, now deputy chief of the managing committee, if it was fair to compare what was produced under Kuomintang rule in wartime conditions with what is being done today.

'From 1940, when what was called Arsenal No. 29 – although it never did produce weapons – was set up here,' he replied, 'until the end of 1949, by which time most of China had been liberated, the plant actually operated for just 398 days. To give one example. It was supposed to produce rails for an old project of linking Chungking with the provincial capital, Chengtu, by train. In all those years only 690 tons of rails were turned out – all of them sub-standard and useless. But there was no shortage of raw materials or skilled workers. Although the Kuomintang blew up the power plant before they left early in 1950, and sabotaged other equipment, we produced 13,000 tons of standard-quality rails in that year. By May 1952, we had produced enough to enable the 505-kilometre-long Chungking–Chengtu railway to be built – the first railway ever to be built in China with our own rails. Within three years of taking over we were producing twenty-three times the weight of steel products compared to the best year of Kuomintang-run operations. The main reason was the difference in the morale of the workers who had taken power in the new society.'

At Chungking there was at least something to build on. Coal and iron-ore mines had been opened up, and there was a nucleus of iron and steel-making equipment and of skilled workers. But at Lanchow, in West Kansu, the small Tungkang Iron and Steel Works had been started from scratch during the Great Leap Forward. Closed down under Liu Shao-ch'i's recession measures before it was even in production, it started working after the Cultural Revolution, turning out 10,000 tons of steel in 1969. By the time we visited it in 1973, this had been stepped up to an annual rate of 45,000 tons, due to rise to 60,000 tons in 1974, 100,000 tons in 1975 and on to 150,000 tons, at which level the management hoped to be meeting anticipated regional needs.

There is no doubt that Western cost-accountants could fault almost everything connected with small and medium-scale steel production and regional and county industry – and, indeed, many other aspects of the Chinese economy. As we are not economists, we cannot argue. But knowing something of China's sufferings at the hands of foreign invaders, we can appreciate the economic–military logic of a Chinese contact of ours who reflected top-level official thinking, when we mentioned how impressed we were at the extent to which diversified industry was flourishing even in the remotest regions.

'Within the first few hours of another war, we must reckon with the destruction of traditional heavy industry centres such as Anshan and others in the north-east, and in the coastal cities,' he replied. 'We must foresee that the bridges over the Yangtze and Yellow rivers will be destroyed, cutting China – for a start – into three distinct economic regions: north of the Yellow river, between the Yellow and Yangtze rivers, and south of the Yangtze. So each of these regions should become completely self-supporting. Within each of these regions, the heartlands and the back country must be independent of the coastal cities as far as industry is concerned. The coastal cities should be independent of the heartlands as far as foodstuffs are concerned. Down to the smallest units possible, each should be capable of feeding, clothing, housing – and defending – itself. If we can achieve this we are invulnerable no matter what happens.'

By now it is probably clear to readers that in all developments described so far, from Taching to Tachai, from the setting-up of communes to the vast expansion of county industry, the master strategic mainspring was the Great Leap Forward. This probably comes as a surprise, because in the outside world there was a general impression that it was one of Mao's failures – a viewpoint which was discreetly encouraged by leaks to journalists from official Chinese sources, not to mention those by diplomatic contacts in Peking who had obvious axes to grind.

According to our own on-the-spot observations at the time and follow-up investigations ever since, the Great Leap Forward was an epoch-making success, the full dimensions of which are only dimly being realized in the outside world.[2] Much that surprises visitors in the post-Nixon visit era has its origins in economic foundations laid during the Great Leap Forward. Virtually all major irrigation and road-building projects, all key economic developments, including the tremendous upsurge of regional industry reaching into the remotest corners of China, had their genesis in this imaginative movement. Mao, in keeping with his style, said nothing publicly to rebut his critics, preferring to let history record the final verdict.

Among other things, the Great Leap Forward served as a great school for breaking old conventions and adopting new methods all over the country. On the technical side, it gave peasants confidence in their ability to do things which they previously thought only urban workers could do. The fact that iron and steel was made all over the countryside – though the

2. My investigations at that time were limited to visiting communes and other economic enterprises in the immediate vicinity of Peking. Rewi Alley, however, travelled very widely in China in 1958–9 and recorded his findings in a little-known book: *China's Hinterland in the Great Leap Forward* (New World Press, Peking, 1961). It was published in a very small edition, after great difficulties and delays – explicably only later when the full extent of the hostility of Liu Shao-ch'i and the Communist Party leadership of the Peking Municipality to the Great Leap Forward became known. This book remains the only eye-witness account of what went on in widely separated areas of China, and the reference material included is one of the precious aspects of Rewi Alley's contribution to the present work.

quality was often very low – had tremendous value even if it was only to de-mystify the secrets of technique. Some critics used to point to stacks of unused iron and steel ingots in many parts of the countryside as an example of the futility of it all. But very quickly such stocks disappeared, transformed into such things as cart axles, rims of wheels or plough-shares. After all, it was never intended as armour-plating for tanks or battle-ships!

That peasants could smelt iron and steel in primitive furnaces in their own backyards was a revelation, a starting-point in mastering technique from which they never turned back. The backyard furnaces, which, as we reported at the time, were intended only as a temporary phase in rural steel-making, were aimed at giving the country-folk confidence that they could do anything once they put their muscles and minds to it. In this sense the Great Leap Forward represented an industrial revolution which consolidated the country's economic and social system. Instead of moving the countryside to the urban industrial centres, entailing the havoc of a European-style industrial revolution, it put industry squarely inside the countryside. Like the setting-up of the communes, it marked a giant step towards one of the avowed aims of socialist society – to diminish, and finally eliminate, the difference between rural and urban workers, between town and countryside.

It worked at every level. For centuries Chinese village black-smiths had done the sort of things village blacksmiths do all over the world – hammer red-hot iron and steel bars into horse-shoes, hoes and other farm implements. As part of his contribution to the Great Leap Forward, one member of the blacksmith fraternity started banging out ball-bearings in different-calibred hemispheres gouged out of his anvil. Sacrilege! An insult to one of the most sophisticated of engineering techniques! The idea caught on all over China. Banging out assemblies was child's play. The result is that millions of horse, donkey and camel-drawn carts – which still bear the major burden of rural transport in China – now glide, instead of creaking, along the country's myriad highways and byways.

In the book mentioned above, Rewi Alley gives an eye-witness account of the development of industry during the Great Leap Forward:[3]

'The Great Leap Forward had its genesis in China's Second Five-Year Plan for 1958–62, which set a high rate for economic expansion, with the target sights repeatedly raised during 1958 on the basis of performance during the early months of the plan. This culminated in Mao's call to "go all out, aiming high and achieve greater, faster and more economical results", as part of the programme for building socialism in China. People at all levels responded.

'Shortage of trained technical personnel was acute. But one technician trained twenty others. City blacksmiths, for instance, were concentrated to help the countryside make, for a start, deep-ploughing ploughs, small one-horse reapers for hilly areas, drills for sowing, pumps for irrigation, ball-bearings for everything with wheels.

'This was child's play compared to what followed. Nearing Wuwei, in West Kansu, the ancient capital of the sixth century Western Liang kingdom, we found carts and people converging on a stretch of stony waste ground west of the city wall where a row of tall furnaces was beginning to grow and foundations for many others were being laid. The big Ming Dynasty bricks from the old city wall were being brought over to the site by streams of carriers – city lads, lasses and farmers. A long train of *la-la-che* (rubber-tyred carts with truck axles, drawn by three camels) was bringing in refractory bricks. Then came a line of small donkey-carts mounted on what once might have been ricksha wheels.

'In near-by villages we found broken cooking pans being smelted into metal for ball-bearings, the latter produced in hand-operated presses, then hand-polished and case-hardened. To casual observers these small industries might not seem to amount to much – perhaps just a few farmers turning out chemical fertilizer in the corner of a compound; a batch of women hammering out ball-bearings; some middle-school students turning out packages of artificial medical cotton from

3. See p. 163 note. Some of the paragraphs which follow have been altered slightly for present purposes.

wood for the local hospitals; a small paper mill; a little hydro-electric plant beside the stream and a porcelain kiln turning out insulators and cleats for electric wiring on the bank above. But altogether they are the start of an interlocking system of local industry that will increasingly bring the machine into the village, changing outlooks, creating a new unity between town and country, worker and farmer.

'Continuing our tour, we arrived at night at Tzuchang, north of Yenan in Shensi province. Before turning in we had a look around. It was bright moonlight and all around the sides of the valley flames of charcoal-burning and iron-smelting leaped up. The smoke haze floated even up along the rear valleys. Some of the coke ovens looked like long dragons coming down the hillside. Real "leap forward" dragons.

'We arrived at Taiyuan (Shansi) on 31 October 1958, just as the local iron and steel works was about to celebrate the "final high wave" of steel-smelting in the area. We set off for the works. The big compound was full of smoke and flame. Bessemer furnaces shot their flames upward and molten steel poured. The local works manager came up to explain that the little band of twenty-year-olds, with helmets and blue denims, were proud of the fact that they were getting steel in a ten minutes' blow instead of the usual fifteen or twenty minutes. From the administration buildings we went to the big steel works themselves. Every available bit of space in the compounds was occupied by gleaming Bessemer-type furnaces, and even local adaptations of electric ones, turning out steel. Above them electric lights were festooned, and with the background of the steel works in action behind them, they presented a vivid and unforgettable picture, rich in fierce colour and action, with helmeted figures, towels tied around their necks, stepping out of the shadows into the brilliant flashes given off by the smelters. There were literally thousands of folk working, most of them off-duty steel workers. Having done their regular eight hours in the works, they were now with family members, friends, neighbours – all of them making steel, fast and surprisingly efficiently.

'We went through and watched both steel- and iron-smelting.

As the furnaces were about to be tapped, the drums and cymbals brought into the works for the occasion crashed out in welcome to the river of steel that shot down into big buckets below. Steel-making in that memorable year became an object of national pride – every heat a victory to be celebrated.

'The Shansi target for steel that year was 1,500,000 tons, of which the Taiyuan works were to produce one third. On the day of our visit, at the crest of this effort, 10,000 tons had been produced, no less than 60 per cent of which came from the small temporary furnaces, and 40 per cent from the great modern works.

'Towards dusk we went off to the historical museum set in modernized ancient ruins. The leap forward had also meant the better conservation of historical and cultural evidence and this museum had done splendidly in its display of the materials unearthed by new construction. Iron rollers in a bronze casing for hub bearings were certainly a new discovery from the Warring Kingdoms Period (475–221 B.C.), as were the saw-tooth cogwheels of a kind we had not seen before. One of the most magnificent pieces in the T'ang Dynasty (A.D. 618–907) exhibits was a large glazed pottery camel, with a jaunty Middle Eastern trader wearing a high horned hat sitting on top of the load. Shansi province is rich in minerals, especially in coal, iron and copper, and perhaps this throws light on the riddle of how man in the early historical period got his metal to make the significant bronzes, unique in our world, which we saw displayed in another museum housed in an old temple.

'Approximately 40 per cent of the total population in southeast Shansi had had a direct hand in the iron and steel programme by the time of our visit. When the iron-smelting began there it was tentatively decided that 100,000 tons should be smelted in 1958. This target was changed at a meeting of the leaders of the people concerned to 210,000 tons, then to 280,000 and finally to 530,000 tons. By 31 October, at the end of the first high wave, production totalled 530,000 tons and by the end of the year would exceed 700,000 tons; 122,280 tons of steel had been made in this same area, much in advance of the 70,000 tons first aimed at. It was something to learn that sixteen communes in the area had each produced 10,000 tons of iron in their best day on the last wave forward.

'It should be understood that there were two kinds of steel production in each county. The first was the long-term plan which set out to make all-weather tall furnaces, improving them with each bit of experience gained, adding better blowers, hot blast and so on, furnaces that would make the base for the regular iron and steel works. The second was the temporary mass movement for smelting, rising in great waves, that came to a climax in set periods, one county competing with another, one commune with another, showing what can really be done when all get together on a set job. On the way to Yangcheng county we had noted that the piles of iron and steel by the highway had grown in the few days since we had passed through the area and that the big heaps of scrap, old pots and pans had decreased. One no longer had to wait for years in what popular magazines used to call "Old Unchanging China". Two or three days were enough!

'The picture was the same in fourteen provinces and two municipalities we visited during the Great Leap period, from Kansu in the north-west, Liaoning in the north-east, Szechuan in the south-west. Kwantung in the south-east and many points in between. At Hofei, in Anhwei, adjoining the coastal province of Chekiang, we watched iron ore coming down the Huai river from Fengyang to the city wharves and being literally hauled by the population to the smelting fields in the outskirts. There is no other way to describe the sight of every kind of cart pulled by every kind of person – farmers, traders, bespectacled city folk, men and women – converging on the seventy new semi-modern furnaces. All the latter had hot-blast and modern blower equipment, and most had automatic feeding hoists. The area in this particular field is large, the furnaces are well constructed and evenly spaced. The year 1959 would bring to this plant five 250-tons-per-day iron smelters as well as a large steel furnace. Production would then be half a million tons of iron a year. The steel target for 1959 was set for 200,000 tons, with two rolling mills to be installed and 30,000 workers compared to the 2,000 at the time of our visit.

'At Hofei itself, everyone had seemed to be on the move; the new railway station was crowded with people coming and going. With the cold weather starting, more bedding and clothing had gone into the roll each person carried, people and baggage sorting themselves out automatically and either getting clear of the station or onto trains and away. Hofei, famous for its role in the battles of the Three Kingdoms period and as a place where the Taipings fought a century earlier, had now changed from a relatively small county centre of around 70,000 to become the provincial capital with a population of over 500,000 – a city of wide streets and modern buildings.

'The dismantling of many of the smaller commune furnaces later was hailed by the critics as proof of the failure of the "backyard smelters". It was, in fact, part of the planned development. Not far from the big Hofei Iron and Steel Works, around which scores of satellite iron and steel works had sprung up, we had seen for the first time, in the spring of 1959, big groups of commune folk dismantling the small iron-smelting furnaces which had been erected in their thousands the previous September and levelling off the ground for ploughing again. It was another stage. China by then had not only its iron and steel giants like Anshan in the north-east, Paotow in Inner Mongolia and Wuhan in Hupei, but also great fields of modern small furnaces, with fuller mechanization than the old, that had grown up out of the movement to make iron and steel.

'We had seen from the road one of the first of these new fields, climbing up from the Anhwei plains into hills ringing the valley of Chaotouchi, described by our driver, whose home village was there, as having been one of the poorest spots in the whole region. Now the valley was dotted with steel furnaces, abundant deposits of iron ore, asbestos, gypsum and dolomite having been found – not to mention coal, which is plentiful in North China. In Chaohsien, another Anwhei county, three more such modern steel works had been set up, serving another 150 industrial plants in the county, all built during the Great Leap.

'As a last example of industrial development in the unlikeliest and most remote area, we could take that at Hsiakuan, just off the Burma Road, about half-way between the Burmese border and Kunming, capital of the south-westernmost province of Yunnan. A big new industrial complex of seven factories had sprung into life here by the time of our visit in the spring of 1959 – a rolling mill turning out steel rods, other plants for ball-bearings, electrical appliances, glass-making, agricultural implements and a sugar-refining mill. And the biggest of them all, an iron and steel works.

'Started during the height of the Great Leap Forward the previous year, with small native furnaces, it had already developed into the embryo of a modern plant, staffed by 1,336 workers, representing all the nationalities of the region. As was so often the case, it was run without a single engineer, the workers from peasant stock having trained themselves. They were operating a battery of Bessemer converters and a rolling mill made by themselves – a more modern one was being installed at the time of our visit – and they had just finished building a battery of modern iron smelters. Finding that waste marble from the marble quarries, plentiful in this area, is the best kind of limestone, they were cracking it up by hand hammers for the furnaces, pending the making of crushers. Management and most of the workers were living with peasants from an adjacent village, no time or labour-power yet having been diverted to building accommodation. In their work-clothes it was impossible to distinguish a Pai from a Han, or a Hui or Yi – six months of working together on iron and steel making made them look alike. Iron-ore comes from communes in the northern part of the region; other raw materials are on the spot. Planned steel production for 1959 was 20,000 tons, half of which was to be converted into steel bars.

'Further east, the road to Kunming from a big iron and steel works at Amning was lined with factories, some completed and in production, others being built. The spreading, modern workshops of the machine-tool works were similar to those in other provincial centres. The foundations of another mighty industrial hub, whose influence would be felt in every commune of multi-national Yunnan, were being well and truly laid, the spade-work done by ordinary men and women, who with all their human virtues and failings were universally alike in one thing, their desire to work hard and create a new land.'

A major result of the ambitious undertakings of the Great Leap Forward was a re-shaping of the whole economic infrastructure, including a re-shaping of the outlook and technical capacities of the hundreds of millions of Chinese from every strata of society who took part. Nothing could ever be the same again. A new dimension was added to the peasantry and this dwarfed into insignificance any material wastes and losses.

There was also the vitally important aspect of the decentralization of industrial development as a factor in national defence, mentioned earlier and well summarized in a book by Jean Esmein.[4] A former officer who had served as naval attaché at the French Embassy in Tokyo long before his appointment as press attaché in Peking, Esmein looks at this aspect through the eyes of a professional soldier. His judgement, based on analysis of published material available in Peking, fits in with our own, based on exhaustive on-the-spot investigations.

'If the whole country is made up of independent cells, leaving between them a sort of loose-knit fabric into which the invasion forces could flow,' writes Esmein, 'but which have solid nuclei, relying only on themselves for supplies and making their own weapons, playing hide-and-seek with the enemy and rendering occupation untenable, the country is capable of a very long resistance war. Decentralization, industrialization spread everywhere at the lowest level, the good technical education of small agricultural communities acquired in learning to repair agricultural machinery – these are elements in preparation for resistance.'

Esmein notes the difference between Western strategy, which relies on long-range warning systems and the increased range-effectiveness of their defensive forces to protect established industrial, communication and other nerve centres, and Mao's

4. *La Révolution culturelle*, by Jean Esmein, Éditions Seuil, Paris, 1970. The quotes which follow are from pp. 34 and 36. Esmein also cites the experience of North Vietnam in dispersing its industry in tunnels and grottoes to maintain production, the success of which we can confirm by our personal investigations.

defensive strategy 'based on the cell-like fabric and dispersal of industry in the countryside'.

One must add to this the fact that wherever the People's Liberation Army is garrisoned, and this applies especially to sensitive coastal and other frontier areas, it has organized contact with the People's Militia of the communes. Each company has contact with a production team which itself has a militia unit. The P.L.A. company helps to train a proportion of that militia unit as military specialists. At a higher level the P.L.A. units runs general staff courses for militia leaders. Once or twice a year, according to the region, the same unit conducts large and small-scale military manoeuvres with the commune militia units.

The key point of Mao's military strategy – that in the long run the decisive element is the capacity of the people to survive, to feed and defend themselves and continue production – was embodied in the achievements of the Great Leap Forward and consolidated during the Cultural Revolution.

CHAPTER ELEVEN

THE NEW RULERS

We had a glimpse into Mao's thinking a good three years before the Cultural Revolution shook the country. We have a diplomat friend who has had long discussions with Mao Tse-tung and we spoke to him during a rare leave from his ambassadorial post abroad. Mao, we were told, had been pondering over the causes of dissension with the Soviet Union and the course which the Chinese revolution was taking. He told us of Mao's concern that there was now a generation of Chinese youth without any experience of revolutionary struggle. And was Marxism–Leninism a valid theory for the present day and age? If not, had they the courage to say so? If so, had they the courage to go ahead and put theory into practice? Were the differences between town and countryside, between urban and rural workers, between workers and intellectuals, being diminished? How likely was it that a self-perpetuating élite would emerge and provide the basis for revisionism? How could this be prevented?

'These are the sort of questions occupying Chairman Mao's mind at the moment,' said our diplomat friend. 'He is particularly worried by the last question. One way of preventing the development of a ruling-class ideology among administrative workers is to send them off to the countryside for one month in the year to plant trees, work on dam-building, help with the harvesting and so on. But often they regard that as a sort of holiday and go back to their offices with the same ideas with which they left. Mao is deliberating over various ways to try to remedy that – six months in the office, six months on factory or farm, or half a day in the office and half a day of physical labour, so that administrative workers can really get close to the workers and peasants.

'Take my case,' he continued. 'I came into the revolution straight from being a student. Afterwards I became a professional revolutionary. I have never worked with my hands. Until those discussions with Chairman Mao, I had never put my nose inside a factory, although one of my jobs at a certain period was to be a leading trade-union functionary! A factory seemed a strange, fearsome world to me. I went and had a look. The first thing that struck me was the terrible noise. I wondered what I could ever do in a factory. But looking round I saw things that even I could do – sweeping up metal shavings from lathes, for instance. It's not just about me and cadres in the administration that Mao is worrying, but also the managers of factories and communes. At all costs he wants to prevent the crystallization of a privileged managerial class.'

When we suggested that perhaps the availability of higher education to the children of workers and peasants would mean a continual injection of fresh blood into management, our diplomat friend laughed and said: 'That was our old mandarin system. In theory everyone who passed the exams could become an official, but once that happened, whatever his social origins, he identified himself with the ruling class.'

While we cannot guarantee the accuracy of our friend's interpretation of Mao's thinking in the autumn of 1963 – when the conversation took place – it did help us to make sense of the Cultural Revolution when it exploded, a major result of which was a revolution in factory management. Whereas the People's Communes are collectively owned co-operatives, the big factories are state-owned. There are now parallel systems of management – by the Communist Party branch committee, which decides overall policy within the framework of the state plan, and by the revolutionary committee, which handles executive management. Members of the latter are elected at general meetings of the workers, and in the period immediately following the Cultural Revolution this was done on what was called the 'three-in-one' formula of an equal proportion of workers, technicians and former administrative cadres. Members of the management committees receive the same wages as they had earned at their factory bench or whatever work they had been engaged in, and spend about one third of their time – in rotation – working at their usual job. Normally they are elected for a one-year period, but they may be voted out of office at any time if a majority of workers feel they have fallen down on the job. (It is rare that this happens, we found, because the rank-and-file workers elect only those who have proved by their work and attitude to fellow-workers that they are worthy of confidence.)

Wages in the factories are fixed according to three criteria: technical skill, length of service, and attitude towards work and fellow-workers. A worker, for instance, whose own productivity is not very high, but who devotes much time to helping younger or less skilled workers, would get a higher rating than another who concentrated on high output but neglected helping others to catch up. Wage levels are set by the revolutionary committee on the recommendations of the rank-and-file workers.

In the scores of factories we visited following the Cultural Revolution we invariably found that the highest wages went to veteran workers – at about the age they would be retiring in many Western factories – for their skills and the accumulated experience they were passing on to younger members. They would usually receive almost twice the pay of the average member of the revolutionary committee, who tended to be younger men, although there was usually a sprinkling of veterans.

At the Chien Shih Machine-Building Plant at Shanghai, for instance, the highest-paid worker was a veteran getting 137 yuan per month; the lowest – in his first year after apprenticeship – earned 42 yuan. The average for the whole plant was 65 yuan. If one excluded apprentices and workers in their first post-apprentice year, the average wage taken home was 70 to 80 yuan. In comparison with pre-liberation wages this was enormously high, but if translated into any Western money at the official exchange rate, incredibly low. On the other hand, rents and other living costs translated at the same exchange rate seem even more unbelievably low. Ling Hsiao-ssu, turner and fitter and member of the revolutionary committee at the Chien Shih plant, earned 78 yuan per month, his wife 62. Monthly rent was 3·30 yuan, another 2·70 went for lighting, heating and cooking.

He paid 12 yuan per month for three meals a day at the factory canteen, working eight hours per day, six days a week. Medical treatment for his wife and himself is free, and their four children are treated at half-price. At sixty, he could retire with a pension of 70 per cent of his wage at the time of retirement, which lent added importance to the system of highest wages for veteran workers. His wife could retire on the same basis when she reached fifty-five. Two of the children received free schooling at a secondary school, the others at primary school. He owned a wrist-watch, bicycle and radio and had a little over 1,000 yuan in the bank, earning $3\frac{1}{2}$ per cent interest. After visiting workers' homes in Shanghai, Peking, Nanking, Chungking, Harbin, Lanchow and many other places, we became satisfied that Ling Hsiao-ssu was China's Mr Average Worker in 1972–3. Mrs Ling had fifty-six days' paid maternity leave when the children were born. Had she been doing heavy work, she would have had seventy days off.

'Of course, the criteria for my salary is the same as for any other worker,' Ling Hsiao-ssu replied to our question. 'We are promoted to management by the workers, so it is natural that we get the same wages.' In that plant, apart from returning to the work benches for a three months' spell every year, management cadres also did their ordinary factory work two days a week. 'In this way,' explained Li Fu-ling, the burly chairman of the revolutionary committee, 'it is impossible to lose contact with the workers and the real problems of the factory.'

One continually runs into the same slogan in every factory: 'Maintain Independence: Keep the Initiative in Your Own Hands: Self-Reliance' – the national guide-line in all branches of activity since the Cultural Revolution. We asked Li Fu-ling what that meant in practical terms.

'The principle is to ask the state for as little help as possible – none at all if you can do without it. It means to raise the spirit of the working group in such a way that they will design and build the machinery needed in your own workshops. It means keeping the factory as self-reliant as possible, the economic region as self-reliant as possible. It means the opposite of the Liu Shao-ch'i line, which was to have industry grouped in big trusts under central ministries, financed exclusively by state investments and with the highest stress on specialization.'

At the Peking 'East Is Red' plant for making jeeps, we were given other examples of the difference in approach to industry. We had a discussion with several members of the revolutionary committee, together with the heads of most of the workshops, and, as we went through the plant, we spoke to workers at their machines. Until the Great Leap Forward it had been a vehicle-repair plant, but with the release of energy and initiative that the Great Leap produced everywhere they succeeded in turning out a car – just to show it could be done. From then on it was transformed into a motor-car plant. It was explained that from 1961 onwards Liu Shao-ch'i had visited the plant several times and gradually changed its functions to making certain assembly parts, relying on other specialized plants scattered all over the country for many others. 'There were constant bottle-necks in production,' explained Li Chan-wei, who worked in the equipment department and was a member of the revolutionary committee. 'There was a constant lack of things we wanted and a surfeit of things we had never ordered. The workers demanded that we make everything ourselves. But casting and forging was neglected. The specialists were in control and there was no contact with the workers, no channels for initiative from below to come up to the designing boards of the specialists. Management and specialists were physically and mentally separated from what went on in the workshops. During the Cultural Revolution, the workers rose up against this system and demanded that the plant become an autonomous unit, making all assembly parts and the necessary tools ourselves. The specialists came from their offices to the factory floor. We elected our own management. With veteran workers and specialists working as a team, we soon developed all sorts of technical innovations, designed and built our own machines and started turning out jeeps.'

In the assembly workshop we came across a group poring over large blue-prints spread over a work-bench. One was a be-spectacled technician graduate from Tsinghua University of Technology, another a member of the revolutionary committee putting in his two days a week on the job, the two others were rank-and-file workers. They were going over the final details of a new assembly line on which the two workers would eventually serve. Technician Yang Yu-chan said: 'In the old days I used to design tools in my office, the way I learned at the university. The first time I actually went into a workshop, I found that lots of my tools had been set aside and the workers had made simpler, lighter and more efficient ones. The idea of specialists in ivory towers has gone for ever. I can be helpful with some theoretical knowledge, but the workers can be more helpful with their practical know-how. Working together, there is nothing we cannot do.'

The ivory-tower role of specialists was one thing that the rank-and-file workers held against Liu Shao-ch'i. Another was the question of material incentives. In a machine-shop, where lines of machine-tools, a high proportion of them made in the factory, were humming away, we asked Hou Fa-hsin, a vice-chairman of the revolutionary committee, what was the real objection to material incentives: 'It was poison and created lots of dissatisfaction. Take old Liao there for example,' and he guided us towards a multiple drilling machine, where an old worker, with a lined face, was intently watching a diminutive young girl, very pretty in her white cap and trim blue denims – streaks of grease on her rosy cheeks. 'Every worker that passes through old Liao's hands can be tabbed "excellent". He takes the greatest pains with the young workers. Because of that his own productivity was always low. Under the material-incentives system, he rarely took home more than 60 yuan a month. But the training of young workers is invaluable. Now he is the highest-paid worker in this shop, taking home 108 yuan a month.'

We asked if old Liao's wage-rise was not in itself a material incentive to concentration on training workers rather than production. Hou Fa-hsin did not agree. 'It's the workers who propose the wage-scales. Old Liao had been training young people and helping less skilled workers ever since he has been here, taking lower wages without complaining. If anyone suddenly switched to training young workers just because he saw how

old Liao's wages had jumped, this would be noted. This is
where the question of overall attitude towards work and your
work-mates counts. During the material-incentives period, a sort
of money-grubbing attitude did develop among a few workers
– not many. But it hurt the ordinary workers to see someone
like old Liao being discriminated against although in the long-
term he was the most valuable worker we had. If he had just
concentrated on production – which was what material incentives were for – he could have doubled his wages, but the
state would have suffered because of lowered qualifications of
younger workers. Such examples can be multiplied by hundreds.
The main proof that the system was no good was the tremendous upsurge in production when it was abolished.'

Seventeen-year-old Miss Ssu-yi, at the multiple borer, explained that her father was a noodle maker. She had come to
the plant straight from junior middle school. 'I love my work
and I love old Liao,' she told us. As to what she wanted to do
later, amidst many blushes as if we had asked about marriage,
she confided with downcast eyes, 'I would like to design
machine-tools,' which we thought in itself was a tribute to
old Liao.

It is in fact rather moving, when visiting factory workshops,
to see young workers and veterans working at the same job – to
see the obvious respect and affection of the youngsters for the
veteran workers, and the serious, responsible attitude of the
latter in passing on their skills. It was something which inevitably provoked Rewi Alley to recall the old days when
apprentices were treated like dogs, and thrown on to the scrap-
heap if illness or accidents impaired their working capacity in
the slightest.

Production figures were quoted to prove that things were
going well. The original plan had called for 5,000 jeeps and
30,000 spare parts yearly, but actual output was 10,000 jeeps
and 100,000 spare parts. One third of the 8,000 workers were
women. The Cultural Revolution, far from impeding production, had released creative initiatives and enthusiasms which
were the secrets of the plant's rapid progress into a self-reliant,
economic unit. The average age of workers was below thirty,

because the plant itself – in its extended form – was young.
Apprentices were taken in from the age of sixteen for a three-
year period. They started at 16 yuan per month for the first
year, 18 for the second year and 21 for the final year, plus
free meals, work-clothes and transport. In the first post-
apprenticeship year, they received 34 yuan per month and then
moved up to regular wage-scales as recommended by their
fellow-workers to the revolutionary committee.

A constant feature of every factory we visited was the extent to which the workers designed and made their own equipment. Even at the Shanghai Yimin Foodstuffs Factory, we found
that workers and staff had invented and designed, without outside help, over forty types of wrapping and packing machines
and all sorts of electronic-control instruments to supervise their
work. In this case, machines and instruments had been made to
their specifications outside the factory.

Another aspect is the extent to which the factories are
themselves technical training institutions. Thus at the Harbin
Measuring and Cutting Tools Plant, which specializes in what
Chiao Chu-sen, the chief engineer, called 'the eyes and teeth of
the machine-building industry', as much emphasis was placed
on the output of technicians as on production: 'We have trained
and sent out over 1,000 skilled workers and technicians to other
factories,' explained Mr Chiao, a big, jolly-faced energetic
northerner. 'That is why the average age here is only around
thirty. We have helped many new factories in our branch with
machines, technical know-how, cadres and workforce. We consider this one of the most important aspects of our work. With
the rapid development of socialist construction, we need more
and more such plants; new plants need workers and technicians
and we are happy to contribute them. We were one of the first
such plants in China and we received much help from other
factories in the spirit of mutual support. Now it is our duty to
repay by helping others.'

He was proud of the fact that the plant – a huge affair with
a total labour force of 5,300 – had made 300 big machine-tools
for its own use as well as supplying large numbers for the new
'babies'. The plant made everything from tiny 0·25-mm. drills

for watch-makers and measuring gauges to ·001-mm. precision to heavy presses for hammering out the chassis of instrument tables. Like virtually every other factory we saw, the Harbin plant had links with the local university, students coming to do their practical work in actual production, and technicians taking technical or refresher courses at the university. The plant also received a quota of high-school graduates every year who would earn the right, after two or three years of practical work, to be recommended by their work-mates to go on to university. The criteria would be similar to those used in deciding wage-scales – technical proficiency and attitude towards work and fellow-workers, which implied ideological attitudes. The time-gap between finishing a secondary education and starting higher studies – always filled by several years' work at factories or farms – was another of those built-in safeguards against the emergence of a professional managerial class.

For a closer look at this danger we had long discussions with leading cadres, teachers and students at Peking's Tsinghua University of Technology and Science. It had been one of the pioneer storm-centres of the Cultural Revolution. For the purpose of this book however, we were more interested in the aftermath. Ma Wen-tsung, a very bright young man, relaxed and confident, who had played a leading part in the original revolt in which the whole student body took part and which had included expelling Madame Liu Shao-ch'i (Wang Kwang-mei) and her 'work-team' from the university campus in the early stages of the Cultural Revolution, was now a representative of the teaching staff on the revolutionary committee. He explained some of the ups and downs and the fundamentally new attitude of university training.

'During the Great Leap Forward,' he explained, 'Chairman Mao proposed the idea that education should serve proletarian politics and be combined with productive labour. This resulted in revolutionary change in educational methods. Workshops were set up in universities, including this one. Contractual links were established between the various faculties and factories. Teaching, designing and engineering work was carried on in factories outside the university. It was an exciting period, in which bourgeois concepts in education were directly attacked. This lasted only a couple of years, before Liu Shao-ch'i, taking advantage of the temporary difficulties in the economy, attacked this concept as diverting education on to a harmful course. He maintained that physical labour only lowered the general standard of education and insisted on reverting to the classical bourgeois yardsticks for measuring the results and methods of teaching. As a result the production workshops run by the university were closed down and the links with factories outside were ended. Emphasis was shifted back to intellectual, theoretical knowledge and examination results were regarded as the highest criteria of learning. Objectively speaking, the aim was to train successors to bourgeois society. Students were greatly affected by this poison.

'During that period, we continued to take in students of worker-peasant and soldier origin, but during their studies they began to desert their class, some becoming ashamed even of their own parents. There was an ironic sort of saying that in the first year such students continued a plain, simple life, in the second year acquired bourgeois tastes, and in the third year no longer recognized their home folk. The idea of exam results became obsessive. To fail meant that life held no future – or so they were taught. There were even some suicides – very few, but occasionally it did happen when exam results were posted up.'

Ma Wen-tsung went on to explain that the majority of students and very many of the teachers were unhappy about the trends and eventually this discontent gathered into the storm that shook the whole country and gave this generation of Chinese youth a taste of revolution. The signal shot, as far as the students were concerned, was fired by Mao Tse-tung on 7 May 1966, when he directed that the schooling period should be shortened, that 'there should be a revolution in education and the leadership of education by bourgeois intellectuals should no longer be tolerated'. After the storm of the Cultural Revolution which followed had subsided and a revolutionary committee had been set up in January 1969 to run Tsinghua University, new standards were adopted:

'The essence,' continued Ma Wen-tsung, 'was to turn out

graduates to serve a proletarian and not a bourgeois state. According to Chairman Mao we should aim at turning out students with a high socialist consciousness, morally, intellectually and physically fit. Ideologically, students and graduates should identify themselves with workers, peasants and soldiers and consider themselves also as ordinary members of the public. Professionally, they should have adequate scientific and technical training to be able to undertake designing, production and scientific research. They should be technical and scientific all-rounders, capable of analysing and solving whatever problems in their specialities are put to them.'

To implement this a number of unorthodox measures were introduced.

(1) The 2,600-strong teaching body, in rotation, was to go to the communes and factories and establish real contact with peasants and workers, while checking up on its own professional and vocational knowledge.

(2) Veteran workers of unusually rich experience and skills were to be recruited as full-time teachers to form the nucleus of a truly proletarian teaching body.

(3) An 'open-door' policy of contact with industry was adopted. Workshops and laboratories were set up within the university, contacts were established with over forty factories. Such faculties as Civil and Hydraulic Engineering conducted their courses on actual construction sites with students and teachers participating in the work. (A new teaching structure was in the process of being set up, comprising three elements – teaching, scientific research and production, a typical three-in-one combination – at the time of our visit in March 1972.)

(4) The method of accepting students was changed. Previously they came directly with leaving certificates from secondary schools. Now they came directly from the ranks of workers, peasants and soldiers. From secondary school they went to factories, communes, the People's Liberation Army. Only after graduating in 'real life' could they be selected for higher education.

The general criteria for selection were: to have shown high socialist consciousness during two or three years of practical work; to have completed secondary school; to have good health; and to be in the very early twenties and unmarried. University entrance applications had to be endorsed by the people with whom the applicant worked and submitted to the next highest authority – commune, county or factory management – who forwarded the applications to the university for the final decision. For veteran workers seeking higher education, questions of age, marital status and extent of secondary education were waived.

'Entrance exams have been abolished for the moment,' said Professor Chang Wei, vice-chairman of the revolutionary committee at the time of our visit. 'This is right. Experience proved that very often it was not those with high marks at an entrance exam who turned out to be good in science and technique after they graduated. The quality of new students is infinitely higher. Before, they came from secondary schools with some book knowledge and copied down what they were told. Now, after a few years in practical work, they have a basis for serious and productive discussion with the teachers. This has forced the teachers to be up to the mark also in up-to-date practical knowledge.'

Tuition was free, students getting a small stipend, but those who had worked for five years were paid at the same rate as in the factory or other enterprise from which they had come. All students enjoyed free textbooks, board and medical care. The length of training courses had not been finally decided then but had provisionally been set at three years instead of six as previously. A lot of overlapping in the various classes had been eliminated and out-of-date materials that had automatically been taught in the past had been scrapped. 'Before,' said Professor Chang Wei, 'we used the "forced feeding" method – like fattening Peking ducks – cramming in theoretical knowledge. Now it is by what we call "intuitive discussion", with teachers and students solving problems together, working together in the laboratories on the real scientific and technical problems that confront our industry. We are constantly on the look-out for the latest scientific achievements to ensure that our standards are kept at an advanced level. Revolutionary education is a new emerging thing, still in an experimental stage, with many problems yet to be solved.'

The thirty-one-member revolutionary committee included seven members each of students and the teaching faculty, representatives of the administrative staff, students' families, factory workers and the People's Liberation Army. Formerly the university had been run by an administrative committee comprised exclusively of teachers, 'very aloof and very authoritative', as Ma Wen-tsung described it. 'Discussions within the revolutionary committee are now very comprehensive, with everyone giving his opinion.'

The electronics workshop which we visited looked like the real factory that it was. Students and teachers designed and produced a whole range of automatic control instruments, 'teaching, experimenting and producing at the same time', as the cadre in charge explained. There were instruments for micro-miniaturization, ultra-sonic microscopic welders, digital frequency meters, instruments for making integrated circuits, diffusion furnaces for stretching mono-crystals and dozens of others made in the shop of a quality up to the best Japanese models, we were assured. There were small transistorized computers, designed and built on the spot for their own use, the other products being handed over to the state for distribution. 'Many of the instruments you see here,' explained Professor Chang Wei, 'China had tried to buy from abroad but failed because of embargos or just plain ill-will.'

It was the same in the Precision Instruments Department, where Ch'ao Feng-shan, a former technical worker, now in charge of the department, showed us programme-controlled milling machines of a type China had unsuccessfully sought abroad, but had now been made at the university. The programme control unit built with integrated circuits was much more compact than the advanced models produced abroad, according to Ch'ao Feng-shan.

'Study what you do; do what you study; conduct scientific experiments – that is Chairman Mao's approach to education, and that is a basic guide-line for us these days,' said Ma Wen-tsung. 'In addition we can make concrete contributions to the national economy, to the building of socialism.'

We wanted to know how old-time university professors, with their classical, academic backgrounds, adapted to these revolutionary changes. It was a question we put to Professor Chien Wei-ch'ang, a chubby-faced man in his early sixties with all the earmarks of an old-time intellectual. Graduating from the California Institute of Technology, he had come straight to Tsinghua University in 1946 and had been there ever since. His speciality was strength of metals.

'I consider the Cultural Revolution of paramount importance to my life, a real turning-point,' he said, speaking in effortless English. 'Forty years ago I studied in this university. Later I spent eight years in the U.S.A. I considered myself rather perfect. I knew my subject. I taught natural science, and I maintained this was based on certain laws that were the same the world over – in the U.S.S.R. or the U.S.A. or Japan – and so teaching methods must be the same. What I overlooked was that what I was teaching and the way I was teaching it were way out of line with the needs of the new society developing around me. I refused to see that students who are being trained to serve a proletarian, socialist society must be treated differently from those in a bourgeois, capitalist society. I retained my totally bourgeois outlook and infected my students with this. Get good degrees, I told them, and you can get good jobs anywhere in the world. I never dreamed of telling them: study well so you can help to build up a socialist society.

'When the Cultural Revolution started, I was one of the chief targets of criticism, right from the beginning. *Ta tze pao* were posted up everywhere attacking me – on the walls of the corridor leading to my living quarters, even on the floor and on my door. They were mainly directed at erroneous views as expressed in my lectures and in conversations with the students. I began to feel that there must be something to all this, but my main concern was whether I would ever be able to hold on to my job.

'Later on, when the students split into two factions, there

seemed only one point of common agreement – that Professor Chien Wei-ch'ang was a hopeless die-hard. So chuck him out. Suspend him for a start, settle accounts with him later. Neither of the factions wanted to have anything to do with Professor Chien. During that time I made little effort to find out what the Cultural Revolution was all about – I was worried only about my own future. Things started to change after the workers moved in with their propaganda teams.[1] After they had persuaded the students to settle their differences, some of them came to talk to me and explain Chairman Mao's policy on intellectuals. We went through some of Mao Tse-tung's works together. Of course I had read Mao in the past, but in the way I would study natural science – to memorize certain laws. But this time, the workers advised me to study them in relation to my own problems. This led me to consider my own attitudes during various stages of the revolution. What side had I taken when concrete issues came up? It did not need much reflection to see that I had always taken a reactionary line. I had always based my stand on personal factors. In fact, I was a firmly entrenched bourgeois intellectual – no two ways about it. I had been completely out of touch with the times and out of sympathy with the great revolutionary changes that, objectively, I knew were taking place.

'When all this was clear I made a self-criticism – quite complete – in front of the students and staff. I went over my whole life. Why had I made so many mistakes? Because I was so conceited and thought myself above everyone else – the only one who was always "right". This self-criticism was very well received, the chief comment being that it was a "good beginning", and this greatly encouraged me. It was in line with Chairman Mao's advice for intellectuals to learn from workers, peasants and the People's Liberation Army. I decided to see what really went on inside a factory.'

Our thoughts inevitably went back to our ambassador friend and his setting-foot in a factory for the first time. Among the

1. At the height of the storm, thousands of workers moved into Tsinghua to unite the students on the basis of discussions of Mao Tse-tung's works.

workers' teams, Professor Chien had made friends with Liu Ming-yi, a worker from a plant making special steels, a workers' representative on the university's revolutionary committee at the time of our visit. Professor Chien asked his new-found friend Liu to arrange for him to work in his plant for a while.

'During the past few years I have worked five times in three different factories,' he continued. 'In the past I had no friends from among the working class. I ignored their existence. My friends were exclusively intellectuals like myself. The first time I set foot in Liu Ming-yi's factory I was worried about the way the workers would criticize me, but they welcomed me and gave me some light work to do just so that I could get used to the place. There were plenty of friendly heart-to-heart talks. "You lived in an ivory tower and looked down on us before, like Liu Shao-ch'i," one of them said on my first day. "But now you've come down among us. Welcome!"

'I still had very subjective ideas. The first time I watched steel-making, I noticed a worker writing something on an ingot before the metal set. I supposed he was writing his name. In fact it was the technical description of that batch of steel. But such a mistake was typical of my state of mind.'

We asked what type of work he did. 'At first I just wandered around and did anything that I thought would be useful, cleaning up bits of scrap metal, or helping to classify different batches and types of steel. Once I was asked to locate a certain batch of high-carbide steel. I couldn't find it. At the university we use an instrument that weighs about 5 tons to make what we call a "tensile test". But there was no such instrument around. While I was wondering what to do, feeling highly embarrassed, a worker came up and asked if he could help. I explained the problem. He took a long rod and started tapping the steel bars on various heaps and quickly found the high-carbide type. He could tell by the sound. I felt very ashamed. For years I had been lecturing on how to recognize the properties and capacities of steel, but such a technique was not in any of the text-books. "Don't worry," the worker said, when I started to explain about this. "Before, you were divorced from practice, even though you were hot stuff on theory. But now you've come to us, we're very glad to have you. We can learn together." But in the two weeks I was there, I never did master the art of distinguishing steel by that method. It comes from long practice.

'Until then I had thought that the idea of "learning from workers" was something I could go along with, but that it applied only ideologically. I never really believed that I could learn anything about steel from ordinary workers until that moment. Practical work was rather painful for me at first, but it soon became very pleasant as well. I will soon be going off again for a few weeks and I can assure you that I am greatly looking forward to it. Friendships formed with workers have opened up a new world to me, even if it is late in my life. My outlook has been transformed through practice.'

If the Tsinghua University represents a typical example of a traditional centre of higher learning completely remoulded, the Gungda Communist Labour University Centre, in Kiangsi province, represents an entirely new concept. Formed in 1958, as part of the Great Leap in educational methods, it is designed to provide ideologically motivated technical cadres for the communes and county industry. Through branches in every county throughout Kiangsi province, 50,000 students were affiliated to Gungda at the time of our visit, over 80 per cent of them of worker-peasant origin. Of the 120,000 graduates, 90 per cent had returned to their own villages or local industry. Great stress is laid on ideological education based on the classic Marxist works and those of Mao Tse-tung. The centre and its branches run their own factories and various types of grain-producing, livestock and forestry farms, students dividing their time equally between study and productive work. They are entirely self-supporting.

Students and staff are supposed to practise 'four goods' – good in political ideology; in contact with the masses; in a simple style of living and working; in mastering technique. They are also taught to be expert in military affairs. The major orientation is to head off any spontaneous tendencies towards capitalist ideology in the countryside and to pave the way for a transition to a communist society.

With such a considerable labour force at its disposal, Gungda goes in for building roads, power plants and broadcasting units, irrigation works, soil and forestry amelioration, experimentation with new agricultural techniques, etc. It has over 4,000 acres of arable land at its disposal and manages 140 farms and 100 small factories.

Self-sufficiency had been imposed by necessity. Originally it had been supported by the state, but as Liu Shao-ch'i opposed such 'heretical' establishments Gungda was treated as an 'illegitimate child' and when the three bad years set in orders were given via the top authority in Kiangsi province to close it down. The staff and students objected, so all supplies were cut off, including money to pay the teachers. The student body was cut back by some 20,000 and the 116 branches reduced to sixty-two. The result was a 'five-selfs' movement – to become self-sufficient in grain, edible oil, meat, vegetables and running expenses. And not to take a cent from the state. It was this that led to the setting-up of farms from land reclaimed from swamps and hillsides and factories started with bare hands. Thus necessity reinforced the fundamental self-reliant outlook of the university and the half study–half work concept.

Before the Cultural Revolution, Gungda was essentially an experimental university on a national scale, with students from over a dozen provinces. Later the student body came exclusively from Kiangsi province, with cadres coming from outside Kiangsi to study the experience and set up similar centres in their own provinces. Gungda, in other words, seemed like another of those efficient, built-in safeguards to prevent the revolution 'from turning into its opposite', a means of ensuring that peasants in the communes, like factory-workers in the towns, were really equipped technically and politically to run their own affairs.

CHAPTER TWELVE

FROM THE BOTTOM UP

A body-blow at one of the most strongly entrenched fortresses of bureaucracy in orthodox socialist planning is the system of planning from below in all sections of the Chinese economy. The state plan is not initiated by top-flight economists with batteries of computers but by farmers and workers with stubs of pencils and well-thumbed notebooks. Computers are used at the top, but only to collate the production estimates which are supplied from rice-roots and factory-floor levels and to integrate these with overall requirements. In this planning from the bottom up, full play is given to creative initiatives and the results of scientific experiments at the base. The resulting national plan represents one of the most complete exercises of democratic power. It becomes a matter of honour and public morality for the various units to accomplish what they themselves have proposed.

A vital element in planning, especially in keeping the increase in foodstuffs ahead of population growth – 4 to 5 per cent for food-grains against 2 per cent for population[1] – is the nationwide response to Mao Tse-tung's appeal for scientific experiments at all levels and in all fields.

Thus every commune, brigade and team has its unit responsible for scientific experimentation. It is not surprising, with tens of millions of people taking part, that there have been some astonishing results. No aspect of production is considered too lowly to escape the attention of the experimenters. A nationally publicized example of the ideal method and approach is that of Yao Shih-chang, a production leader from Shantung province. Almost half of the brigade land was devoted to peanuts. After failing to increase production by copying

1. According to official figures released in Peking on 20 September 1973.

methods which had given fair results elsewhere, Yao Shih-chang decided to apply dialectics to peanuts, pin-pointing the main contradictions to resolve them. He started by going to the fields at night, literally to watch the growth process. His first discovery came just before dawn one morning when flowers opened on the first of his test clusters. More early-morning vigils and he discovered that this was a law – the flowers all opened just before dawn. Knowing that the pods begin to form as the flowers begin to wither, he continued watching the flowers, hanging a label on each stem with the date on which the first flowers appeared, continuing his night-watch over sixty nights, by which time he had accumulated a vast amount of peanut lore, the test plants being covered with labels. He discovered that the time between the opening of the flower and the ripening of the nuts was sixty-five days, and that the first pair of branches produced 60 to 70 per cent of the nuts, the second layer 20 to 30 per cent, while the mass above produced nothing except empty pods.

The following season, by pruning off the unproductive upper branches and changing cultivation methods to provide maximum nourishment for the first and second branches, Yao Shih-chang managed to boost output from 3·65 tons per acre in 1958, when the Great Leap Forward inspired him to start his experiments, to an average of 8·5 tons on the whole 330 acres devoted to peanuts, with up to 15 tons in some places. We do not know whether brigade-leader Yao has made any contribution to the science of growing peanuts, or whether he could have saved many sleepless nights by reading scientific literature on the subject – it is beside the point. The important thing is that he discovered secrets of peanut growth by his own efforts in a spirit of genuine scientific inquiry, with a patience worthy of a scientist, and provided another object lesson for commune farmers all over China to probe into the mysteries of plant growth to boost agricultural production.

The results of such experiments, once they have been thoroughly tested out, are among the vital data used in drawing up the yearly production plans.

In late May 1973, we drove from Wuhan, the provincial capital of Hupei province, north from the Yangtze river along roads which led through fields bordered by rows of wheat interspersed with cotton. The heavy green-golden heads of wheat nearly ready for harvesting contrasted strangely with the fluffy white bolls decorating many of the brown cotton plants. At the headquarters of the Hupei provincial revolutionary committee, Li Chin-ha, in charge of the foreign-affairs section, explained that the almost simultaneous harvesting of rice and cotton was possible because a commune experimental team discovered that undeveloped cotton bolls continue to develop normally even after the plant is pulled up.

'In this area,' he said, 'winter wheat is sown in September for harvesting in May. But to raise cotton on the same fields it must be planted out in March, which means some very special treatment of the seedlings to get them ready in time.' When we looked into it, 'very special treatment' seemed an under-statement and represented another illustration of the creativeness of the Chinese farmer once he gets his teeth into a problem. The cotton seedlings, we found, are grown in cones of stamped earth, prepared and dried by the tens of thousands. They are placed together on the sunny side of a dyke or road cutting or in sunny places in village compounds. Sand is scattered over them if the weather turns cold and they are covered over with plastic sheeting. The cotton plant grows well in its earth cone and can be planted out between the rows of growing wheat in spring, or at least be ready for transplantation at the time of the wheat harvest. Harvesting the cotton goes on through the autumn months, but when the time comes for late-autumn ploughing for wheat the plants with the last residue of bolls on them are pulled up, tied in bundles and stacked away until the bolls are fully ripe and time is available for final picking. Some other commune teams found by experimentation that they could harvest an early crop of oil-bearing seeds, then two more of rice. At the county level, when a plan like this was submitted, it was thought that the second rice crop was included by mistake, so it was struck out. The team members were angry and planted the second crop anyway. It did well and many other communes now do the same. This just shows the way the farmers are thinking. Old customs have gone by the board since all the teams have started going in for scientific experimentation.

We asked to what extent such experimentation had become a generalized practice in the area.

'Despite the natural conservatism of the countryside,' replied Li Chin-ha, 'there is already great respect for those engaged in scientific experimentation. Each year's planning is based on the previous year's harvest. The opinion of those engaged in seed and fertilizer selection at team level and weather forecasting at county level is sought and their opinions are reflected in the plan. In 1971 for instance the consensus of weather forecasters was that there would be drought conditions the following year. The acreage allotted to the various crops, the types of drought-resistant seed and suitable fertilizers were decided accordingly, and the estimated yield was somewhat down-graded. The drought came, but the communes got about the planned yield. Also, thanks to good work by the scientists, we have developed seed strains which give high yields but short, sturdy stalks which are unaffected by the strong winds that sweep the Hupei plains during the growing and ripening period. The farmers say that, even with planning based on scientific experimentation, if the skies decide to take a hand against them, there can be some difficulties, but they can at least reduce the havoc which may be caused.

'It is because the results were speedily apparent that everyone supports the experimental teams,' Li Chin-ha continued. 'At times everyone takes part. If insects attack the crops, for instance, there are plenty of volunteers to turn out at all hours to study their habits and trace their origins as the basis for a massive extermination campaign. Nothing is left to guesswork these days. The farmers want to know the real truth about what happens if such and such a seed or such and such a fertilizer is used. They want to see the results in the experimental plots first.' He pointed out that, because of the multi-crop system, problems of management have become much more complicated.

'At all levels those in charge have to be thinking in several dimensions at once. Before, there was plenty of time between harvesting one crop and planting another,' he said. 'Now there is an uninterrupted cycle of productive activity. A commune becomes more and more like a big enterprise working on a three-shift basis. This in itself helps to eliminate the difference in outlook between rural and urban workers. Largely because of the educative work of the scientific teams, farmers have become aware of the importance of timing, and this has brought a new sense of alertness to the villages. Team members know they can always get a crop of some sort but that yield often depends on timing. Nowadays, as soon as harvesting has progressed far enough, compost is spread, ploughs and harrows follow on, turning in both compost and stubble and breaking up the clods, while behind the harrows are teams ready with the seed. Everything has to be done with the precision of an automatic line in a factory.'

Pondering over the vast enterprise of preparing the annual national plan for agriculture, the results of which dominate the rest of economic planning, our minds go back to computers. The basic elements of the programme rely on the input of people like the modest young chap from the scientific group of the Tungfang brigade of An Lung commune, in Kwanhsien county in far-away Szechuan. His job was to collate the results of experiments in seed selection. Several years' results were set out in many scores of neatly labelled jars, placed in rows on a long table at the team headquarters, which looked out over experimental plots. When we met him he had just returned from a visit to scientific teams from other brigades and was entering their results in a big ledger. In his ledger, jars and experimental plots, he had the basis for his report to the team's technical committee, and on the basis of that report a plan was drawn up after each year's harvest and presented to a mass meeting of team members. After intensive discussion, the plan would be passed on, with whatever modifications the majority decided on, to be incorporated into brigade, commune and county plans, the relevant portions of which would be filtered back to the Central Planning Commission in Peking. Even at team level, all the necessary statistics would be there, including expected population increase, the amount of compost available, the pig population – the latter very important because of their contribution to natural fertilizer.

Scientific experimentation is not carried out in a vacuum. Teams exchange experiences with other teams and communes with other communes. The communes are linked with regional or provincial agricultural scientific research stations, such as one we visited in the outskirts of Chungking. It had five departments, specializing in grain, livestock and veterinary affairs, soil improvement and fertilizers, anti-disease research, and vegetables.

Director Hu Ch'i-tso, a gnome-like person who spoke with the affection of a father about the various seed strains developed by the station, explained that it had been set up during the Great Leap Forward and maintained contacts with seventy other such stations all over the southern part of China. It had 40 acres of experimental fields. Of the 190 working personnel, forty were agricultural specialists. After detailing the various types of grain and vegetables developed for the surrounding communes, director Hu said: 'One of the most important aspects of our work is that we have trained 6,200 technical personnel from the communes who have themselves returned to carry out scientific experiments based on local conditions. This enables planning work to be done with great precision and ensures a steady rise in productivity.' The station had regular contacts with 150 scientific research groups from the surrounding communes, each with its experimental plots. They had three main tasks: to produce improved seed strains; to carry out soil-improvement work based on soil analysis; and to discover optimum conditions for stable high-yield crops in their respective areas.

'One of the problems is to generalize the two-crop system in an area which traditionally used single cropping,' he said. 'Since 1963, when we succeeded in regularly producing two crops per season on our experimental plots, we have sent our own technicians and workers to live and work with thirty-four different production brigades to help them to switch to double-cropping. There is also a constant flow of scientific groups from the communes to study our methods of close planting, giving the rice seedlings a good start by covering them with plastic sheeting and other innovations for this region. One of the important things in introducing double-cropping here is to change the farmers' outlook. They were used to processing grain immediately after the harvest, but now the stubble has to be ploughed in immediately and the second crop sown. Radiating out from this centre, however, more and more communes are moving over to two crops – and the local scientific research groups are the prime movers in this.'

Hu Ch'i-tso was convinced that once commune members had adjusted to the idea of two rice crops per season, it would be possible to add a third crop of wheat. A rapid increase in the pig population would provide the necessary fertilizer. 'But the move from one to two crops, and from two to three, can only come when the overwhelming majority of commune members really want this – and have sufficient fertilizer,' he said. 'Chairman Mao has said that: "People are the real heroes. We should rely on them. If we don't, we'll accomplish nothing." We stick strictly to this principle. With our scientific work we can demonstrate what is possible. But only the masses of the farmers can decide whether to adopt the new ways. In this, it is the work of the local team that is decisive.' Decisive also is a rapid increase in the pig population to provide the necessary fertilizer, and in many areas this depends on finding alternative sources of domestic fuel. It has been discovered that straw, corn cobs and other agricultural left-overs traditionally used for fuel can be ground into a flour-like powder which, after a little fermentation, makes excellent pig-fodder. (In India, the habit of burning dried cow turds for fuel has been a major factor in the continuing impoverishment of the soil. In China they have never been wasteful of human or animal manure, but it is now seen that the country-folk have been burning sources of fodder for those invaluable grunting fertilizer factories that the pig population represents. While not exactly an 'energy crisis' in the Western concept, the problem of domestic fuel in areas where there is no abundance of local coal presents its problems.)

When we asked if samples of new strains of seed or new types of fertilizers had to be submitted to the Ministry of Agriculture before they were used, in view of the key role they played in crop estimates, Hu Ch'i-tso replied: 'Not at all. The decisive thing is that the commune members approve them. If they do, the Chungking Municipality agrees automatically. In the national interest, reports of all new developments are forwarded to the Ministry of Agriculture through its local organs. But the decision on choice of seed, as on all other matters, rests with the general meeting of members at commune, brigade or team level.'

It is the fact that the commune members run their own lives and work, responsible for the thing that concerns them most, drawing up their own production plans and accepting responsibility for fulfilling them, that has given the farmers a new stature. One is aware of this the moment one sets foot inside a commune. They feel that not only do they run their own affairs but that their voice is heard in Peking in deciding the dimensions of the national plan. It is this new status, acquired since the Cultural Revolution, which prompted Joan Robinson to comment that before the Cultural Revolution bureaucrats in Peking believed 'in dictating to the people instead of consulting them . . . [They] thought that all that was needed could be done with three instruments, the computer, the telephone and the typewriter. They dealt with statistics, not reality; they thought in terms of materials and forgot about people.'[2]

Planning in industry follows some of the basic principles of that in agriculture. Each year's plan is primarily based on the previous year's production and the details are decided on the factory floor. Apart from five categories of industry which are run by the counties, communes and brigades to serve agriculture directly (small mines for coal, iron-ore and other minerals; small iron and steel plants; small cement works and hydro-electric power plants; small fertilizer plants; and small machine-shops producing farm implements, various types of spare parts and the machines to make them) all the rest of industry is integrated into the state plan. Obviously overall freedom to choose

2. *Economic Management: China 1972*, p. 17.

what to produce cannot be the same in a state factory as in a commune because its roles are different. A major task of the collectively owned communes is to produce all it can to supply the daily needs of its members in foodstuffs and the tools and services necessary for that. Surplus production is a welcome contribution to support those who are not direct food producers. The publicly owned factories are not producing goods for the use of those that produce them but for society as a whole. Thus the initiative of what to produce lies at a higher level, but how to produce and in what quantities remains basically an initiative of the workers in the various plants.

As a result of the Cultural Revolution, industries formerly under the administration of centralized ministries were transferred to the competence of the provinces where they were located, as part of the drive for regional economic autonomy and decentralization within the 'prepare against war' concept. Chou En-lai told Edgar Snow in 1970 that, as a result of the decentralization measures, ninety departments formerly directly under the central government had been reduced to twenty-six, and administrative personnel from 60,000 to about 10,000.

The overall five-year-plan is drawn up by the State Planning Commission in consultation with the provinces, and is based on existing plant capacities and the production schedules covered by the period of the plan. Approximate quotas are passed down to the various provinces, where they will be discussed at meetings with representatives of the plants concerned. Once the master plan is agreed, the question of its year-by-year implementation becomes very much the concern of the workers in all the plants concerned. When we asked at the Harbin Measuring and Cutting Tools Plant what was the significance of the management's announced intention of fulfilling the 1973 plan forty-five days ahead of schedule, chief engineer Chiao Chu-sen replied: 'That this means extra production of about 12 per cent is quite important, but still more important is that we will have more time to prepare the plan for 1974. We have no hope of fully meeting the increasing needs of the country for our products, but we must find means to bring into full play the enthusiasm and initiatives of the plant personnel.'

We asked if the management knew roughly what would be required for the following year.

'More of everything that we produce this year,' he replied. 'But we like to propose more sophisticated products which we know the country needs and which are not being made. Through technical literature we know what is being done abroad and it is up to us to keep abreast of the most modern techniques so as to find short cuts for our own industrialization programme. This keeps our workers, technicians and administrative cadres on their toes through scientific experiments and technical innovations to propose more interesting production plans every year. Such initiatives from below are highly appreciated at the higher echelons.'

At the near-by Harbin Electrical Machinery Plant we asked Liang Wei-yen, a leading member of the revolutionary committee, how the actual planning was done. 'We receive a draft plan from the government,' he explained, 'handed down to us through the provincial authorities. Workers, technicians and administrative cadres discuss this plan and give their opinions, and it goes up again through the provincial revolutionary committee to the State Planning Commission and comes back to us in final form.'

The factory had come into operation at the end of the Korean War, in 1954, having been originally designed to build medium-sized hydro-electric generators. During the Great Leap Forward it had been greatly expanded to build big thermal power stations as well. We asked – as it was a highly specialized plant – to what extent it worked to a 'vertical line', turning out equipment for a central ministry to be distributed all over the country, and to what extent to a 'horizontal line' of serving the province.

'Chairman Mao,' he replied, 'appealed for two initiatives – from the centre and from the locality. Our aim is to push for both, supplementing initiatives from the centre with our own for the province and pushing ahead to build socialism. Last year, for instance, the province proposed to build a 1,600-kilowatt power station in the near-by Wuchang county. It was not in the state plan but we took it in our stride and supplied the equipment without interfering with our programme for the state.

'Producing electric power equipment comes under the First Ministry of the Machine-Building Industry,' he continued. 'This ministry takes into account the whole country's power-building capacity before allotting tasks, keeping that capacity constantly under review. For instance we used to specialize in 2,500-kilowatt generators but we have moved up into much bigger fields – 300,000 kilowatts for hydro-electric and 200,000 kilowatts for thermal-power generators. Our capacity for the 2,500-kilowatt type has been transferred to a plant in Peking. But the location of plants like ours is also taken into consideration – contracts for any new projects within our province or neighbouring provinces would be allocated to us.'

On the question of who decided about plant expansion, Liang Wei-yen explained that if the expansion was relatively small it could be carried out by a decision of the plant concerned, in consultation with the provincial authorities. It could be financed from a residue of the original state investment, which was paid off in annual instalments, with a proportion retained for minor expansion or investment in new equipment. Any major expansion would have to be approved by the provincial authorities and then submitted to the State Planning Commission. If the plan was approved, the question where and how to build would be decided by the Harbin Municipal authorities, in accordance with the very strict anti-pollution safeguards enforced by all municipalities and which no directives from the state could over-ride.

When we asked to what extent workers' initiatives played a role in production, Liang Wei-yen smiled and said the fact that the plant was now building very big power generators entirely designed and made within the factory was only possible because of the wealth of initiatives from the rank-and-file workers.

'They have solved engineering problems on a level comparable to that of the most technically advanced countries,' he said. 'By introducing, for instance, a special water-cooling system for 200,000-kilowatt thermal-power generators, we were able greatly to reduce the size compared to advanced foreign models of the same power, resulting in a big saving of raw materials. Scientific research groups have produced plastic tubing to replace copper pipes; synthetic resins to replace mica. They have solved many difficult technical problems which still plague the power-making industry of technically advanced countries.' He pointed to a number of big Soviet machines and mentioned that, although the withdrawal of Soviet technicians with their blue-prints in 1960 had been a bitter blow at the time, it had put their own workers and technicians on their mettle and forced them to adopt the policy of self-reliance. 'It was the case of a bad thing turning into a good thing,' he said. 'The fact that we are now working on a 600,000-kilowatt hydro-electric generator, designed by ourselves, speaks for itself.'

A cheerful and dynamic trade-union representative, Peng Hang-shen, took over the discussion to say: 'When we speak about workers being the masters, this has been literally true since the Cultural Revolution. We are in fact the management at all levels. Apart from the revolutionary committee, elected from the factory floor, there are work-teams in every department in charge of quality control, safety precautions, material supplies, planned unit production, economic use of materials, welfare and political work and women's affairs. Trade-union cadres play a leading role in such teams, and also in leading political education – the study of the Marxist classics. It is from the rank-and-file workers that the initiatives come for technical innovations, for more economic use of materials and for greater efficiency.'

As the trade-union movement had only recently begun to emerge again after its dissolution during the Cultural Revolution, we asked about its specific role and its relationship to the factory's Communist Party committee.

'The trade union is the mass organization of the workers under the leadership of the Communist Party,' replied Peng Hang-shen. 'It is a school for studying communism and the trade-union committee carries out its work under the Communist Party's factory branch, in accordance with the central tasks as defined by party policy. An important function is in helping the rank-and-file workers in ideological and political education. It also takes responsibility for factory safety and workers' welfare projects.'

We asked what was being studied at the moment and were told that cadres were studying Engels' *Anti-Dühring*, while the main body of workers were studying Lenin's writings on Marx and Engels, and Stalin on Lenin. Another important function of the trade unions was welfare work, we were told.

'If members seem to have problems we try to find out what they are,' explained Peng Hang-shen. 'If they are reticent, some trade-union cadres will visit the family to find out what it is all about. If there are financial problems – too big a family to support in relation to the total income – we have a special fund on which we can draw to help. In any case we visit workers in their families to listen to advice and criticism as one of the means of improving working conditions. An important function of trade-union work is to ensure very strict control over safety precautions. If there are any deficiencies, they will be taken up as a matter of urgency with the revolutionary committee. We also keep an eye on the factory canteen, the kindergartens, sports and cultural activities – on everything that affects the daily life of our members.'

As a quarter of the workers were women, they were represented on the trade-union committee in the same proportion, occupying one of the three posts of vice-chairman. We asked why there was as yet no trade-union committee at Heilungkiang provincial level.

'Because, like everything else in China,' replied Peng Hang-shen, the trade-union movement must be built from the bottom up. Only when all enterprises throughout the province have functioning trade-union committees will there be the basis for electing a committee at provincial level. And only when there are committees in every province will there be the basis for restoring the All-China Council of Trade Unions.'

The question of the role of trade unions in a socialist society, especially in one such as China where the rank-and-file workers were so obviously masters in the factories, was one which had long intrigued us and which we were able to take up at as high a level as existed in mid-1973 – that is with the Peking Municipality General Trade Unions. Among the officials who received us was the vice-chairman, Ch'ang Shih-chung, who had led the 'Work Team for Propagating Mao Tse-tung's Thought' into Peking's Tsinghua University at a decisive moment in 1967. A small, slender man, calm and soft-spoken, he was an alternative member of the Central Committee of the Communist Party. We remarked that militant trade-union leaders in the West often returned home less than satisfied after visiting socialist countries where the trade unions seemed to be integrated into the ruling bureaucracy as glorified cheer-leaders to ensure that targets were reached in the current economic plan. Ch'ang Shih-chung replied:

'The trade-union movement is a mass organization of the working class to carry out class struggle and further the interests of the working class. In the past, in our country as elsewhere, it was organized against the bourgeoisie. As a tool for carrying out the class struggle, the proletariat must use it to liberate itself politically and economically and overthrow the bourgeoisie. After political power has been seized, the workers have complete political power, they are masters of their fate, they have become the leading force. But, although the situation of the proletariat has changed, they still have to march forward to continue the revolution. Chairman Mao has taught us that: "In the long historical period of socialism, there will still be class struggle. There will still be the choice of taking the capitalist road, the risk of the restoration of capitalism." Thus the basic line must be to continue the dictatorship of the proletariat and in this concept strengthen the trade unions and develop their organizational role.

'According to the classics of Marx, Engels, Lenin, Stalin and Chairman Mao, as an arm of the Communist Party, vanguard of the proletariat, the trade unions should play their role in three fields: as schools for learning communism; as pillars of the dictatorship of the proletariat; and as transmission belts linking the Communist Party with the masses. Within this framework, we have advanced seven tasks for the trade-union movement: to study the classics of Marxism and Chairman Mao conscientiously; to repudiate bourgeois ideology and revisionism in order to consolidate the dictatorship of the proletariat; to further the revolution and promote production and progress in all fields so as to build socialism in a faster, better and more economic way while preparing against war; to educate workers and employees to supervise cadres at all levels to ensure that they carry out the party's line and policies and adhere to a socialist orientation; to train outstanding workers actively and send them as cadres to party and state organs; to show great concern for workers' living conditions, paying great attention to labour protection and safety as well as to the technical and cultural education of the workers; and to educate workers in a spirit of proletarian internationalism, helping them to foster the lofty idea that only by the emancipation of all mankind can the proletariat finally liberate itself, thus ensuring that Chinese workers make their due contribution to the world revolution.'

In this first exposition to Western writers of the new role of the Chinese trade unions following the Cultural Revolution, Ch'ang Shih-chung made it quite clear that it was to play a leading role in educating and preparing Chinese workers for a communist society. The historical tasks of trade unions he defined as: 'To overthrow the bourgeoisie and all exploiting classes; to strive for the replacement of the bourgeoisie by the proletariat; to replace capitalism by socialism and finally to achieve communism ... In order to achieve communism, it is necessary to inculcate people with a communist spirit. This is also a historic task of the proletariat and therefore it is necessary to make the trade unions a school of communism.' He laid great stress on the educative role of the trade unions and the need for the working class to remould itself while remoulding society to ensure that it remained highly qualified to maintain its vanguard role.

'Veteran workers, comparatively speaking, have a high degree of class-consciousness,' he continued, 'because they were so exploited and oppressed during the pre-liberation era. They have a deep class feeling for the Communist Party, for Chairman Mao and the socialist motherland. But these sentiments are no substitute for the scientific knowledge and lofty ideas of

Marxism–Leninism and Chairman Mao's works. On the other hand, there are a large number of educated young people who have reinforced the working class in the factories, but their ideology is not necessarily that of the working class. They have no experience of the bad old days. They were born in New China, brought up under the Red Flag and came direct from school to the factories. They need to be educated not only through the Marxist classics and works of Chairman Mao, but by learning about the revolutionary struggles and traditions of the Chinese working class. Only thus will they become worthy successors of the latter.'

We asked if the new trade-union leadership felt that there were infallible safeguards against the trade unions becoming extensions of administrative organs without any creative life of their own, or of turning into autonomous bureaucratic institutions with too much life of their own. Ch'ang Shih-chung thought this danger did exist up until the Cultural Revolution, which was why the trade unions had been repudiated to a great extent by workers who by and large stuck to basic party policies. Point four of the seven tasks was also an effective safeguard.

'One must not confuse China after the liberation with the old China,' he went on. 'It would be wrong for the trade unions to organize struggle simply for economic gains, just as it was wrong – and futile – in the past to take only a peaceful road to get political power. The working class are the masters now, so it would be wrong to fight against themselves, but it is right to consolidate the dictatorship of the proletariat by exercising controls, by taking part in management, co-operating with and supervising the implementation of policies at various levels. To ensure this really does happen, large numbers of working-class cadres have been assigned to work in party and state organizations – about 20,000 in Peking alone since the Cultural Revolution.'

Asked to define what was the most important change in the role of the trade unions brought about by the Cultural Revolution, Ch'ang Shih-chung replied: 'The worker from his factory bench has moved up through the trade unions into the superstructure.' And he cited the names of those who had been elected to the Central Committee of the Communist Party at the Peking and national levels. 'The trade unions have moved out of the narrow role as an integrated part of a bureaucratic ruling system that Liu Shao-ch'i had allotted them, into that of creative organizations which encourage and stimulate the leading role of the working class, marching forward towards communism along the basic lines set forth by the party and Chairman Mao.'

Regarding welfare activities, Ch'ang Shih-chung said that it was the duty of trade-union cadres to ensure such things as the application of provisions for maternity leave, care for the old and disabled, and the proper functioning of collective activities at the factories, such as canteens, crèches and kindergartens. He pointed out that in the early days after liberation only one in a family of five, on the average, was a rice-earner. This had since increased to two per family of five. But it was the job of trade-union cadres to check up to ensure that the total income of members of a family corresponded to the family needs. If not there would be an individual application of the communist creed of 'to each according to his needs' and a subsidy would be paid directly to the family. 'Most of the workers have a high political consciousness,' he explained, 'and even if they are in difficulties they will not ask for help. That is why direct visits to the families are essential.' Another form of financial help comes from the 'Mutual Financial Help' fund also organized by the trade unions. Workers contribute small amounts to this mutual fund and when somebody needs a relatively large sum – perhaps for a long trip because of a death in the family or other reasons – he can draw from the fund.

When we remarked on the dramatic changes in the status of workers that we had seen, Ch'ang Shih-chung said: 'In Peking in the pre-liberation days, workers were at the bottom of the social scale. They were always on the verge of starvation. They had no political power, not even the right to form trade unions. Peking in those days was considered a "consumer city". But what could workers consume? At one small mill, they spoke of their "three scrap" living standards – a scrap of matting for a bed, a scrap of brick for a pillow, a scrap of maize to eat. Now a decent living is guaranteed, and politically those who were at the very bottom are now the political masters of the state, exercising real power at all levels. They have won this right by carrying on their shoulders the burdens of revolution and production.'

We asked when the All-China Council of Trade Unions would be reconstituted, and he replied: 'The rank-and-file trade-union members and the leadership of all organs reconstituted hope this will happen very soon. The important thing is that there is consolidation at the base and the new leading organs are built from the bottom up.' At the time of our visit, leading organs had been set up only in the Peking and Shanghai Municipalities and eight provinces, but the tempo of forming leading committees at provincial levels was speeding up. It was a question of building up from the factory benches – not just nominating functionaries from above – organizations in which the workers had total confidence.

One aspect of the newly reorganized trade unions is that many more women have been elected to leading positions than ever before. This follows a general trend in national policy whereby more and more women are elected to executive positions at all levels. Women's liberation is a progressing cause in China today, very much part of the changing quality of life of the whole Chinese people. The fact that twenty women were elected to the 195-member Central Committee of the Communist Party at the Tenth Congress in August 1973 and that, of the 124 alternate members, twenty-one were women emphasizes this trend at the highest policy-making level.

CHAPTER THIRTEEN

WHAT MAKES CHINA LEAP?

Amongst the most honoured figures in old tales of Chinese history and folklore – perhaps *the* most honoured – are the hydraulic engineers. Wherever there is a great river or ancient waterworks, there was a temple to Yü Ta Wang, more popularly known as Yü the Great, a leader who about 4,000 years ago carried out great flood-control works. Where the Min river hurtles down from the 15,000-feet-high mountains in the Apa Tibetan Region in West Szechuan to debouch on to the Chengtu Plain at Kwanhsien – a mere 1,000 feet above sea level – there is a temple to Yü the Great on one side of a diversion canal and on the opposite bank another to Lin Pin and his son, famous hydraulic engineers whose flood-control works date back to the Han Dynasty period, two millennia after Yü the Great.

At Shaoshing in Chekiang, the province where Yü the Great is popularly believed to have been buried, there is a tomb ascribed to him. In the same province there is a temple to an eighth-century A.D. official who gave up his post as Grand Secretary of Rites and returned to his flood-plagued native village. Using his influence at court to secure a suspension of tax payments for three years so the inhabitants could concentrate on flood-control works, he led and personally worked with them to confine the trouble-making and meandering Pai Sha river into a single bed; and he dug lateral canals to drain off surplus water in flood periods. On his death-bed he requested that his real name should not be perpetuated and that he should be known only after the name of the river. So grateful villagers erected an image of him as Pai Sha Ta-ti (the Great Pai Sha One) and built a temple around it. Here the local people have rendered homage throughout centuries in the ninth month of the lunar year. Deservedly so, as here we have an early example of serving the people in the crucial task of controlling the waters.

With the setting-up of the People's Republic, great attention was focused on finding radical solutions to end the periodic floods, with the enormous human and material losses that came in their wake. One of those placed in overall charge of such work was Fu Tso-yi, one of Chiang Kai-shek's former generals. Entrusted by Chiang to hold all of China north of the Yellow river during the later stages of the war, he fought hard but unsuccessfully against the People's Liberation Army. As a reward for his patriotism in surrendering Peking to avoid war damage, and as a tribute to his capacity to handle men by the millions, the new government made him Minister of Water Conservancy, a post he has held ever since, at times concurrently with other posts, untroubled even by the tempest of the Cultural Revolution. (A reminder of the solidity of the offers from Peking of reconciliation and integration still open to those holding the highest posts in Taiwan, not excluding Chiang Kai-shek if he had a change of heart in time!)[1]

Some eighteen months after the People's Republic was set up, we spent a few weeks at the sites of the first vast undertaking to bring China's waters under control. On 14 October 1950, following a disastrous flood in the Huai river valley – which caused the loss of 5 million tons of grain among other things – Mao Tse-tung signed a decree initiating works to bring the rampaging Huai under control. Situated roughly mid-way between the giant Yellow and Yangtze rivers, for many years the Huai had been one of the greatest disaster-makers. Within eight months of the signing of the decree, 3 million peasants directed by about 15,000 technical workers shifted 185 million cubic metres of earth, two and a half times as much as that moved in building the Suez Canal and about equal to that in building the Panama Canal. It was the greatest mobilization of man-power we had even seen till that time. A Huai River Harnessing Com-

1. Fu Tso-yi died in Peking on 19 April 1974 at the age of seventy-nine, holding till he died the post of Minister of Water Conservancy and Power, power having been added to the original ministry a few years before his death.

mission was set up – the name a correct description of what it did – and the result was an astonishing organization of manpower and resources, and co-ordination of effort.

We visited the headwaters areas in the western mountains of Honan and Anhwei provinces, where dozens of big and medium-sized reservoirs were being built simultaneously to trap and control the rate at which the waters would rush down to the middle reaches. We watched work on smaller reservoirs and dams in the middle reaches, the gouging-out of deeper and wider channels in the tributaries, the building of hundreds of miles of dykes and installation of sluice gates, the hacking-out of a completely new outlet to the sea and strengthening of dyke walls in the lower reaches. To some who visited the project, it was a frightening exercise of 'blue ants', but each of these 'ants' had been actors in tragic human dramas, which explained the fervour with which they threw themselves into the work of hacking and carrying earth, hewing stone or working on whatever fragment of the gigantic mosaic to which he or she had been allotted. We recorded many of these passionately human stories at the time and published them, as facets of the living history of China. One such was that of a model hacker and carrier of earth, Ma Fu-cheh, who looked absurdly like a priest, with his shaven head and a white padded collar broad enough to cushion the weight of his carrying pole on his shoulders. After telling of the tragedy of his village in which only five out of thirty-six families survived one of the Huai floods, the six members of his own family wandering from place to place as beggars, he continued:

'We heard that Red Army people were in our village and that they were good. We heard that if they stay in a peasant's home they help to cut firewood and carry water. We heard too some rumours about the land being divided up, so we decided to come home. That was two years ago. But half our village never came back. From the family next to me six went away and only two came back. The rest died. My uncle's family all died. We were given 2½ acres of land last year, but of course it was flooded in the autumn. When Chairman Mao sent out the call for volunteers to stop the floods, I simply got terribly

excited. I made two baskets and waited for the day to set out.'
Wasn't he worried about the farm at home? 'The mutual-aid
team are looking after it and they won't take a cent for the
work. The government gave our family a loan and we pooled
it with two other families and bought an ox to make it easier
for the women to do the work.'

Apart from some work done in Shanghai factories, such as
making sluice gates and fittings, the state invested just 50,000
tons of rice in the whole Huai river project – enough to feed
the peasants who willingly gave of their labour to end the
greatest scourge of their lives. One sixty-five-year-old peasant,
wrinkled and brown like an old walnut, with enormous ears
and a tuft of wispy beard, was introduced to us as 'Old Huan
Chung', from a character of that name in the *Three Kingdoms*
novel who never knew he was old. He told us a harrowing life-
story from childhood on, of being at the mercy of floods and
landlords until liberation brought with it 1½ acres of land as a
start, and until land reform (not then completed in his province)
made the final distribution.

'That old turtle Chiang broke the dyke and the Yellow river
flooded our province.[2] We must now build dykes and dams so
that the land in both high and low places will yield good grain.
All will have plenty to eat and a good life. When the dyke is
finished we'll have land reform. We'll have bigger crops and
we'll be able to send part of it to our brothers in Korea and
to our own volunteers there ... How could we have a better
arrangement than this? We work for ourselves and eat government grain!' And he grinned so broadly that his eyes disappeared behind the wrinkles.

The new concepts touched on by 'Old Huan' (whose real

2. 'Old Huan' was referring to an incident in June 1938 in which
Chiang Kai-shek sent a division of troops to Hua Yen Kou, at the Yellow
river bend, to blow a forty-five-foot gap in the dykes, at a moment when
the water-level was 9 feet above the surrounding countryside. His troops
machine-gunned villagers who rushed to try to repair the gap. In this
vain attempt to halt the Japanese advance into Hopei province half a
million people, including many of Chiang's own troops, were drowned,
and over 6 million made homeless. The Yellow river turned south, ejecting
the Huai from its own bed to flood the surrounding countryside.

name was Cheng Hang-shin) were enlarged on by Wang Feng-wu, the Commissioner (the title in those days of the chief official of an administrative sub-region) of the Suihsien region of North Anhwei, one of the most hard-hit regions in the 1950 floods. As the work progressed, he said: 'You can see a peasant's outlook changing from day to day. Like peasants in all countries, the Chinese peasant is an extreme individualist and because of our feudal society the world did not exist for him outside his own family. He comes to the river work at first to earn some relief grain to feed himself and send some back to his family. At most he has accepted the idea that he is working to stop floods on his own land or land which will be his after land reform. He expects to mark out a piece of ground, dig it out and carry it away as an individual, measuring to the last cubic centimetre how much he has cut. Instead of that, he finds it is more convenient to work with a team. If he is on ramming work, he can only work in a team. Two things happen to him. He gets the first idea of co-operative work. He begins to exchange ideas with other peasants. He attends meetings where peasants from other villages and even other districts tell of their sufferings from floods. He sees his work as a larger thing than saving his own farm-land.

'He starts to have a fellow-feeling for his work-mates and sees them working together to save the whole district. He goes to lectures where the cause of floods is explained, and he is told that hundreds of miles away there are more peasants working, building dams, and he begins to see that only by the united labour of peasants over wide areas of the country can floods be stopped. Step by step, by his own experiences on the river site, he begins to think of the village instead of his farm, the district instead of his village, the county and region, and eventually he grasps the conception of China. From that it is not a big step for him to understand the danger to China by what is happening in Korea, and he begins to acquire a world outlook.

'And that is not all,' continued Commissioner Wang. 'The only reason he can work on the river site is because of organization at home. His wife and children and aged father have combined with other wives, children and parents to plough the land, sow the crops and reap the harvest. They have pooled their animals to get the work done. Where there are no animals, groups of them combine together to pull ploughs and harrows. Here at the front and in the villages in the rear, the first steps are being taken in co-operative work. The peasants will never go back to the old individualistic way of thinking after these experiences. They become receptive to the new forms of co-operative work, to co-operative farming of which the mutual-aid teams are the first step. So you see', he concluded, 'we are not only changing nature, but we are changing the outlook of our peasants at the same time.'

During the twenty-two intervening years, as Huai river-type projects greatly reduced – and eliminated in many areas – the danger of catastrophic floods, the accent on hydraulic engineering shifted to irrigation projects, carried on without state investments, at county or commune levels. The model for such projects is the Red Flag Canal in Linhsien county in the northwest corner of Honan province, referred to in an earlier chapter as an example of the development of county industry in the wake of water.

Another of the Great Leap Forward projects, it was born of the failure of previous efforts to solve the problem of water in Linhsien county. Three big reservoirs and a 7-mile canal had been built by county co-operatives in 1957, but as there was a big drought in 1958 the reservoirs remained dry. After the formation of the communes that year it was decided to work out a radical solution, and by 1959 an audacious ten-year plan was drawn up to tap the Chiang river at a high point in the Taihang mountains in neighbouring Shansi province, hacking out a twenty-five-mile-long canal, 20 to 25 feet wide by 12 feet deep, out of the plunging cliffs to lead the water around the mountain and down to the plains. Three subsidiary canals would branch off the main trunk canal to bring water to every commune field throughout the county, turning small hydro-generators on the way. Altogether a total of 1,000 miles of canals, and everything to be made on the spot – lime, blasting-powder, crow-bars and chisels, with human muscle-power substituting for machines. Work started in February 1960, the local county Communist Party committee ignoring orders from Liu Shao-ch'i, four times in three years, to halt the work on the grounds that valuable man-power was being diverted from agriculture. By June 1969, the plans were completed and peasants came from far and wide to gaze at the miraculous plenitude of water in Linhsien county.

By any standards it is a major engineering work. The three main subsidiary channels totalled over sixty miles and altogether the project meant cutting 180 tunnels totalling fifteen miles, building 150 aqueducts to span gullies and canyons, and displacing 16.4 million cubic metres of stone and earthworks, which someone calculated was enough to build a mini-Great Wall 3 feet high by 12 wide north to south across the whole of China from Harbin to Canton!

The Ta Feng (Bumper Harvest) aqueduct, for instance, spans a gully over 500 yards wide, carrying a 14-feet-wide channel and rising 50 feet above a highway. Built of massive bluestone rocks, quarried and dressed by members of commune work-teams, moved to the spot in convoys of donkey carts and hauled into place by ropes and improvised winches, it is a magnificent piece of work, with massive buttressed arches, through which double rows of traffic pass, supporting the whole thing. It was built in sixty days by 700 members of nine work brigades, paid on work-points and thus financed from the normal commune income.

At the time of our 1973 visit, finishing touches were being given to the Nankutung reservoir, one of the three originally built in 1957, but now greatly expanded to form a beautiful lake over four miles long with a storage capacity of 67 million cubic metres. It is no longer conceived as a primary source of water supply but as a reserve, to be filled up at leisure, just in case the Chiang river unprecedently dries up. A dam, over a thousand feet wide at the bottom and sloping up to form a 45-feet-wide roadway at the top, towered 250 feet from the bed of the Lo Shui river, which was gradually filling the lake.

In every direction there were lush fields of maize, apple and pear orchards, and glistening lines of water-filled canals, an orderly example of the 'waterproofing' process that is spreading over much of China.

What had happened at Linhsien was of particular interest to us, because it was the very centre of the terrible Honan famine of 1942, of which we had witnessed some of the horrifying consequences. It is estimated that in 1942–3 between 3 and 10 million people died. If it was not much publicized at the time, this was because it started in the early stages of Japan's entry into the Second World War, and, in order not to encourage the Japanese to exploit the disaster, journalists more or less accepted the bland Kuomintang assurances in Chungking that there was no such thing as a famine. After the Second World War, there were several accounts of the horrors and extent of the Honan famine, stressing the fact that Chiang Kai-shek, despite a well-documented account from the very conservative Catholic Bishop Paul Yu-p'in, never lifted a finger to alleviate the sufferings. Some of our own impressions were as follows:

'The Kuomintang made no attempt to help the people, who were hit with a combination of flood, drought and plagues of locusts. I visited the area at the time and saw tens of thousands of living skeletons staggering along the roads and dying by the wayside. There was not an ear of grain or a blade of grass left on the brown earth for thousands of acres, not even leaves or bark left on the trees. Anything which could be digested by the human stomach had long been eaten, including bark, dried grass and leaves, which were sold as food in the village markets. A great exodus from the stricken parts started with millions of peasants leaving their native villages never to return. They sold up farms, implements, wives and daughters in an effort to stave off disaster, hoping to buy them again when times got better. They ate their seed stocks, their oxen and donkeys, the dried-up grain stalks in the field, and even tried to stop their hunger pains by eating the earth itself.'

This account was based on what happened in Shansi province, which adjoins Honan to the south-west and to which millions of famine victims made their way in hope of relief. Finding nothing to eat in Shansi, they crammed on to the tops of trains, squatting dangerously also on the undercarriages until they were too weak to cling on.

In all, four provinces were hard hit by a three years' cycle of floods, drought and pests lasting from 1941 to 1943, like the cycle almost exactly twenty years later. Of the four, Shantung, Hopei, Shansi and Honan, it was the latter which was hardest hit, and within Honan it was Linhsien county. But, as Phuong Chen-chi, of the Foreign Affairs section of Linhsien county, explained, if 125 rainless days on end in 1942 provoked a mortal catastrophe, 300 rainless days on end in 1972 caused hardly a dint in production. Had 1942 been a normal year the grain yield would have been 600 pounds per acre; as it was a drought year, it was nil pounds per acre. In the bumper year of 1971 the per-acre yield was about 1·5 tons, with about 50 pounds per acre less in the record dry year of 1972. A spectacular success for 'waterproofing'! Even in the early years after liberation, Phuong Chen-chi assured us – and we had confirmation of this in scores of conversations with the local people – three hundred of the county's five hundred villages were without drinking water. It had to be carried by humans or on donkeys for anything from one to six miles. The region had two peculiarities – that people begged for water as they did for food in other areas, and that they hired themselves out to landlords for wages paid in water.

On the question of what the revolution has done for the Chinese people, the experiences of the Linhsien people are instructive, to say the least – especially if, as we did, one probes into the lives of those who played outstanding roles in building the Red Flag Canal. Their sufferings, however, were only some degrees more dramatic than those in many other areas where the endless cycle of floods, droughts, insect plagues and resulting famine was broken only by the sweeping away of feudal fetters and bureaucratic indifference.

Having seen an excellent documentary film of the canal-building, we tracked down some of those whose exploits had been visibly spectacular.

One episode in the film which had the audience gasping is that in which a figure, dangling most perilously at the end of a rope, swings out over a deep ravine, using his legs and body like a swimmer to propel himself against the sheer cliff face, where, like an eagle attacking its prey, he pecks away with an iron bar to lever off a piece of rock. Then, pushing powerfully with his feet, he swings out into space again as far as the rope will go, then comes in again for another attack. Again and again he repeats this, and each time a rock goes hurtling down into the ravine. We found him on solid earth – Jen Yang-chang, a slight man, with a cheerful, triangular face from Ku Chan village of Linhsien county. What he wanted to talk about first was that Chen Yung-kuei, that stubborn hero of Tachai, was from the same village, their two families having left about the same time during the 1942 famine. This was further fascinating confirmation for us of what goes into the making of a hero in China! But we wanted to hear Jen Yang-chang's own story.

'In the days of the great famine,' he said, 'conditions were terrible. No food grain, no water, not even any fuel for the cooking pots of those who still had some reserves. As a kid, I went up to the mountains looking for fuel to sell – and for my family to use. Things got to the point where there was nothing. Trees had completely disappeared, the fields were bare of grass. But peering down into the ravines, I could see there were tufts of grass growing in clefts in the rock face. Together with some friends we weaved rough ropes, taking it in turns to let each other down to get that grass.' He pointed to a gap in his teeth and said: 'A bit of rock fell once and knocked out four teeth. When the canal work started, I thought of the danger from falling rocks to the young people working from ropes to hack out the first footholds for building the canal. I suggested that, to protect them, we must first prise off all the loose rocks above where they had to work. It was agreed and I was very proud to lead a team of thirty volunteers to continue this until the job was done. But this time we had proper strong ropes, checked every morning before we started work.'

Sixty-three-year-old Lu Yin, tall with a dome-shaped head, is also in the film. He is seen getting levels for setting explosive charges – not by a theodolite, but by sighting along bars of small frames floating in enamel wash-basins. 'During the great famine,' he said, 'we had to leave our native Kuo Chia Yao village and go begging for water and food. We were nine altogether and I carried the smallest children in baskets at the end of a carrying pole. We headed for Shansi, where we heard it was easier to get land to cultivate. But things were scarcely better there. I worked for a landlord for half a cup of grain per day. How could a family be fed from that? We collected leaves from hillside trees and dried and powdered them. But the family still starved. I was forced to sell my three-year-old son for 50 kilos of millet and 25 kilos of rice husks – to keep the others alive. My younger brother then tried to sell his son, but he was so skinny that nobody would buy him. He died. We poor peasants were saved only when the Eighth Route Army liberated our area in 1944 and carried out land reform. How could we not agree enthusiastically when the idea was put up to build a canal and solve the water problem?'

Explaining why he had headed the group in charge of explosives, Lu Yin replied: 'For three generations my family have been quarry workers. At county and commune level, they asked me to work on the canal. I wanted nothing better. We quarry workers put our heads together and discussed all the problems. We are not technicians, but the advice of the older people is respected and we learned from each other. We were used to handling explosives in the straightforward way you do in quarrying, and we had to work out new techniques for cutting a canal out of the rock face and especially for tunnelling. But we managed because everyone was determined to solve the water problem once and for all.'

The tunnelling was a major problem. The further the tunnellers progressed, the longer it took for the fumes from the black powder explosives to clear away. Without any ventilation or mechanical smoke-evacuating equipment, it took longer and longer between charges before the workmen could get in to clear out the fallen rock. As tunnels up to 4,000 yards long had to be driven though, the problem seemed insoluble, until Wang She-tung got the idea of blasting out a series of 'chimneys' down to the canal-bed level, wide enough for workers to be lowered to set the explosives, and then working out in both directions until the base of the 'chimneys' were linked up. The fumes would thus be evacuated by natural draught and the 'chimneys' filled in later. For the 4,000-yard tunnel, thirty-four such 'chimneys' were blasted out, with Wang She-tung in the vanguard – lowered down, level by level, to set their first explosives, hauled up before the fuses set off the charges, until he got to the levels calculated by Lu Yin with his wash-basin 'theodolites'. Five feet in diameter and almost 200 feet deep in the centre of the tunnel, the vertical shafts were blasted out and the dynamiters and those who cleared the debris lowered and hauled up by improvised winches until bedrock level was reached and the shafts had all been linked up to permit the horizontal clearing and stone-facing work to continue. Another of the documentary 'film stars', Wang She-tung looked older than his forty-three years at the time we met him, with his cropped hair and a sun-tanned, lean face which lit up into wrinkled smiles when he touched on a particularly hair-raising incident – a hitch in the winch with the fuse sputtering away below him! What had motivated him?

'Apart from the usual exploitation by the landlords when I was a lad,' he said, 'there was always shortage of food – and practically no water from the time I can remember. I am from Lu Gia village, one of the poorest in this terribly poor county. Now it is part of Tungkang, a very prosperous commune. We had a bit of land, but in 1942, when I was only twelve, we were hit by the drought and our family had to leave the land and go begging – for water more than food. My father and older brother found work for a short time with a landlord in a neighbouring county. I got work near by looking after a landlord's seven cows, from dawn to dusk. For that I earned two buckets of water a day. Some other refugee peasants got together and started digging a well in some common land near by. When they struck water, the landlord I worked for took it over, putting in a cement cover through which only his special oval-shaped bucket would pass. He put his men on guard day and night and only those who gathered fodder for his animals all day would be given one or two buckets, according to how much fodder they gathered. That's how some of us survived. Thirty households went off from Lu Gia village and not a single member returned. Perhaps some of them survived in Shansi or Shensi – we don't know. But no one came back. Of my family of thirteen, eleven died. Most of them set off for Shansi, where there was supposed to be grain. There was none. People ate leaves, then bark from the trees and finally a sort of soft white earth that was supposed to be edible, but those who ate it soon died. When Chairman Mao says "Water is the life-blood of agriculture", that is something we could all understand. Sometimes when things went wrong in the tunnelling – a charge failed to explode and I had to go down to see what had happened – I thought what an unimportant thing it would be if I got blown up in comparison to the great work that was going on to serve the generations to come.'

To complete the group of those we were able to contact from the documentary film there was Han Yang-ti, a bobbed-haired young woman of twenty-six, very relaxed and self-assured, typical of the young people who had invested their muscle-power, enthusiasm and idealism in building the canal. She had headed an 'Iron Girls' team, working under Wang She-tung in blasting out the vertical shafts. In the film, she is seen lighting a score or so fuses and then being hauled up to the surface in what seems a hair-raising, dangerously slow ascent as the camera switches to the sparks snaking their way along to the explosive charges. The commentator explained that Han Yang-ti was always the last of her team to be hauled up after the fuses had been lit and the first to be lowered to check up and fan away the smoke.

She was a toddler of two at the time of liberation and knew only from family lore that thirteen relatives had left for Shansi during the 1942 famine and had not been heard of since; others survived by slaving for local landlords – who expropriated the abandoned farms. As a child after liberation she recalls members of the family spending much time fetching water from a stream five miles distant.

'It took up most of their time,' she said, 'but I accepted that as just a normal fact of life. Later I often listened to my parents talking about life in the old days with the lack of water always the centre of discussion. When the canal project was announced, of course I volunteered immediately. When I asked to work with explosives, older people in the village shook their heads and said: "Blasting rocks is no work for young girls. It's beyond their strength – no good can come of it." Finally they changed their views, until now they like to talk about the village girl who made a contribution.' When we asked what she wanted to do later on in life, she replied: 'Continue as a farmer or a worker – both are fine as far as I am concerned. What is important is not what you do but how you do it.' At the time we talked to her, Han Yang-ti was in charge of maintenance work on a section of the main canal, but 'Whatever the revolution wants me to do, I'll do' were her last words to us.

We drove up into the Taihang mountains to the corner where Honan meets Shansi and Hopei provinces, rising above what was left of the chocolate-coloured Chiang river, which creamed swiftly down its rocky bed with the majestic mountains soaring above, green where there were slopes, ochre-coloured where they broke off into sheer cliffs, alternate layers of green and ochre until they disappeared into swirling mists. The part of the river which had not been diverted into the canal had been reduced to a point at which the commune members in the valley had been able to reclaim land. Behind walls built in the river bed, they had filled in the space with soil in the Tachai manner. At the height of a thousand feet, walking the last few hundred up steps carved into the cliff-side, we came to the main canal, where the main body of the river now flowed deep and placid in contrast to the foaming rush of the river we had followed from the plains – there had been torrential rains for three days on end before our 1973 visit. We came to what is called the 'Youth Tunnel' where the canal waters disappeared into an arched passage, 20 feet wide at the bottom and 16 feet to the tip of the arch, hacked and blasted out of cliffs rising another hundred feet above the tunnel, a silvery waterfall hurtling down in bursts of spray in the background. The tunnel, 650 yards long, had presented the same problem of smoke dispersal as the longer versions. The youthful builders cut five downward-sloping lateral shafts, 6 feet in diameter and from 10 to 20 yards long, to get the workers in and the fumes out. It was built by 300 young commune members working for seventeen months. When one looked up at the vertical cliffs, with not a foothold for the most daring mountain goat, one could only marvel at what had been done with blasting powder and coal chisels – and that only two youths had lost their lives on the job. It was a spot from which to admire the grandeur of these wild mountains, so friendly to the guerrillas, so hostile to Japanese and Kuomintang invaders, with remnants of bandit fortresses on their ridges. The 'Lin' of Linhsien means forests – literally county of forests – but these had disappeared over a century earlier, perhaps because the tree bark had been consumed during the periodic droughts! The crumbling bandit fortresses, naked in the misty sunlight, had once been protected by tall trees, now replaced by stunted shrubs.

It should not be thought that the Red Flag Canal is the only one of its kind. Even in the prefecture in which it is situated, that of Anyang, Honan, there is already a new large-scale one called the 'Victory' being built. The Chinese farmer knows well enough what water control means to him. Give him the chance to organize to get water or control it, and he responds with all his immense collective might.

No country in the world has done so much in water conservancy over the past two decades as China has. Every winter off-season, in all parts of the land, a great number of commune folk mobilize groups to go off and work on such projects. The conservation of the Hai river basin in Hopei, for instance, following a natural disaster in 1963, took 300,000 commune members each winter for the succeeding decade to build enough big-dyked diversion channels all the way across the plains to the sea. Shantung and Honan provinces have seen similar great movements.

In the Szechuan 'Red Basin' practically the whole of the ancient irrigation system there has been re-dug and the land re-moulded into rectangular flat fields, making the project irrigate five times its original amount. The Wei valley plains of Shensi from Paochi eastwards have been irrigated with a large-scale system entailing many new bridges and highways. In Hupeh, along the Yangtze, the whole of the Hung Hu region is now controlled with a new system of dykes, sluice gates and canals, while a new giant flood diversion basin is being built there. Such projects, small and big, are now current in every part of China. It is hard to think of any region we visited, whether up amongst the Miao folk of west Hunan, down with the Tai along the Lao border, with the Korean minority folk along the cliffs of the Tumen river below Chang Bai Shan, or anywhere else in this vast land, where there are no new irrigation schemes. Their building has been one of the most outstanding proofs of the success of the Chinese revolution.

Having seen the Red Flag Canal and its myriad subsidiary works and visited other grandiose flood-control works, including several inspired by the Red Flag Canal, and above all having talked with the builders at all levels, we felt that Yü the Great, Lin Pin, Pai Sha Ta-ti and other great hydraulic engineers throughout the millennia could rest content that water control was in the hands of worthy successors.

PART FOUR

THE QUALITY OF LIFE

CHAPTER FOURTEEN

CHINA'S HEALTH

Americans visiting China in the wake of Nixon's ice-breaking trip in early 1972 always comment on how healthy and relaxed the Chinese seem to be. What poor subjects for doctors and psychiatrists! This was an aspect of the new society which we had long taken for granted, but, faced with repeated requests for the whys and wherefores, we decided to raise the subject with our old friend, Dr George Hatem, or Dr Ma Hai-teh as he is known to millions of Chinese. Conveniently we found him at the Peitaiho seaside resort, where we had met to compare notes after our separate travels. Coincidentally, when we first found him he was dissertating on this very subject to a younger sister, freshly arrived from the United States, whom he had not seen for forty-odd years and who had immediately started pestering him about why people looked in such good shape when they obviously worked hard and owned little.

As it would be inappropriate to quote from Dr Ma without introducing him properly and establishing his credentials, we must digress somewhat to present a rare and remarkable foreign participant in the Chinese revolution.

With a brand-new medical degree in his pocket, George Hatem arrived in Shanghai in 1933, fresh from completing his formal medical studies at the University of Geneva, via the American University of North Carolina and the Rockefeller Hospital in Beirut. He was the guileless, good-hearted, apolitical son of a Lebanese migrant steel-worker who had settled in Buffalo, New York State. (Nearly forty years later, as the naturalized Chinese doctor Ma Hai-teh, he was to return to Geneva at the head of a medical team to ease the final days of his great friend Edgar Snow, then dying of cancer.)

Why Shanghai? The reason was as casual as that which had brought Rewi Alley there six years earlier.

'I thought I would learn a little tropical medicine in China, before completing my world tour and returning to the States to start practising.' What had 'turned him on' to the extent of completely identifying himself with the revolution?

'I was appalled at the conditions in China. Nothing I had read prepared me for what I found. Poverty, disease wherever you looked. Nothing a doctor could do about it. You could diagnose, write prescriptions, but the people you wanted to help had no means of paying for the medicine. It was hard enough for them just to avoid starving to death. Many couldn't even do that. Getting enough to eat was their main problem. Buying medicine was beyond their dreams.

'Then there were the executions all the time. It was a fashionable week-end spectacle for some foreigners to go to the big Lunghua pagoda – where Shanghai's international airport is now – and watch young men and women being decapitated or shot. It impressed me how calm they were, and always shouting "Long live Communism" before they were cut down.'

What were his first steps along the forty years' march with the Chinese revolution?

'I used to pick up some books at a left-wing bookshop run by a Dutch woman, Irene Wertemeyer, and there was a German, Hans Schippe, who I discovered was the "Asiaticus" whose articles had attracted my attention in the Shanghai English-language press. He was a frequent visitor to the shop. They introduced me to Agnes Smedley, who had just written *The Red Army Marches*, and she put me in touch with Rewi Alley. At that time he was Chief Factory Inspector of the Shanghai Municipality and at one of our early meetings he asked me what I knew about "chrome dermatitis". I said, "Not much, but I'm willing to learn." Rewi was indignant about the conditions under which teenage boys were working over open chromium vats, without any exhausts to draw off the poisonous fumes, in the chromium-plating industry. He was right to be indignant. Conditions were horrifying. Chrome holes in their nostrils, chrome sores all over their bodies, the poison eating right into the bones of their fingers and in between their toes. They were living skeletons who slept alongside the vats and machines for lack of lodgings. I looked into this for several months and wrote a report which was published as a monograph by the Lester Institute in Shanghai under the signature of its director. The result was some minor reforms. At least it attracted some attention to the scandalous conditions. It was for trying to agitate against this sort of thing that youngsters were being executed at the Lunghua pagoda.

'Through my contacts at the left bookshop, through Agnes Smedley and Rewi Alley, I kept hearing about the Red Army – communists who were said to be really doing something for the people. And I couldn't get out of my mind the bearing of those young people shouting "Long live Communism" before they died. I felt very frustrated as a medical man, surrounded by the most urgent problems about which I could do nothing.

'When word came through via Rewi in early 1936 that the Red Army needed a Western-trained doctor, I was delighted. By that time there were only two things I wanted to do – go to help the Republicans in Spain or go to serve with the Chinese Red Army. Rewi's message was decisive. So I started out to find the Red Army with Ed Snow, a journalist having also been asked for.'[1]

After many adventures, the travellers finally made contact with the Red Army – in the form of a black-bearded Chou En-lai – and were escorted on to Mao's headquarters, at Pao An in North Shensi at that time. One of George Hatem's first tasks was to give Chairman Mao a thorough medical check, pronouncing him in excellent shape – at a moment when he was variously reported killed in battle or dying from tuberculosis. Towards the end of 1936 after the Fourth Front Army under Chu Teh and the Second Front Army under Ho Lung had joined up and were completing their part of the Long March, Dr Hatem joined them, very impressed by the fact that the two legendary commanders – Chu Teh was Commander-in-Chief

1. The fact that George Hatem shared the adventures of crossing into the Red Army areas with Edgar Snow was not mentioned in the early editions of *Red Star over China*, as the fact that there was an American doctor at Mao Tse-tung's headquarters was a closely guarded secret for many years.

of the Red Army – marched with their troops, carrying their own gear, having given up their horses to wounded army men. He accompanied the Second Front Army to Yenan, where the Red Army headquarters was set up and George Hatem was to join his medical headquarters and help to direct – among other activities – a training centre for medical cadres. When Ed Snow left some four months later with his notes and photos to return to Shanghai and write his first great classic on the revolution as it had unfolded until that time, George Hatem had already decided to throw in his lot with the revolutionaries, locating himself in the brain and nerve centre of it all from that time on.

In the early 1940s, Rewi Alley – by then in Chungking – received a terse telegram: 'GETTING MARRIED STOP SEND MONEY STOP GEORGE.' The money was sent; George married a very beautiful, intelligent political activist in the revolutionary theatre – Ssu Fei – and Rewi Alley was interrogated at length by Kuomintang agents as to why he had again sent 'funds to Mao Tse-tung's headquarters'. (He bluffed his way out of it, but it was one of the charges later used to get him sacked as Chief Technical Adviser of the industrial co-operative movement.) That was the beginning of the metamorphosis of the American son of an immigrant steel-worker into a Chinese citizen and, eventually, member of the Chinese Communist Party, who reversed the name Hatem into Ma Hai-teh, Ma (horse) being the most typical Moslem surname in China, appropriate to someone of Lebanese origin.

When the People's Liberation Army moved its headquarters to Peking in 1949, Dr Ma obviously moved also, as a cadre in the Public Health Ministry. Within a few years he was to be known in the outside world as an outstanding epidemologist who had played a considerable role in the field during nation-wide campaigns to eradicate a whole range of epidemic diseases in China, one of the most notable successes being the total elimination of venereal disease, especially syphilis, which had wrought havoc among the minority peoples.

In the years following liberation, Ma Hai-teh has worked with medical teams in virtually every province in China, even 'pursuing the spirochete over the grasslands of Inner Mongolia', as he remarked on one occasion, in campaigns to eradicate everything from elephantiasis and leprosy to shistosomiasis, including malaria, cholera, smallpox, bubonic plague, kala-azar and others in between, with results that have made the international medical fraternity sit up and rub their eyes.[2]

So much for the credentials of Ma Hai-teh. Asked what he considered the single greatest success in the field of public health, Dr Ma replied: 'The provision of medical services to the grass-roots – the constant day-to-day availability that works year in and year out, that continuing drip-drop that brings the steady results. The campaigns are more dramatic, but it is the day-to-day follow-through work that results in the eradication of disease. This was in addition to keeping a tab on the general state of health of the whole population. People are very healthy now. They get a good start through proper nourishment, infant care and more generalized knowledge of how to look after children, so that you get a healthier youth growing up from the start. But the secret of the glowing health that visitors remark on in the streets is this constant day in and day out availability of health care. People know the service is there – and they use it.'

How is it done in practical terms in view of the enormous population and the terribly backward state of Chinese medical services at the take-off point?

'By a tripod of measures,' explains Ma Hai-teh. ' "Barefoot doctors",[3] traditional medicine and co-operative medical aid provide a solid foundation for the grass-roots medical services. In a country like China with so many people it is impossible to provide that scope of on-the-spot medical service in any other way. There are over a million barefoot doctors, so you reach at least 90 per cent of the commune brigades through these three

2. Striking confirmation of the phenomenal success of these efforts can be found in *Medicine and Public Health in the People's Republic of China*, published by the U.S. Department of Health, Education and Welfare, in June 1972 (DHEW publication No. 72–76).

3. 'Barefoot doctors', sometimes described as neighbourhood first-aid workers, receive a few months' basic medical training, followed up by regular refresher courses. They can handle most of the petty ailments and call in fully trained doctors for cases beyond their competence. They are part-time medical workers, part-time farmers.

measures. Co-operative medicine means that commune members pay very small fees, the barefoot doctor is paid on the work-points system out of brigade funds, the brigade buying some specific medicines like antibiotics out of the fees paid, but the majority of the medicines used are herbal, grown on the spot, gathered by commune members or bought at insignificant prices out of brigade funds from the state pharmaceutical companies.'

We asked how the idea of barefoot doctors originated. Dr Ma thought it was a continuation of a practice introduced by the Red Army. 'In those days, our medical schools in the Chinese Soviet areas turned out medical workers in seven to eight months. Until the end of the anti-Japanese war and the start of the liberation war,' he continued, 'you could count on the fingers of both hands the number of modern university-trained doctors in the Liberated Areas and with the Red Army. Virtually all the medical work was done by the people we trained ourselves in these short courses. So there was a long tradition of training various para-medical personnel. "Qualified" in those days meant a different thing to us. The idea of barefoot doctors was alive then but under a different name. Those people with seven or eight months' training could handle simple surgery, limb amputations and so on, but chest and internal surgery was very complicated owing to the lack of instruments and anaesthetics. Acupuncture anaesthesia had not been developed at that time.'

The four fundamental principles on which the approach to medical care were based Dr Ma defined as: 'Serving the workers, soldiers and peasants; emphasizing prevention; integrating and unifying traditional Chinese medicine with modern medicine; and cultivating a mass approach to health work and methods. The first point did not imply that workers, soldiers and peasants were to be cared for and other sections of the population neglected; it was a corrective for the old concepts in which the poorer sections of the community were totally neglected, not only because they had no money but because it entailed 'loss of face' for a traditional doctor to treat the poor. On 26 June 1965, Mao called for radical improvement in the rural health services. According to a version published by a group of Red Guards during the Cultural Revolution, in the statement accompanying this call Mao delivered some pithy remarks regarding the Health Ministry and the attitude of many of the doctors. 'The Ministry of Public Health works for only 15 per cent of the country's population,' he is quoted as stating, 'and of this 15 per cent, mainly the lords are catered to. The broad masses of the peasants get no medical treatment – they have neither doctors nor medicine. The Ministry of Public Health is not that of the people and it had better be renamed the Ministry of Urban Health for the Overlords.' Mao called for placing the focus of medical work in the rural areas.

There was a tremendous response to the call and by the autumn of 1965 some 150,000 medical workers left the cities to bring their skills to the rural areas. Hundreds of thousands more followed in subsequent years.

'Some of them went on a temporary basis from six months to a year,' Ma Hai-teh continued; 'others settled down. They worked in rural hospitals, but, more important, they gave short training courses at county and commune level, so that the communes could handle the overwhelming majority of their own medical problems.' It was around November 1965 that the term 'barefoot doctor' began to be used. (Some foreign visitors to brigade clinics were surprised to find the white-gowned, white-capped barefoot doctors invariably wearing sandals or canvas shoes. The term arose spontaneously, because half the time they do field work like other commune members, which often means working knee-deep and barefoot in rice-field mud.)

'They go through almost continual automatic refresher courses,' explained Dr Ma. 'They are in continual contact with city-trained doctors at commune or county level; they go up to the county seat several times a year for one- or two-day courses and if any new disease shows up in their area they are called in for special courses where they learn how to cope. The same thing happens if some more effective way has been discovered to cure old diseases. Some are taught to specialize in just one thing if it happens to be a problem in the area – shistosomiasis for instance, which is eradicated in most parts of China but still exists, especially in areas where seasonal flooding has not yet been eliminated.'

A revolution in doctor–patient relations was brought about by the massive influx into the countryside of the university-trained graduates. China had suffered no less than most other countries from the tendency of the medical profession to congregate in the cities, and in his 26 June 1965 directive Mao had commented ironically on the doctors' habit of donning gauze masks before examining anybody, thus creating a psychological barrier between himself and his patient. 'Is he afraid of communicating his own disease to other people? I think the main reason is that he is afraid of being infected by the people.' This sort of barrier disappeared overnight when the doctors went into the communes, where many of them got to know the peasants for the first time in their lives. The American writer Mark Selden, who made a special study of the situation in 1971, reported that: 'By January 1971, more than 330,000 urban medical workers, including the most recent graduates of medical colleges, had settled in the countryside and 400,000 more had participated in mobile medical teams.'[4]

This typical massive Mao-style concentration of forces Ma Hai-teh believed was the secret of the overall success on the health front. Regarding the eradication of syphilis he pointed out that, according to recognized authorities, syphilis had shown a marked increase in recent years in 75 out of 105 countries and territories, and that authoritative American sources claimed there were 1·2 million untreated cases in the U.S.A., where the incidence of syphilis had continually increased since 1957. People's China got off to a bad start with an incidence of syphilis of up to 20 per cent among Kuomintang troops, who spread it like wildfire in every town and village through which they passed. Statistics showed that the incidence of syphilis in small towns and rural towns was in direct proportion to the size of the Japanese, American and Kuomintang troops units and the duration of their stay. The overall national percentage however was highest (10 per cent) among the national minorities,

4. 'Health and Revolution. The Chinese Medical System', from *Essays on Contemporary China*, Peck, Schurmann and Riskin, New York, 1972.

with a staggering 48 per cent of 163,000 people examined in Inner Mongolia (where the traditional hospitality of the women-folk to visiting males was a major factor), compared to 5 per cent in the cities and – except for areas particularly ravaged by war – 1 to 3 per cent in the countryside.

Dr Ma pointed out that a single injection of neosalvarsan in pre-liberation days would cost a national minority herdsman a horse or cow; and that poverty, ignorance, illiteracy and un-employment, which forced the daughters of the poor into prostitution, provided the propitious social climate in which syphilis thrived. A major factor in treating the disease was eliminating the social and economic causes. The economic roots of prostitution were cut, facilitating elimination, rather than the 'control' often favoured in the West. Brothels were closed, the inmates separated from the owners and organized into groups for examination, education and free medical treatment, after which they went back to their villages or were found jobs in the cities. This in itself was a major blow at syphilis because it struck straight away at a major source of infection. The prob-lem, as everywhere in the world, was to locate the latent cases, the one in a hundred or one in a thousand. 'In this the Mao Tse-tung concept of putting "politics in command" was decisive. The problem of syphilis had to be explained on a political basis – a legacy of the old society." Our People's Government wants to help us get rid of this disease. It is no fault of your own that you are afflicted and no shame should be attached to it. If you have any of the symptoms – skin lesions, falling hair or genital sores – come for an examination. Comrades, we cannot take syphilis with us into socialism." That was the line we took in a mass campaign to get people co-operating. And it worked.'

This campaign was launched shortly after the People's Gov-ernment was set up and was headed by medical workers like Ma Hai-teh and others from the old Liberated Areas. By January 1956, Dr Ma said that specialists from eight major cities – in-cluding Peking, Shanghai and Tientsin – had reported only twenty-eight cases of infectious syphilis in the four years be-tween 1952 and 1955, and by 1964 the rate trend of early-infection syphilis in these same cities was estimated at less than twenty cases per 100 million people, with none at all in Shanghai or Tientsin.[5]

Regarding mental health, Dr Ma said that psychiatrists from the West generally agreed that the country was in good shape as far as psychiatric problems were concerned. 'Peking has 700 beds in mental disease hospitals,' he said. 'That is virtually all there are for the whole of North China and these beds are far from being all occupied. This is partly because the attitude to treatment is different, but mainly because the socio-economic system is such that people are not subject to the same strains and stresses that produce the depressive type of mental ailments that are so frequent in the West, nor to the sort of contradictions that give rise to schizophrenia. Treatment is based on getting people back to normal, familiar surroundings as soon as possible, back to their families or the collective. People are encouraged to get together, to talk over their problems. But there is no Western-style compulsion to try to keep up with the Joneses. Of course there are economic problems in some families, but these problems are settled within the collective.

'Bringing up all one's problems and speaking out frankly about anything from bringing up the children onwards is a way of letting off steam – psychiatric therapy if you want to call it that – which eases emotional strains. It is not my field, but every doctor has to have something of a psychologist in him, and professionally speaking it is not a problem that comes my way, or that of my colleagues. So in general it is not a problem. There are some rare cases of schizophrenia, usually brought about by suspicions of wives or husbands about the fidelity of their spouses during long separations. But these are extremely rare. The type of schizophrenia which exists in the West because of contradictions between what one learns of moral right and wrong as a child and what you have to do in real life, just to get by, does not exist here. After living and working here for so

5. Part of the above material on how syphilis was eradicated is from a report by Dr Ma Hai-teh, *Mao Tse-tung's Thought as the Compass for Action in the Control of Venereal Diseases*, published by the Institute of Dermatology and Venereology, of the Chinese Academy of Sciences, October 1966, and made available to us by Dr Ma Hai-teh.

many years, it was difficult for me to realize the strains under which people live in capitalist society, especially in the United States, as my sister described them. The basis for so many of the fears – the disaster that can hit a family in case of illness or accident; teenagers going on to drugs; insecurity in the streets and parks; obsession with sex – simply do not exist in China. This is because of a collective, or socialist, rather than individual outlook.'

For a more detailed study of how mental problems are handled in China, Dr Ma referred us to an article, 'Mental Diseases and Their Treatment', by Ruth Sidel.[6] She discovered that there were 20,000 hospital beds altogether in China for treating psychiatric and mental cases. The average length of stay in the Shanghai Mental Hospital was seventy days, and the author comments that: 'Because of the recent disclosures of the political use of psychiatry in the Soviet Union, the process of psychiatric hospitalization seemed an important one to understand. The doctors at the Psychiatric Ward of the Third Hospital in Peking said that hospitalization is nearly always through persuasion by relatives, friends and colleagues at work. Occasional commitment is by force, but this was thought to be exceptional.

'After admission the patient needs to be persuaded by the personnel to remain and receive treatment. The technique of welcoming new patients by old patients and the old patients helping the new patients to adjust, was considered important in this beginning phase of hospitalization.' Ruth Sidel referred to the practice of group discussions in which the patients are encouraged to discuss their problems with each other, the technique of occupational therapy – rolling bandages and other light work – the great effort to create a normal family atmosphere and the importance of the fact that when a patient was discharged he or she was placed under the 'special concern of members of the revolutionary committee in his neighbourhood, as well as his family and friends, and this community concern, plus the assurance of a job and family waiting for him, helps to ease the transition from hospital to community'. Among her conclusions after a month's investigations in China was that the

6. In the book referred to in note 2, p. 231.

'belief in the malleability and perfectability of man "through education and re-education" is the foundation on which many of the new techniques such as Mao Tse-tung study groups are based'.

Another example of the use of mass methods to deal with drastic problems, which are now a nightmare in some Western countries, was related by another foreign doctor, also now of Chinese nationality, Dr Hans Müller, a leading cadre at Peking Union Medical College, who, during his medical studies in Basle, had been persuaded by Swiss progressives of the Chinese Red Army's need for doctors. Following the Japanese surrender and throughout the civil war, Hans Müller, a tall, thoughtful man whose speciality is internal medicine, was in charge of a base hospital in what was then known as Manchuria. It was a time when the Manchurian puppet troops, with no more Japanese to pay them, had disintegrated into landlords' armies in units averaging two to four hundred each. As land reform, in one stage or another, followed in the wake of what was now the People's Liberation Army and the power of the landlords was greatly reduced – even if they were subject only to rent reduction and cancellation of old debts – their private armies started switching their allegiance to the P.L.A. (When the Kuomintang started moving into certain areas, many changed their allegiance again!)

'A major problem was that these new recruits were almost 100 per cent opium addicts,' Dr Müller told us. 'Jehol (now part of North Hopei and Liaoning provinces), where I had my hospital, was the centre of opium production. It was the staple crop – any grain brought in was bought with money obtained from opium, which was the main cash crop. The landlords paid their private armies exclusively with opium. Every soldier had an improvised syringe made from copper tubing or cartridge cases, with cheap needles. They took the raw opium, dissolved it in hot water and injected it in their bodies. It was absolutely unrefined and scabs formed where the needles went in because of impurities which the body tissues rejected. The arms and upper parts of the bodies of these new recruits – or any captured in battle – were covered with scabs according to how long they had been soldiers. First one arm, then the other, then the body. When there was no place left for the needle between the scabs, a soldier reckoned he was about to die.'

The Pentagon's problems in Vietnam were obviously small stuff in comparison, but having in mind the long U.S. Army programmes for nursing addicts back to normalcy, we asked how the P.L.A. coped.

'By a mass attack on two fronts,' replied Dr Müller. 'By cutting off supplies to the recruits and by land reform. As soon as the troops came over, we isolated them in special compounds, for weeks or months if necessary. We gave them some political education and plenty of decent food for the first time. Completely cut off from supplies, the overwhelming majority of them quickly lost the habit. Once land reform was carried out, the peasants planted food crops, as they had always wanted to. It was only the landlords who were interested in opium production. They trafficked with it in the cities, where it was refined into heroin and other derivatives, which they sold to the Japanese who exported it all over the place.' (In Harbin alone, at the time of Japanese occupation, there were seventy-six opium dens and 58,567 – the 1940 figure – registered Chinese opium addicts.)

We had always been led to believe that addicts had to be slowly weaned away from the drug habit; that a sudden cut-off was medically dangerous.

'Nonsense,' was Dr Müller's reaction. 'A tiny proportion had to go to hospital, mainly because their systems had become so thoroughly poisoned and not because of the sudden cut-off. The physical changes were quickly remarkable – cheeks regained a healthy lustre, eyes lost their dullness and the former addicts were soon normal healthy lads again. But it was a wild time,' he mused. 'Many of them had become so used to looting and raping that they had difficulty in adjusting to the strict discipline of the P.L.A. When the Kuomintang started pushing in, some of them killed their P.L.A. cadres and crossed over to the Kuomintang, where they were encouraged in their old habits. It was a time when a fast horse made the difference between life and death. Under the Kuomintang, many of the former puppets started playing the same role as they had with the Japanese. But they were bad fighters, the Kuomintang troops little better. In one battle, 15,000 Kuomintang and puppet troops were captured together with all their new U.S. equipment. On one occasion, at our base hospital where we had only 150 personnel including the cooks, we had to take charge of 400 captured Kuomintang officers.'

Apart from his base hospital, Hans Müller had to organize hospitals in the whole vast area of the north-east, and he recalled a momentous occasion when an entire thousand-bed missionary hospital fell into P.L.A. hands, together with large amounts of urgently needed supplies. 'It was a confused period,' he recalled. 'Apart from troops switching sides all the time, there was the great mobility of the P.L.A., which meant having to be ready to switch from one area to another at very short notice. But as far as the opium problem was concerned, we knocked that on the head in a very short time. It never was a problem within the regular P.L.A.'

Dr Müller is a great enthusiast for acupuncture anaesthesia. It was only at his insistence – being somewhat squeamish at watching scalpels slice into living flesh – that we decided to convince ourselves that a different sort of needle from those used for opium injections could replace chemical anaesthetics.

At Shanghai's Hua Shan hospital, after donning white caps and gowns, we were ushered into an operating theatre where a middle-aged man was lying on the operating table, his close-shaved head an egg from which the top was to be removed. Four needles had been inserted, two in his right hand, near the thumb, two more in his face. They had been placed and left there – no twiddling or twirling, as is often the case. He chatted away to nurses, smiling and saying he felt 'quite comfortable' as work started on cutting open the scalp. We watched his face intently as the doctors, with something remarkably like a carpenter's brace and bit, continued boring holes through the top of his head. Into one hole and out of the other, a wire-like, fine saw was inserted and, as this was pulled back and forth to saw the skull through from underneath, he was asked if he felt anything. He replied: 'It seems as if someone is pulling at my head.' It was the understatement of the morning! Eventually the rectangular piece of skull – not entirely severed along one of its edges – was turned back like the lid of a can of sardines, and there was the brain pulsing away beneath the membrane like the stomach of a newly hatched bird. The patient was still chatting away with the nurses as the work of slicing through the membrane started and Dr Tsu Shi-chih, the chief surgeon, suggested that as it would take some time to remove the tumour we might like to continue the tour and pop in to see the brain tumour case a little later.

In another operating theatre an attendant was twiddling two needles, stuck into the outer side of each of the patient's feet just below the ankle, while a surgeon was sewing up a big gash in his stomach, from which a half-pound tumour had just been removed in an operation that had lasted two and a half hours. His face had nothing of the greyness one is used to seeing after such a time on the operating table. He said he had felt nothing except a 'slight tugging' when the tumour was removed. He looked quite normal and was clearly not in any pain, nor was he under any hypnosis, which some Western sceptics have suspected is used in such operations. The next case was a woman who was having a growth removed from her throat. There were four needles, two on each side of her hands near the thumbs, which were gently twitching. She said she felt 'fine' and gave us a 'Long live Chairman Mao' when she saw that we were foreign visitors, and said that she 'was very pleased to meet foreign guests'. Work had started on sewing up her throat as she said this. The last case we saw before looking in on the brain tumour was another woman who was being operated on for a glandular growth at the side of her neck. Four needles, all on the same side, two near the thumb and wrist joint, one just above the wrist and another in the upper part of the forearm, linked up to an electronic vibrator. We noted that her thumb was also gently twitching. She assured us that she felt no pain at all.

Part of the brain tumour had been removed and the surgeon in charge was going after the rest – rather deep inside the skull. The patient said he felt fine, but asked the nurse if he could have some more bottled fruit, so she started feeding him some with a spoon, while the surgeon probed around in the depths of his skull.

By that time we were feeling rather more emotionally exhausted than those on the operating table, so we were escorted into a rest room for discussion.

'Some 300 nerve points where needles could be applied,' explained chief surgeon Tsu Hsi-chih, 'were known to us from ancient anatomical charts prepared over 2,000 years ago. We have since discovered some more. About half the total are just beneath the nerve points and half of the others are within half a centimetre of the nerves. There are a few dozen points that can be used to produce an analgesic effect, or anaesthesia, which for practical purposes we have reduced to about half that number.' At that moment the two women patients, Meng Feng-fen and Wang Tsai-feng, whom we had left fifteen minutes earlier on the operating tables, walked in, smiling and giggling, with thick bandages on their throats and in blue dressing gowns. They were both textile workers. By their comportment one would have thought they had just come from a ping-pong match. The stitches, Dr Tsu told us, would be out in three days and they would leave the hospital in a week – unless an unexpected complication occurred. While we were taking their photos, Chang Kuo-hsin, the man from whose stomach a tumour had been removed, was wheeled in, grinning all over. Everyone said they felt 'fine' and Chang Kuo-hsin said he had just dropped by to show us how workers are looked after these days. The two women said they had felt immediate relief after their tumours and thyroid glands respectively had been removed and Dr Tsu warned them that within a few hours the effect of the needles would wear off and they might feel a little pain which could be relieved by traditional, herbal-based medicines, given by injection, or by more needles if the pain got severe.

It was during the upsurge of scientific experiments in the field of medicine during the Great Leap Forward that acupuncture anaesthesia was discovered, said Dr Tsu Hsi-chih. Until then it had been used exclusively to treat and cure a wide range of maladies. One of the great advantages was the absence of the toxic effects of classical anaesthetics, which meant that the post-operational period was greatly reduced. Also, because the patient was fully conscious throughout, bleeding was reduced and in certain types of operations the patients could co-operate with the surgeons by describing sensations.

Some half million operations under acupuncture anaesthesia had taken place at the time we visited the Hua Shan hospital, 1,200 of them at that hospital, where the practice had started only in 1967.

'We can say that such operations are 90 per cent successful,' said Dr Tsu, and he went on to explain that there were three different yardsticks of success. 'We consider it "excellent" when the operation goes off without a hitch and the patient feels no pain at all; "good" when at a certain stage a patient may feel a little pain but not enough to need some classical anaesthesia, and "fairly good" when the patient feels some pain and anaesthesia is needed. We have 98 per cent "excellents" when the operations are above the abdomen, 85 per cent only for operations on the abdomen and below. We do not yet know the reason for this. We are still doing a great deal of research into such questions.'

The hospital's chief anaesthetist, Dr Wu Wei-ming, said: 'One thing is certain. Acupuncture anaesthesia is one of the great developments in the history of medical science. It provides a vast new subject of study, with elements of biochemistry, physics and anatomy all involved. There is a group which controls and co-ordinates the activities of a number of other groups each studying different aspects.'

Some remarkable results of limb surgery were also shown to us at the same hospital. A fourteen-year-old lad had had a malignant tumour in his upper right arm, a condition normally requiring amputation. Only the upper section of the arm with the tumour was removed, and the rest was joined up, so that apart from one being 6 inches shorter than the other he has the complete use of his right arm and hand. Even more dramatic was the case of a nineteen-year-old peasant lad who had had a tumour in the upper left arm. After a first operation, the malignant tumour continued to spread. The whole upper forearm was then removed and the lower forearm joined directly to the shoulder. He has the use of his hand and can move his arm parallel to the body. The last example of this type of surgery was an extraordinary case in which a forty-two-year-old lathe worker had suffered an accident in which all fingers of his left hand had been severed. Attempts to provide him with artificial fingers were unsatisfactory. Finally, six months after the accident, a group of eight doctors, in a mammoth operation, succeeded in grafting his big toe and one other toe on to his wrist, to provide him with a workable thumb and index finger. 'It took eighteen hours to stitch the blood vessels together,' said Dr Tsu. 'Some of them were thinner than matches, but all had to be sutured.'

'The main thing is that I'm back at the lathe,' said the young man, and, giving his trouser belt a powerful hitch with what remained of his left hand, he continued: 'With my new thumb and index, I can hold things with my left hand as well as ever. I have to thank the doctors here for putting me back into production.'

'It isn't just the question of putting people back into production,' commented Dr Tsu. 'It is making them feel they are useful, normal citizens again. It is our way of serving the people, not just in some mechanical way by doing a competent job of surgery, but in a creative way to give each human being who passes through our hands the possibility of maximum self-fulfilment, which in today's society means service to the people. Even had it been technically possible in the old days to undertake such an operation, who could have afforded it? Certainly not a lathe-worker!'

In our final meeting with Ma Hai-teh, after all we had learned and seen – from the 'barefoot' doctors' clinics to the big city hospitals – he made a claim which no China-born cadre would have done. But with his Western background and the fact that he keeps abreast with what is going on in medicine all over the world, we felt he was justified when he said:

'If you consider that the whole population has medical services at its disposal at negligible cost then you will realize that China has a better medical service than any other country in the world. Nowhere else can the population be reached to the same degree. People are taught how to fight against disease, so that there is collective immunity, born of knowledge, against a whole range of diseases which continually crop up in the rest of the world. Emphasis on personal hygiene, grass-roots medical knowledge of how to struggle against disease and the sources of disease, the absolute devotion of the medical profession to serving the people – all these give China a great advantage over countries which have advanced medical services but lack the assets of China's revolutionary approach.'

CHAPTER FIFTEEN

'SERVE THE PEOPLE'

Five ideographs in Mao Tse-tung's inimitable calligraphy adorn markets, factories, hospitals, schools and army barracks. They are painted or scrawled up in more vulgarized forms on village walls, bridge archways and railway sidings, on banners of work teams in the communes or at construction sites – wherever any human activity justifies the slogan 'Serve the People'. The words seem to have been absorbed into the national blood stream as the most concise formulation of Mao's concept of the ultimate aim of the revolution and the method of advance to a communist society. It was tempting at first to shrug it off as just one more slogan – one of the watchwords of the Cultural Revolution – when it was difficult to know which of the many battle-cries were of tactical, and which of long-term, strategic, significance.

When one travels round and probes deeply, one is struck by the extent to which the concept seems to have been accepted not only as a guide to people's daily activities, but as a yardstick to measure attitudes towards life in general, towards work and fellow-workers, towards study and fellow-students and towards one's neighbours. It is not just the 'one good deed a day' credo of the Boy Scouts, but 'only good deeds every day and always' that is expected of people in their attitude towards society as a whole and within that microcosm of society where each lives, studies or works. 'Serve the People' dominates the approach to all aspects of running the economy, being accepted as the principal guide-line at all levels, from planning heavy industry to selling peanuts. The attitude towards pollution, for instance, is an example.

At Nanking, we raised the subject of the general approach to pollution with Wang Hsing, the elderly vice-chairman of the city's Municipal Construction Organization. He had been ex-plaining various types of equipment installed in the Nanking Petro-Chemical Works to deal with what the Chinese refer to as the 'three wastes' (waste gas, waste liquid and waste solid residue), so we asked whether the aim was to improve the economy by retrieving what was economically useful from the 'three wastes' or to deal with them for social and health reasons.

'We cannot tolerate a situation in which the "three wastes" prejudice the people's health,' he replied. 'We are a socialist state, so industrial enterprises exist not to make profits but to serve the people. The workers at every level are concerned if there is any risk that production at their factory could harm the people's interests, so they display all sorts of initiatives to eliminate this harm but in such a way that the overall economy suffers as little as possible. For instance, the equipment to deal with polluted water at the petro-chemical works was very ex-pensive and caused regular losses to the department concerned. The workers were certainly not going to try to recover those losses from the communes, which benefited from the water for irrigation after it was treated. In this case the losses were more than compensated for by the recovery of useful chemicals from waste gases in other departments of the same factory. But even had this not been possible, the water would have been treated and the factory would have shouldered the loss.'

Wang Hsing went on to explain that in Nanking, as in other Chinese cities, there was a strict rule that if a new enterprise should produce any of the 'three wastes' it must invest in anti-pollution equipment approved by the municipal revolutionary committee. And if any unexpected 'three wastes' were pro-duced despite the measures, the enterprise was bound to elimin-ate them. 'How would we be serving the people if we permitted the air they breathe to become polluted?' asked Wang Hsing. 'Established plants,' he continued, 'must also eliminate pollu-tion. For instance there were two cement plants in Nanking, producing a great amount of dust. They had to install dust ab-sorbers, which are being paid off by the recovery of 3 to 4 tons of raw materials daily. A petro-chemical fibre plant is being built, with the best-known anti-pollution equipment incorporated. This is a new field for us. Perhaps there will be some pollution at first, but it is the job of my organization to see that it is entirely eliminated. Cost is not a consideration when it is a question of people's health. Whether it is a question of plants run by the state or by the Nanking Municipality, it is our organization which decides on the conditions under which they can be established and run. We have a very active attitude to this and the workers themselves are very vigilant.'

Similarly at the Shanghai Electro-Chemical Works, in a discussion with leading members of the plant's revolutionary committee, following a tour of the plant's installations, vice-chairman Seng Sui-chun explained: 'When what you in the West call "anti-pollution measures" we call the "multi-purpose utilization of the three wastes", we are expressing our basic active attitude towards the problem. We must eliminate the danger from such wastes in order to serve the people better, but do it in such a way that the elimination itself also serves the people. There was a contradiction in what we were doing – making products which are useful, but in such a way as harmed the people's interests, whereas we should proceed in all cases from serving those interests.

'Liquid from one of our departments went into the river, harming fish life and water for irrigation. From another department the air was so polluted that people had to wear face masks when approaching the factory. We sent some workers to check up on the fields. They were horrified at what the polluted water was doing to vegetable production and the effect this would have on the worker–peasant alliance. After thorough discussions, we set to work and within three months and an investment of 10,000 yuan in equipment we solved the problem – almost completely. From waste residue, we recovered 20 tons of calcium sulphate a day. Mixed with powdered slag from a near-by steel plant, this gives us a daily output of 200 tons of cement. From the waste gas of the paraffin-chloride department, we get 30 tons monthly of a chemical used in refining aluminium, but we lose 2,500 yuan per ton because the process is very expensive. For us the essential thing is that the offensive smells have gone – people no longer have to wear masks. The waste liquid, after preliminary treatment here, is piped off to another chemical plant where some important acids are extracted, instead of polluting the irrigation channels. The "three wastes" problem has been solved by about 85 per cent. Our workers will be satisfied only when this is 100 per cent. They are happy at the results because they see this as a practical way of serving the people, which is the overall aim of everything done here.

'During 1971,' continued vice-chairman Seng, 'we succeeded in treating thirty-six types of waste, recovering about 4,000 tons of marketable chemical products, but still about 20 per cent of the waste gas escapes us. The leadership at all levels, from the Shanghai Municipality revolutionary committee down to factory management and rank-and-file workers, pay great attention to the problem. We send groups to other factories and schools to study it and exchange experiences, and scientific institutes send groups to our factory. Factories have no industrial secrets to hide from each other, as I understand is the case in capitalist countries, so it is easy to get to grips with each other's problems. We all have the same aim, to build socialism faster and serve the people's interests better.'

We investigated pollution in scores of factories and became satisfied that the task is not an economic one but one of safeguarding the health of the people, although this should be done as economically as possible.

Changing a 'bad thing into a good thing' is a constantly quoted phrase from Mao's dialectic approach. Tackling the 'three wastes' has given rise to all sorts of new scientific and industrial endeavour. At Shanghai we learned that, in 1971, 70 per cent of waste residue had been found recuperable and that 1·4 million tons of industrially useful chemicals had been recovered. An example was given of the chain-reaction effect, once the problem is decisively tackled. Cotton seeds have been crushed for centuries in China to extract oil – the residue is used as fuel. Once the 'anti-three-wastes' drive was on, workers at an oil-pressing plant began to extract furfural – a valuable chemical solvent used in refining lubricating oils and in the manufacture of nylon and other synthetics – from the residue. From the gas given off in making furfural, acetone was obtained. Glucose was extracted from the residue left after the furfural had been obtained, and glycerin, butanol, alcohol and a food-flavouring essence were extracted from the glucose residue.

At the huge Peking General Petro-Chemical Works, some forty miles north of Peking, employing about 25,000 workers, we found that four out of the thirty-five plants were designed especially to handle the 'three wastes'. It was fascinating to follow the process of purifying a most unpromising-looking liquid covered with thick black scum which came from the petrol refinery – with an annual capacity of 2·5 million tons of refined products. The main pollution materials were sulphur, phenol and oil waste. The process was first to steam-heat the liquid in a de-sulphurization tower to remove and transform the sulphur into aluminium sulphate, then separate the oil from water in a series of flotation basins and finally deal with the phenol, waging bacteriological warfare against it by employing a microscopic bacteria – vorticella – in an aeration pond. The ironic touch, so symbolic of China's frugality and ability to exploit its most improbable assets, is that the natural habitat of the vorticella – surely the lowest on the bacteria social scale – is human excreta. Vorticella and its own excreta have an economically exploitable love-hate relationship with phenol, feeding on it and destroying it and themselves, and providing the final factors in the purification process.

One can see the 'happy ending' in an adjoining basin in which goldfish and plump white ducks – ready for one of Peking's famous duck restaurants – are swimming around. 'After purification,' explained Chao Li, a leading member of the plant's revolutionary committee, 'the water is good enough for ducks and fish and for irrigation – a proportion of it having been recycled back into the refinery.'

Anti-pollution equipment had amounted to only 1 per cent of the total investment in the plant, but the percentage 'would have gone up to any level necessary to ensure the total elimination of pollution,' said Chao Li.

This is not to say that there is no pollution problem. New industrial cities in the interior like Tangshan in Hopei, and Chiaotso in Honan, still have much to do. In creating something from nothing, they have faced immense difficulties which have absorbed all their technical energies. Now, however, they are starting to deal with pollution. The essential thing is that there is a national consciousness on this issue. The daily press constantly reports new successes in dealing with the 'three wastes'.

One finds the more obvious aspects of the 'Serve the People' cult in shops and markets. A good example is the 'Three-Cornered Market' in a triangle formed by the junction of three streets in Shanghai's central Hung K'o district. Yu Hsiao-ying, a bright, apple-cheeked young woman, elected by fellow stall-holders to a leading post on the revolutionary committee, related how the market workers had 'repudiated the profits-in-command' concepts of Liu Shao-ch'i in favour of the 'Serve the People' line of Chairman Mao. Once the new committee had been set up, she said: 'We went around the street committees to find out how we could give better service. People criticized the lack of variety of vegetables, complaining that supply depended too much on the seasons. So we sent some committee members to the vegetable-growing communes and they agreed to build lots of hot-houses. We were also criticized for being open only from 6.30 a.m. until mid-day, whereas many people could do their shopping only after work, in the evening. So we decided to keep open until midnight – and found that a good third of our daily average of 12,000 customers came in the evenings.'

The lively Miss Yu was hailed from all sides as we strolled through the market, itself a convincing monument to the abundance of foodstuffs one sees everywhere in China today. Our guide, obviously a great favourite of the stall-holders, pointed out the quick-service stalls and ones with special foods for pregnant women; another stall where the sick or infirm could order for delivery to their homes; simple visual gadgets for testing eggs before you bought them; money-changing stalls; others where you listed your needs in temporarily unavailable produce which would be delivered to the homes as soon as they were in supply again. It was impossible to look in any direction without seeing the 'Serve the People' signs in varying shapes and sizes. We stopped at a stall where shoppers were downing bowls of steaming noodles:

'We discovered that night customers like buying things easy to prepare for breakfast,' said Yu Hsiao-ying, 'so we decided to make favourite breakfast dishes to take home which would only have to be warmed up. Then we added a stall where any left-over could be heated, so that the shoppers could have their breakfast there. We have also gone in for peeled potatoes and many other semi-prepared vegetables to save the housewives unnecessary work. So many of them have jobs these days. Stall-holders listen to people's criticisms and comments as they talk among themselves – many are too polite or shy to write anything in the complaints book – and they report back to us, so we can continually improve the service.'

When we asked if it was uneconomic to treble the time the market was open when the number of shoppers increased by only a third Miss Yu looked at us as if we were really backward elements, 'capitalist-roaders'. She remarked rather primly that the aim 'is not to make profits but to serve the people in the most complete way possible'. She added that one complaint over-heard by the stall-holders was that the produce was not always as fresh as it should be. Delegates were sent to the vegetable-growing communes and by arranging special early-morning shifts and speeding up transport, matters were arranged so that the maximum time for getting vegetables out of the ground and into the shoppers' nets and baskets was fifteen hours. The fish-breeding communes were approached on the same subject, and, by converting some old barges into tank-boats, freshwater fish were delivered to the market alive. Sea-fish arrived deep-frozen from the deep-sea fishing fleets.

'We are still not satisfied,' said Miss Yu, glowing all over when we congratulated her on the impeccably clean and orderly state of the market, the swift and friendly service, the excellent relations between customers and stall-holders and the holiday-like atmosphere, the stalls gay with flowers and artistically ar-ranged mountains of fruit and vegetables. 'We have to find new and better ways of serving the people and would welcome your criticism and advice on how to do better.'

Most visitors to China comment on the friendly service in shops – not only for foreigners, who automatically get priority on the assumption that they are in the country for a visit and their time should not be wasted behind shopping counters, but for the general public. They contrast it with the poor service in many European socialist countries, where those who serve either consider service in shops or restaurants a demeaning employment, or, if consumer goods are in short supply, feel in a privileged position, conferring favours on customers by handing out hard-to-get goods! The concept of the 'sacred sovereignty of the consumer'[1] is completely lost sight of in a socialist society if there is not the ideological conviction that serving the people is a meritorious task. The attitude towards service in a number of European socialist countries is a major target of criticism. In China, since the Cultural Revolution, the maintenance of high standards of service does not only depend on the goodwill of those specializing in the service trades, although it seemed to us that this goodwill exists to a very high degree. The 'sovereignty of the consumer' is exercised by the consumer through the street committees and neighbourhood units.

Town-dwellers all over China are linked together in street and neighbourhood committees, the functions of which broaden and deepen as life goes on. They are essential fragments in the mosaic of the future communist society. It is constantly stressed in conversation with cadres that, to build a communist society, a communist consciousness or morality must first be created. In this the street committees, the basic unit of urban organization, play a key role. They are as fundamental to ground-level democracy as are the communes in the countryside and worker control in the factories.

As typical as any is the Chuan Ta street committee, in the western district of Peking, one of twenty-five similar committees under the Fang Shan neighbourhood revolutionary committee, which in turn comes under the revolutionary committee of the Western District, one of Peking's nine administrative districts. The average number of households covered by a street

1. The phrase is borrowed from Joan Robinson's *Economic Management: China 1972*.

committee is about 600, Chuan Ta, with 808, being bigger than average. The name comes from Chuan Ta *hutung* where it is situated, one of 125 of those picturesque narrow lanes running through whole areas of one-storey houses with dove-grey walls and curved tiled roofs which characterize Peking. The lanes are faced with the outer walls of the houses, interrupted only by narrow doorways leading into airy courtyards around which the classical red-lacquered rooms are built. Rice-papered windows and sliding doors look into the courtyards, the whole providing a rare warmth and intimacy. Gateways lead from courtyard to courtyard, according to the distance between the *hutungs* and to the size of the family for which the house was originally built.

'What are your main tasks?' we asked Hsiu Tung-chi, chairwoman of the Chuan Ta revolutionary committee. An energetic woman with a ready smile and the usual bobbed hair, she created the impression of the sort of neighbour you would like to turn to in time of trouble. She was seated with four vice-chairwomen and one male staff member in a red lacquered room at the street committee headquarters.

'A major task is to help those families in which both husband and wife are working,' she said. 'We can do their shopping for them, and their laundry, and of course look after their children so they can concentrate on their work without worrying. There are quite a few old people who have no family to look after them. Financially they are supported by the state, but we can do odd jobs for them – do their laundry, clean up the house, escort them to some recreational activities when they want to go, encourage them to take an interest in political affairs. They are kept happy this way, and feel useful in the twilight of their years, because we encourage them to talk to the younger people about life in the old days. All this is looked after by housewives who don't have activities outside the street – that is who are not working in neighbourhood unit factories. In winter-time, after a snowfall, it is our menfolk who clear the ice and snow from around these old people's houses so they can walk around without risk of slipping or falling. This is one way in which we can be of service to the people.'

Fourteen of the seventeen members of this committee were women, as such committees represent essentially housewives and dependants; those who had jobs outside could not be members of a revolutionary committee at their place of work as well as in their street or neighbourhood.

The tireless Mrs Hsiu guided us into a tiny clinic where a 'barefoot doctor' insisted on taking our blood pressures, and on to a well-stocked grocery and vegetable stores. 'Another of our important functions,' she continued, 'is to exercise consumer control over shops and enterprises in our area. We have special teams which check up on the quantity, quality and variety of goods available and the attitude of the service personnel. We can offer advice on how the service can be improved; criticize shortcomings and in this way help the shops to give better service. After all it is the consumers who have the right to say which products are good or bad and whether the service is good or bad. This helps to improve the human contact between producer, consumer and the servicing branches.

'We have a similar system to check on the schools,' she said as she conducted us through a nursery where fat, rose-cheeked children shouted with excitement at the sight of such corpulent, ageing 'foreign friends', as we were invariably described. 'Our representatives can drop in when they like and check up on the leadership, on the relations between teachers and pupils. Our members also help with extra-curricular activities. We consider that contacts between teachers, pupils and parents are vitally important. We arrange for some of the retired workers to talk to children about the old days.'

Of the nursery Hsiu Tung-chi said: 'Nurseries and kindergartens are very important now that in many families both parents are working. Our job is to free the parents from as many worries as possible, so we have a very flexible system. We take in babies at the end of the mother's fifty-six days of paid maternity leave and see them through nursery school and kindergarten until they start regular school at the age of seven. Parents can leave their children for mornings or afternoons only, or for the whole day or for a week, collecting them at the week-end. The parents have no worries, firstly because they know those who are looking after their children and secondly because they have confidence in our committee, which keeps an eye on what is going on.'

Apart from four kindergartens in the area, mainly for children of parents working in neighbourhood unit factories, there were others at the parents' place of work. 'Usually mothers who are working outside prefer to leave their children at the factory or office kindergartens so they can be nearer to them,' said Mrs Hsiu.

When we asked what she considered was the most important function of her committee, she replied:

'These days' – it was mid-1973 – 'the most important thing is to organize the study of the Marxist–Leninist classics and the philosophical works of Chairman Mao and thus guide the people into taking an interest in state and international affairs. It is very difficult because most of us have had little or no schooling, but study groups are organized according to the different levels of understanding. Those who are better educated help those who are backward.'

The 'low-level' group to which she was attached were studying *The Communist Manifesto* and the *Four Philosophical Essays* of Chairman Mao.[2] Others who were better educated were studying Marx's *Critique of the Gotha Programme* and Lenin's *Materialism and Empiro-Criticism*. Were these not very difficult, we asked.

'Very difficult,' replied Mrs Hsiu with a sigh, echoed by the other four vice-chairwomen and male staff member. 'But some study first and grasp the essentials, then help others. Whoever leads the discussion is responsible for explaining the difficult terms. Only when everyone has grasped the point is there a general discussion. We have four groups, each studying different works according to their level of understanding in three sessions of two hours each per week. Such studies heighten our political consciousness and we see the future more clearly. If anyone tried again to put over a wrong political line, like that political swindler Liu Shao-ch'i, we would soon pull him up.'

2. *On Practice, On Contradiction, On the Correct Handling of Contradiction among the People* and *Where Do Correct Ideas Come From?*

We continued along the scrupulously clean *hutungs*, turning off into a courtyard where, behind the lacquered wood and rice-paper door and windows, we found several dozen placidly smiling elderly women, sitting round tables with scrolls of coloured paper, scissors, glue-pots and coils of fine wire, making a great variety of artificial flowers.

'They used to look after their grandchildren in the old days,' explained Mrs Hsiu, 'but now the grandchildren are in the nurseries and kindergartens. We have set up facilities for those who want to do something – embroidering on silk, making artificial flowers, producing medicines from herbs, working in sewing circles and other light jobs. They like the idea of being together and the feeling that they are useful in their old age – not to mention earning a bit of extra money. Of course some prefer to stay at home, but the majority are happy to do something. Many of the younger housewives work in one or another of the seven street factories run by the neighbourhood committee and turning out industrial goods.' We visited one – the Feng Shan Insulating Materials Factory – set up like the other six during the Great Leap Forward. Women accounted for half of the 190 workers. They turned out thirty-nine types of insulating materials, mostly for a wide range of electrical transformers. Planned production for 1973 was evaluated at 5 million yuan.

As we drove back from the factory – a little faster than one normally travels in the *hutungs* – an old chap sitting on a stool at an intersection got up and signalled energetically to us to slow down. He was one of the local 'traffic policemen' – a ricksha-puller in the old days, Hsiu Tung-chi told us. Back at the committee headquarters, we asked about crime in the community. The narrow ill-lit *hutungs* of the old days were notorious hunting grounds for footpads and other nightprowlers. 'Crime is a product of class society,' explained Mrs Hsiu, 'and will exist for a time even under socialism. But it is insignificant and in recent times there has been none at all.' We asked what had been the nature of the last crime committed, and after considerable discussion with the four vice-chairwomen and male staff member Mrs Hsiu replied: 'It was a young lad who shinned up an electric light pole and stole a lamp. He was criticized and turned into a very good lad indeed – so good that later on he was accepted into the People's Liberation Army.' When we recalled the evil reputation the *hutungs* had in the old days, she laughed and said: 'There are no police in our area at all. Now people leave their food on the window-sills at night and nobody would dream of touching it. In the early days after liberation, there were a few bad elements, but they were criticized and educated by the community and there was no further trouble.'

We asked to talk to an old-time resident and were taken into the house next to the committee headquarters to meet Mrs Hsi Chin, sixty-two years old, who had been a resident of Chuan Ta *hutung* for forty-six years. Rather corpulent, with a wrinkled face, her eyes disappeared so far into the sockets that we thought she had dozed off. But when we asked what she remembered of the old days, they popped out. 'My father was beaten to death by the local landlord, just outside Peking, when I was sixteen,' she said. 'My mother and I were turned out of the house and begged our way to Peking. When we had almost starved to death my mother got a job as *pao mu* (nurse-maid), but couldn't take me into the household. She married me off to a man eighteen years older than myself who lived in this *hutung*. He made copper wire for 3 yuan a month – not enough for even him to live on. I took in sewing, so we managed to keep alive. The streets were filthy in those days, full of pedlars and rickshaw-pullers, who hauled their passengers all day long but didn't earn enough money for one decent meal a day. They slept in their rickshas at the street corners. There were fights and thefts all the time and it was unsafe to go into the streets after dark. Life was so miserable that many people could keep alive only by stealing. One night, I got the fright of my life when I stumbled over a corpse in the snow – but to find frozen corpses in the winter was quite common. Of course there was no medical care if you got sick. I had eleven children, four of whom died as babies, but I was luckier than most of my neighbours to be able to save seven. They are all grown up with good jobs now.'

We asked what she thought about family planning – the new ideal of having only two – or a maximum of three – children.

'It's very good,' she said promptly, her eyes again coming out of her sockets. 'I take part in propaganda work for family planning. Women are emancipated now and can work at everything that men can. Once I got married, I hardly set foot outside the house, I was so busy with my children, my husband and doing a bit of sewing. The idea then was to have seven children – five boys and two girls. I remember hanging copper cash on chains round the necks of my first children, with "*wu nan, ehr niu*" (five boys, two girls) engraved on them. It was the older people who insisted on this because they wanted lots of grandchildren to look after them when they grew old. My husband was regarded as a good son because he kept me pregnant all the time; I was regarded as a good daughter-in-law because I bore eleven children of whom seven survived – even if they weren't in the right proportions. Now if you have sons or daughters, it's the same thing. A girl now can get education and marry later – it's very good. She can get a job, earn money and have a couple of children practically without interrupting her work. Not all of the older people see things the way I do. They still want their children to give them lots of grandchildren. But not the young people. They – boys and girls alike – want to be free to serve the country and have their own development.

'I was lucky,' she continued. 'My seven children are very good to me – they send me money so I can work for the committee without any pay. But if I was young again I would want to have a different life – learn a profession and not just be a breeder of children.' And with that rather passionate defence of Women's Liberation, Mrs Hsi Chin's eyes disappeared behind the wrinkles and we took our leave.

Hsiu Tung-chi reminded us of the realistic wall newspaper at the Feng Shan factory illustrating family-planning methods, and said that the committee paid great attention to this subject, Hsi Chin being one of the most tireless propagandists. 'Pushing ahead with education on this subject,' she said, 'is no problem because the street committees are all dominated by women, who also provide 46 per cent of the labour force in this area, and it is the women who are the staunchest advocates of small families.'

At the Wu Lao (Five Aged) Neighbourhood Committee in Nanking, we went into family planning in greater detail. The district had been one of Nanking's worst slum areas, with people living in thatch-roofed hovels, and unpaved streets interspersed with open sewers. There were twenty-nine cesspools, according to the notebook of Mrs Liu Kuei-hsing, who headed the revolutionary committee – twenty-nine foul ponds covered with slime and sewer-borne filth. Flies by day, mosquitoes by night – disease rampant. Diminutive Mrs Liu, beaming goodwill and kindliness behind her thick-lensed glasses, said that perhaps it was because of the past that extra emphasis was placed on hygiene. The old thatch-roofed hovels had long since been replaced by decent tiled-roofed dwelling units, built by the residents themselves. Each unit had electricity and piped water and Wu Lao had been selected as a national model for health and cleanliness.

'People quickly became health-conscious,' explained Mrs Liu. 'Old or young, if they see dust accumulating, they brush it away; if they see any mess, they tidy it up; if they spot pests or insects, they wipe them out. Because of our work in the health field there has not been a single case of infectious disease in the kindergartens for instance for the past seven years (our visit was early in 1972) nor any other sickness worth talking about. We strictly follow Chairman Mao's line in public health: "Use prevention as the main method in medical work. Combine prophylactic work with treatment." '

At neighbourhood-committee level there was a Public Health Station and at street committee level a Public Health Centre, which directed the work of several clinics, run by the housewives with 'barefoot doctors' in charge. We visited one of the clinics, run by a cheerful matronly woman who was setting out various pungent-smelling leaves and roots on a drying table as we walked in. 'We couldn't even pronounce the names of medicines when we set this up,' she explained. 'Now we go to the mountains to select medical herbs and roots. Treatment here is mainly by acupuncture and herbs. We can treat maladies like colds, high blood pressure, arthritis, rheumatic complaints, digestive disorders, various types of fevers, and keep a check on pregnancies. With acupuncture we can even handle cases of partial paralysis and temporary loss of speech.' We asked about family planning, and she escorted us into a tiny room to open up a filing cabinet which contained the health record of everyone in that portion of the street served by the clinic.

'We have a health file on every family,' she explained. 'How many children, when the last one was born, whether the mother is pregnant and from what date, if there were any complications during a previous pregnancy and so on. We carry on active propaganda in favour of small families and family planning but we also pay great attention to pregnant mothers to ensure their babies are born under the best conditions. Means of birth control are available free – the pill taken twenty-two days in the month is the method favoured by most wives. Abortion can be done in the street clinics and merely at the desire of the mother.

'Without a doctor's certificate or written approval of the husband?' we asked, and got one of those withering looks to which we have become accustomed when our questions seemed to reflect a 'backward' state of mind. 'Women are really emancipated in our country,' came the reply, 'and do not need their husband's permission for such things, which are their own concern.'

There was one 'barefoot doctor' on duty at the clinic twenty-four hours per day and the staff included seven public health workers, working on eight-hour shifts round the clock. They could be at a patient's bedside within three to five minutes of getting a call and were in telephone communication with the centre, station or county hospital in case of emergencies they could not handle. The clinic treated ten to fifteen patients in their homes and seventy to eighty at the station each day. 'As we have everyone's health record,' explained Mrs Liu, 'we know when they are due for innoculations, so the street clinics save people a lot of time by giving them their shots at home. At the Street Committee Public Health Centre, there are seven fully qualified doctors for general medicine and surgery. They are immediately available for house visits for any cases that the clinics report.'

As an example of the availability of health services to the

whole population on which Dr Ma Hai-teh had laid such stress, the Wu Lao street clinic was convincing, as it typifies the standard public health unit in every urban centre throughout China. It is difficult to conceive of service to the people in a more appropriate form.

Among the many activities of the street committee was the running of a co-operative factory for making electric hot-plates. Fifty housewives turned out 2,000 units per month, in six different models from 300 to 2,000 watts, very nicely finished. Mostly they are for home use but a proportion were being exported to Hong Kong. The housewives took a little over 30 yuan a month in wages from the profits and the rest went to general neighbourhood-improvement projects.

During our visit, we button-holed a worker who was wheeling his bicycle into the gate of his house as we passed by and he invited us in. There was a big radio and a transistor set in the front room, his bike was new and he was wearing a wrist-watch. He introduced himself at Tou Ah-fou, a former itinerant peddlar, who got his first regular job after liberation and later was trained for his present job as a skilled lacquer painter in a furniture factory, where he earned 71 yuan a month. He showed us a second room, where there was a sewing machine, and a kitchen, where there was another new bicycle. He apologized for the absence of his wife. She had recently taken a job for the first time in her life, working at a radio assembly shop for a starter's pay of 42 yuan. 'She was very impressed by our daughter taking an apprentice's job at a mine where she uses a pneumatic compressor,' he said, 'and now brings home 30 yuan a month.' We asked about the second bike. 'For my son,' he replied. 'He was recently demobbed from the People's Liberation Army and is working in a hospital for a while, where he also lives. I bought him a bike when I bought my own, so it will be there for him when he comes home.' As for living costs, he paid 2·80 yuan per month to the State Housing Bureau for the flat; food for the three at home averaged about 37 yuan per month, 60 cents each for water and electricity per month and 1·30 yuan for cooking gas. Films at the factory cost 5 cents, at the public cinemas 15 to 20 cents, the theatre 30 cents. 'I made a splash recently when my son got demobbed and I bought him a wrist-watch, as well as buying the two bikes, so I only have 200 yuan in the bank at the moment,' was his reply to our question whether he had a bank account.

As he was a frank, down-to-earth person, we asked him whether the slogan 'Serve the People' was something which the working people really accepted as an aim in life, a guide to their day-to-day activities, or whether it was something they just went along with because it was the slogan of the day. 'It's something which has stuck,' he replied. 'How could it be otherwise? Who are the people? We are. So we are asked to serve ourselves. But not just as individuals. We should serve ourselves as a collective. This makes sense to everyone except a handful of selfish no-hopers who wouldn't dare to oppose it openly but try to get by without doing anything for others.'

If the application of this concept at all levels of economic and social activity was impressive, it was even more so because of the long-term implications, as a central theme in education from babies in the nurseries right through to graduation from university. Many times we watched games played by nursery toddlers, pretending to give up seats in trams and buses for the old and weak, helping them aboard with their bundles and baskets. In primary schools children go into the streets and put their play into practice, carrying parcels for the aged, helping them to cross streets.

If it seems that in the nurseries and kindergartens children learn the sort of things one used to learn at Sunday school, the difference is that when the children go out into life the same behaviour is expected in daily activity seven days a week. It is not the 'help thy neighbour' philosophy of Sunday, ignored for the rest of the week. It has become the expected and respected 'way of life' for the whole nation. If Mao can make that concept stick for a quarter of humanity – and our deep conviction is that it has struck root – then a giant step will have been taken towards changing human nature. The example could be a compelling magnet for other peoples!

CHAPTER SIXTEEN

MINORITIES STAND UP

For students of the evolution of human society, some of the national minority areas in the majestic mountains and valleys of south-west China, especially Yunnan, with its long frontiers with Vietnam and Burma, and Szechuan, leading up to the province of Tibet, until recently would have provided living museums. Every stage of society could have been studied if the local peoples would have tolerated it – the primitive communism of the head-hunting Kawa, the slave society of the Yi, Tibetan serfdom, landlordism and all the transitional stages in between. More enthralling even for the non-specialist today is to see how these peoples have sprung in a single mighty leap from the bottom rungs of the ladder of human progress to somewhere near the top.

The national minorities have moved relatively faster up the prosperity scale than the Han majority people, because they started from so far behind and also because they have been given a helping hand to compensate for the wrongs visited on them during centuries of oppression which reached its zenith during the declining years of Kuomintang rule. At the Burma railhead town of Lashio, the starting point of the Burma Road, while awaiting a truck lift on the eve of Japan's entry into the Second World War, we heard persistent rumours of a Kuomintang extermination campaign against 'Lolo' tribespeople living in the mountains on the other side of the border. Squatting in the Lashio market place, bundles of rags and bones, with dulled eyes fixed on the ground, coiled cloth turbans around their heads and at their feet a few dried herbs, tigers' knee-caps and bears' dried gall-bladders – highly prized as medicaments – were 'Lolo' survivors from burned-out villages.

Such stories were repeated to us with more convincing details when we reached Kunming, the beautiful old capital of Yunnan province, by some hard-headed pilots of General Chennault's 'Flying Tiger' fighter squadron, engaged in protecting convoys of U.S. supplies moving up the Burma Road. Their headquarters base was at Kunming but they had forward bases in other areas adjacent to 'Lolo' country and some of them were appalled at what was going on: 'We came here to help Chiang Kai-shek fight the Japanese,' a Texan pilot – son of a former missionary to China – told us, 'but we find he's slaughtering his own people.'

At the time we did not know that 'Lolo' was a term of contempt for the Yi people, who now have their own autonomous counties and regions. Thirty years later, we asked Fankuokuo, a young Yi cadre who had employed the education acquired since liberation to study the history of his people, if he knew anything about that particular incident. A good-looking young man, with the soft, moulded features of his race, wearing a coiled turban with a jaunty sort of cloth spike to it, an embroidered tunic and wide trousers, he explained that he was not even born at the time we were talking of and that he came from the Tao Liang mountains of Szechuan, but that such things as we had heard of went on all the time.

'We lived in a slave society and the slave-owners, although they were also Yi people, were the allies and stooges of the Kuomintang' he said. 'There were uprisings somewhere or other all the time and the slave-owners would call in the Kuomintang troops to wipe out everybody. They could easily get more slaves. My own father was slightly better off than most people in our area, as part slave, part tenant farmer. He had no land of his own and virtually everything he produced, including all the rice, went to the slave-owner. We lived on potatoes, wild strawberries and anything else we could find to eat in the woods. When I was very young my mother was dragged off to work for the slave-owner. She was starved and beaten so much that she could hardly drag herself around. She managed to survive to see us again at liberation, but died soon after. My father and the others walked around like dead men. Life was hopeless – there was only death to wait for. Those that rose up were massacred by the Kuomintang. Any who tried to escape risked having their eyes gouged out and hands cut off. At the very least their bodies would be branded with red-hot irons to show who they belonged to in case they tried to escape again. Anyone had the right to kill a runaway slave on the spot.

'Most of those in our village were totally slaves – bought and sold like cattle in the market. Two slaves for an ox, five for a horse was an average price, but it varied according to the slave's strength. My father watched buyers prodding buttocks, arm and leg muscles of slaves, just as with animals. According to their wealth, the slave-owning households had ten to twenty slaves each.' Fankuokuo's village, in the now autonomous Li county of Leipo, is now a production brigade of the local commune and the former slave-owners are still being 'remoulded by labour', as he expressed it. As in most places in the minority areas, the new development naturally appeared later than elsewhere. The People's Communes were set up only in 1965, the first co-operatives having been formed in 1956.

The provinces traversed by the Burma Road – Yunnan, Kweichow and Szechuan – were known for the harshness of man and nature. Rugged mountains, warlords, bandits, man-eating tigers, sullen, unsmiling faces, above all among the minority peoples who rated lower than domestic animals. Travelling along the Burma Road were the lines of sweating porters, toiling up terribly steep mountain passes, each with a great block of rock salt lashed to an A-shaped frame on his back, with a cleft stick as a climbing aid. Almost every person one saw along the road had a goitre, the size of which seemed to be proportionate to their age. All the salt the porters were carrying ended up in the hands of the warlords or their profiteering agents. Woe betide the porter if the weight delivered to the agents varied an ounce from the original load, which weighed up to 150 pounds and was loaded on to his back at the salt mines. But these were things one was to learn only later.[1]

1. Here I speak for myself, Rewi Alley knowing all about such conditions at the time. We were both in the Burma Road area in 1941, he on Gung Ho affairs, I slowly making my way from Lashio to Chungking, where we were finally to meet.

At the roadside markets, there were hopeless-looking people with downcast eyes like those at the Lashio market, despite the fact that the women often had colourful headdresses, silver ornaments adorning their necks, layers of bangles half-way up their arms and heavy ear-rings. Spread out in front of them were usually jars of brown, treacly opium, medicinal bark, herbs, whitened bones, a length or two of sugar-cane and some woven baskets. The unrelieved darkness which set in soon after the sun disappeared over the towering ridges of the ever-present mountains seemed to reflect the spiritual gloom which hung heavy over the countryside. Except for isolated dim lights in the villages through which we passed, it was total blackness momentarily inhabited by grotesque shapes, left to the imagination to decipher, picked up by the truck lights as we spiralled up and down the series of great mountain walls that lay squarely athwart the Burma Road.

To return thirty years later and find valleys and mountain slopes sparkling with clusters of lights – mostly powered by tiny generators tucked into rushing streams – brightly lit villages, flames and sparks shooting up from the smoke-stacks of county industry, was like entering another world. The minority peoples had learned that iron and steel could be harvested almost like grain. There were no more downcast eyes among those one passed on the road, but smiles and waves of the hand, shouted greetings from people on bicycles – Hans or national minorities it was impossible to tell, as they looked and dressed alike except on special occasions that called for national costumes.

Some 'old China hands' will doubtless sigh and wail – as did the slave-owners at the passing of the old days – when they learn that many of the national minorities are adopting the practical working-day dress of the Hans, especially in the towns where machinery does not take kindly to 'picturesque' headdresses, flowing sleeves and wide trousers, skirts and aprons, no matter how attractive they may look in magazines. But if national costumes tend to be less in evidence except on holidays, when they appear in quantity, colour and quality of cloth undreamed-of in the old days, a new birth to national culture has been brought about, especially by the development of written scripts for those of the national minorities who had none.

As national cultures and village economies developed, old taboos died natural deaths. Doubtless those 'old China hands', if they bothered to look into such things, found it romantic that some of the mountain peoples considered the mountains 'taboo' and inviolate, and that the Kawa people, for instance, believed that snicking off some of the heads of a neighbouring minority people was the only way to ensure good harvests. With education came the revelation that it is water and human manure, not human heads, that bring good harvests. The old taboos went overboard, heads remained on their owners' shoulders and irrigation channels began to snake their way around the flanks of the mountains, disappearing into tunnels on one side to reappear on the other, spiralling their way through the mountains like the old Burma Road, tapped at different levels to water terraced fields and help to produce two and three crops a year.

One remarkable cadre of the T'ung minority, about 800,000 of whom are spread around the border of Kweichow, Kwangsi and Hunan provinces, had some interesting observations on this question. We had met Yuang Chuan in 1951, some months after the Institute of National Minorities was set up in Peking, he being the only T'ung student at the time. Round-faced, diffident and a bit jumpy at that time, he has since developed into a very alert but relaxed cadre who played a leading role in developing a written language for his people, and after much research and travel has written a history of the T'ung minority. Why he had ventured to study at the Institute, he told us at the time:

'At the end of 1939, about the time I was born, the Red Army passed through our area at the beginning of the Long March. They left a big impression on the T'ung people. For the first time we were treated as equals by the Hans. Wherever they stayed, they helped people with their work. As a child, I heard stories all the time about what good people they were; of how heroically they fought against the oppressors, for the people. This contact was never forgotten. When the People's Liberation Army started to move south again, I was a cowherd, but I remembered the good things I had heard about them, so I set out to find them. Because of our long history of mingling with the Hans and some of the other minority peoples – the Miao, Yao and Chuang – a lot of T'ungs including myself can speak the Han and Miao languages as well as our own. So the P.L.A. accepted me as an interpreter. After the war was over I worked at the local Communist Party committee as interpreter, and later I was asked whether I would like to go to Peking to study. I and all the T'ung people in our area were very pleased.' On graduating, he had been invited to stay at the Institute to train other T'ungs, so they could later return to their villages as cadres and teachers. Yuang Chuan had often led groups of students back into the T'ung country to study their society and language, as a result of which the written script and the history of the T'ung people were produced.

'Our people did not want to study before, even when it was possible,' he explained at our meeting in 1973. 'If the Kuomintang took children off to schools, it was to send them back later as agents of oppression, so there was a social conscience against education. We remained backward and isolated in our mountains – no transport, no industry, no machines. I had never seen a truck or train until I set out for Peking over twenty years ago. When the People's Republic was formed and a working team was sent to our area to explain Communist Party policies towards the national minorities, it sounded like a dream. People could not take it in at first. Then they explained that an autonomous region would be set up where we would run our own lives and therefore people must study so as to be able to do this, and the feeling towards education changed straight away. After some social reforms, in my home province, the Miao–T'ung Autonomous County was formed at San Kiang. There is also a T'ung Autonomous County in Kwangsi and two more autonomous counties in Hunan, the T'ung Tao and Sing Tao, in the second one Sing and Tao nationalities being much more numerous than the T'ung. We have a representative from each province in the National People's Congress. There are primary schools at brigade level in the communes and middle schools at county level.

'In Kweichow one of our main activities has always been timber-getting. Our people are skilled at forestry, both in planting trees and handling timber. In the Kuomintang days, this was also the case. But we could keep no timber for ourselves. We lived in miserable thatch huts while all the timber went for others. For us there was bare sustenance – everything went to local big-shots linked to the Kuomintang. Now we all have timber houses and electric light. After land reform, we studied the Han methods of rice-growing and now get an average of 3 tons an acre in two crops a year, instead of less than a ton per acre in the old days. Forestry methods have improved, so that cedars mature in eight years instead of eighteen. All the T'ung communes are linked by roads – the railway runs to Sankiang, the centre of the autonomous county. With all this, our people are clearly delighted. But the main thing is that we run our own affairs and live in perfect harmony with the other national minorities and with the Hans. Kuomintang policy was to keep the national minorities at each other's throats, fomenting artificial disputes to prevent unity. Now we get along like one big family, settling on an equal and friendly basis any problems that crop up.'

Rewi Alley visited San Kiang and T'ung Pao in the early sixties,[2] finding that great progress had been made in improving livelihood and that integration between the various peoples had been wonderfully successful. He has a vivid impression of a commune farmers' mass meeting in San Kiang, with people filing in from the countryside and joining together under a sea of red flags discussing the new season's farming and irrigation plans. He confirmed what Yuang Chuan said about the satisfaction of the people there in being able to run their own affairs, and the fine relations already built up between them and the Han peoples.

In the West, a great deal of printers' ink has been splashed about regarding the 'fate' of the Tibetan people, thanks mainly

2. He described the situation in those regions at the time he visited them in *China's Hinterland in the Leap Forward* (New World Press, Peking, 1961) and *Amidst the Hills and Rivers of Hunan* (Foreign Languages Publishing House, Peking, 1963), respectively.

to the tales of lords, lamas and dispossessed serf-owners, starting with the Dalai Lama and those who fled with him to India after an abortive uprising by this slave-owning, serf-owning upper strata of what we prefer to term Lhasa–Tibetan society. We have not visited Lhasa Tibet – it requires special heart and blood-pressure specifications to support travel in the high altitudes that such a journey entails. As the Tibetans have received far more publicity than any other of China's national minorities, it is important to understand that numerically the Tibetans rank in numbers after the Chuang people of Kwangsi, the Uighurs of Sinkiang and the Yi and the Hui. Also that those who live in Lhasa Tibet, that is in and around Lhasa itself, about 130 miles from the Indian border and within a narrow strip south of there down to the India–Nepal–Bhutan–Sikkim border, represent less than one third of the 3,000,000-odd Tibetan people. Most Tibetans live in the adjoining provinces to the east and north where we have visited their autonomous communities on many occasions.

The March 1959 revolt was fomented by the C.I.A. and the Kuomintang, and prepared on Indian soil – one of the principal bases being at Kalimpong, due south of Mount Everest, close to the India–Nepal border. At an earlier stage Nehru had told the Indian parliament, regarding Kalimpong, that he 'began to doubt if the greater part of the population does not consist of foreign spies ...[3] But he did nothing to exercise Indian sovereignty in this matter and it can hardly be considered accidental that the centre of the counter-revolution was in the regions adjacent to the Indian frontier; nor that the first armed clash between India and China – at Longju, on 25 August 1959, when Indian troops tried to occupy a military post manned by Chinese troops for years previously but which India claimed *after* the incident as her territory – took place within a few months of the counter-revolution being crushed. If China became suspicious that the border war which followed was an attempt by India to achieve directly what the counter-revolution had not been able to achieve indirectly, she could hardly be blamed!

3. In the Lok Sabha (Lower House) on 17 September 1953.

The counter-revolution started when cautious social reforms cast a shadow of events to come as far as the powers of the lamas and feudal lords were concerned. The People's Liberation Army had moved into Tibet in 1950, but because basic policy requires that reforms must come from the local people themselves, things moved slowly. A group of journalists who made a visit to Tibet in 1955 were horrified to see serfs still being whipped in the fields while Han cadres gritted their teeth and pretended not to see. But had the cadres or P.L.A. intervened at that stage the cry of 'Greater Han chauvinism' would have echoed around the world.

As part of the preparation for the revolt, the C.I.A. had recruited hundreds of warrior Khammba tribesmen from the south-eastern corner of Tibet, flying them to a combat training field in the Rocky Mountains in Colorado, where conditions of climate and terrain were closest to those of Tibet. After six weeks' crash courses in guerrilla warfare, they were flown back and infiltrated into Tibet to take charge of an army of around 40,000 Khammba tribespeople, for whom the United States supplied the weapons. In other words the Khammbas[4] were used precisely as the Meos were later used in Laos – as U.S. mercenaries. That such preparations and supply operations could have gone on without the benevolent connivance of the government of the late Prime Minister Nehru is, of course, unthinkable. So much for the 'spontaneous' nature of the uprising which led to the flight of the Dalai Lama and his retinue to India.

4. In the 8 May 1971 issue of the *Far Eastern Economic Review* (Hong Kong), there is a fascinating letter from an Edward Friedman of Illinois, U.S.A. 'Your correspondent G.M.T.,' he writes, 'calls me to task in Review No. 13 for misleading and unsubstantiated contentions about C.I.A. aid to Tibetan rebels by the early 1960s. Perhaps the following quotation from Colonel Fletcher Prouty, who helped organize the Special Operations Force, will satisfy G.M.T. Prouty claims that in the late 1950s "we knew the Chinese were eventually going to come into Tibet, so we started recruiting a resistance force from among the natives. Up to 42,000 Tibetans were put under arms. We flew groups of tribesmen from Tibet to Saipan and from there to the Rocky Mountains in Colorado, where the atmosphere is similar to the Himalayas, for combat training. In six weeks they were back in Tibet and a fairly good force was built up." '

Among those who were not sorry at this turn of events was Tengchen, a slave in the Dalai Lama's household from boyhood until the latter's flight freed him at the age of twenty-two. He is now a teacher at the Central Minorities Institute in Peking. Shangri La is a very romantic name and the huge Potala fortress palace in Lhasa a magnificent architectural monument, but what went on behind those inward-sloping massive walls and the geometrically arranged squares of windows was anything but romantic. 'Even to raise my eyes to look at a lord passing by would mean having my eye gouged out, as I saw happen to others,' relates Tengchen. 'Not to poke out my tongue as a sign of reverence when a lord passed by would be to have it pulled out with red hot pincers or have it slashed off with a knife, as happened to fellow slaves.' To be starved, reviled and whipped was Tengchen's daily lot, but if he got to the point where he was so bashed about or ill that he could not work, he was given pellets made from the Dalai Lama's excreta, the miraculous properties of which were lauded by the lamas as a cure-all.

Missionaries in the West, raising money to support the Tibetan exiles in India and making impassioned declarations about the suppression of 'religious freedom' in Tibet, should understand that as far as those in India are concerned they are talking about members of a dismantled aristocracy who were thrown out, or simply walked out, after their attempted counter-revolution failed and their rotten and reactionary social order started to be taken apart. Many of the slaves and serfs, taken with them to carry their loot, have since returned. A special reception office was opened long ago in Lhasa for the purpose of settling them on the land or training them for jobs, whichever they prefer.

For an inside account of what it was like to work under the Dalai Lama, we talked with Tzejen Shanto, who, like Tengchen, had come as a student to the Peking Central Minorities Institute and remained as a teacher. With a stern, sombre face, withdrawn eyes and dark leathery skin, Tzejen Shanto grew up in Alidjada county, near the border with India. Born into a family of serfs, he said, 'we lived the lives of beasts of burden, crushed into the ground by the system of serfdom', and went on to describe how tragedy hit his family one winter when a sudden blizzard, the worst for a century, wiped out most of the 500 sheep which his grandfather tended for the local lord. Almost all livestock in the area was lost, his grandfather barely managing to stagger back to the village, three-parts dead, to face the fury of his lord and master.

'Even without that our lives were unbearable,' said Tzejen, his already sombre face darkening as he recalled the past. 'No wages were paid at all. For food we used to boil bits of yak-skin or sheep-skin and drink the soup; or grind up bones flung out from the serf-owners' table. We never got proper food-grains, but a sort of bran from barley and in summer wild grasses that filled the stomach but made the face swell up. For clothes, we had bits of sheepskin with holes for the arms – no sleeves, so your arms were always half-frozen in winter. Grandfather tended the serf-owner's sheep, and my father was in charge of the lord's caravan of fifty yaks which went back and forth between Lhasa and Chengtu, in Szechuan. Our home was a pile of stones, our main possession one battered old cooking pot.

'I was only a baby when the blizzard struck but my father told me many, many times exactly what happened. The serf-owner came and after having one of his men give my grandfather several strokes of the whip, he demanded compensation – the equivalent of 10 yuan for each sheep. Of course we had no money and he knew this before my grandfather told him. After several more strokes of the whip, the serf-owner said that if the money was not found by the following morning my grandfather would be flogged at the rate of one stroke for every yuan.

'Father was home at the time. He and my grandfather talked things over and decided that the only thing was to run away. As soon as it was dark in the afternoon, we fled – grandfather, father, my sister of six and I, a baby in my mother's arms. Another brother was living with an uncle.' In five days, they covered about sixty miles, in wild, mountainous country, heading towards India. On the morning of the sixth day, the serf-owner and a gang of his men caught up with them.

'They started to tie up my father and drag him off, lashing at him with their whips. My grandfather was indignant and shouted: "I've worked for you all my life, all the year round for nothing, and now you drag off my son. You want money for your sheep. All I've got is a bit of the skin of a sheep to cover my old bones." The serf-owner's bullies ripped off his sheepskin and tied him to a tree, naked in the freezing cold. "We'll warm you up and see if there's any fat in your old bones," the serf-owner shouted. They piled yak turd around my grandfather's legs, and lit it and burned him to death.' He turned his face away and wiped his eyes at this point, with the sleeve of his long Tibetan gown. A few embarrassing minutes went by while he tried to control his voice.

'When it was over, they took my father away. My mother did not know where to go; we had nothing left to eat – so she headed back towards our home village. She and my sister got weaker and weaker and it took them ten days to cover what they had previously done in five. My mother found a dead lamb and fed some of the raw meat to my sister, but she herself did not eat. Next morning we found her asleep and we could not wake her up. A few days later, my uncle came and found my sister and me huddled against her cold body. He took us to the village, where neighbours found someone to feed me milk. They advised my uncle to replace my father, whom the serf-owner had taken in place of grandfather, so he could come and look after us.

'My uncle agreed – he was a very kind man, my father told me. A few days later, my father was carried in, blood dripping from the lower part of his body. He had been given 500 lashes and there was nothing left of his buttocks. He had been forced to go down on all fours like a dog, his legs and arms bound and a heavy weight around his neck while the whips cut away at his buttocks.

'It was a year before my father could walk again. About that time, word came that my uncle was dead. Some said that he had been flogged to death, others that he was dropped down a dried-up well by the lord for being "rebellious". With my uncle dead, the serf-owner again came and demanded payment for the sheep. As we had nothing, he took my father to weave carpets – as he could hardly walk but could use his hands – my brother, who had returned after my uncle went to work for the serf-owner, to tend sheep and my sister to work in the house. One day while my brother was tending the sheep, he tripped over a stone and hurt his foot so that he couldn't move for a while. By the time he caught up with the sheep, some had been eaten by wolves. When the serf-owner heard, he had my brother brought back and tied up to a rafter. A fire was lit under his feet and he was beaten so brutally that he lost one eye.

'When I reached the age of six, the serf-owner took me from the neighbours who were looking after me. I had to serve as a yak-herd by day and as a sort of horse for his son in the evenings. He would pull my hair like a horse's mane when he wanted me to stop and beat me with a short whip when he wanted me to go faster. Once he fell off and started bawling so his father came and knocked me unconscious with a stone, claiming I had beaten his son. If the stone had killed me it would have been all the same to him. On another occasion, he set his most savage dog on me, then locked me up in a sheep-pen so the blood would not stain his floor.

'When my father protested and said at least he should give me some food, the serf-owner shouted, "You still owe me for my sheep," and had him whipped in front of me. I tried to crawl towards him but fainted. For about six months I could not stand up, the serf-owner coming every few days to kick me in the ribs to make me stand up. That is what the lives of the serfs were like. Can you wonder when we compare Chairman Mao to the sun?'

During the land-reform movement, he was given a job as messenger boy and later worked in a telecommunications office at the district administrative committee. 'They insisted on paying me wages,' he said. 'I tried to refuse, telling them that life was so much brighter that I would be glad to work all my life for nothing. In 1967 I was invited to go to Peking to study. I asked the neighbours, and they thought it was a very good idea. People started to hear about this all over the country. I was so excited that I wept. People said: "It's not just for your happiness but for ours that you go to study. You must go and study for us all." So I came and studied hard so that when other young people came I was able to help them. I am paid wages even to study!

'It is difficult for you to understand how ignorant we were, and what study means. The morning after a P.L.A. team with a portable projector had shown us a film about the Patriotic War, some of us went around the back of the screen hoping to pick up the bullets! Where there were only yak-tracks before there are now highways. There are clinics in every village and hospitals at county and district levels. You don't even have to go to the clinics – medical teams come to the houses. There are schools at commune level, some with teachers that I helped train here.

'We read in the newspapers,' he concluded, 'that there are people in India and elsewhere who would like to put the Dalai Lama back in Lhasa and the lords and serf-owners back inside the country. There are all sorts of schemes to divide the country and the people. You can tell such people that we, former serfs and slaves, will fight to the last drop of blood to prevent this. All our people have seen the difference between a Dalai Lama and a Chairman Mao and we have made our choice. No force can turn our people back to the old times.'

We collected many stories similar to that of Tzejen Shanto from Tibetans who had left the Lhasa–Tibet area for other provinces, but his was the most articulate, as he had acquired an excellent command of Mandarin Chinese. With such first-hand accounts from ex-slaves and serfs we thought we had touched rock-bottom as far as exploitation and oppression in Tibet was concerned. But we came across another, also at the Peking Institute of Minorities.

It was a very brief account by a seventeen-year-old lad, Malakun, of the tiny Teng minority from Ta Yi county, south of Chayu, near Lhasa Tibet's south-west frontier with India. A small chap, with a close-cropped, long head and a very solemn expression, he spoke Chinese with difficulty after eighteen months at the Institute. One had the feeling, by some grimaces he made, that he had not yet learned to smile. The Teng was an outcast minority discovered after the P.L.A. entered Tibet, with a still lower status than serfs and slaves.

'We lived in bark huts in the mountains,' explained Malakun. 'It was forbidden by the local lords for us to come down to the plains. Any caught doing so were beheaded on the spot. There were thirty "do nots", each punishable by death. We could not walk on roads or dig up wastelands. We had no written language and information was recorded by cutting marks into trees. Most had no clothes, only bits of bark to cover the back and hips. Any clothes were patchworks of old rags. We grew maize by dropping seeds into holes made by poking sticks into the ground after burning a patch of forest. Men carried a long knife on the right side, a pipe on the left, stuck into a jungle creeper that held the bark in place. People wore their hair long, twisted in old rags and piled on top of the head.' This information about what is probably China's tiniest national minority – unless the 'abominable snowmen' are finally proved to exist – did not come out in a connected account but in questions and answers, the answers often accompanied by gestures when Malakun's knowledge of Chinese and Tibetan ran out. (Tzejen Shanto helped out as interpreter when this happened.) His mother had died when he was a baby, as often happened, he explained, and his father died shortly afterwards. Some years after the P.L.A. moved in, the Communist Party sent in some cadres who tried to explain the policy towards minorities, and advised the 700-odd Tengs to move out of their mountain-slope forests into the warmer foothills and valleys.

'Most people were afraid,' continued this painfully extracted account. 'They feared their heads would be cut off. But after several visits and much talk, some of the younger people went down. They were told they could look at many places and decide where they would like to live. They were shown some places and went back to explain to the others. Many people were very surprised that their heads had not been cut off and that they had come back. That was in 1966 and I was only ten, but I went down too. Everybody was excited when we got back. Most people said: "That's fine." Some more went down and said where the first village should be. A warm river valley was chosen and then we were asked what sort of houses we would like. There was much talk about this because we had no idea about houses at all. We lived in shelters of bark leaned against the trees. The Communist Party people drew pictures and so it was said what houses there should be. They were built in 1967 and some P.L.A. people came and put some metal wheels and things in the river and there were lights in the houses much brighter than from pine torches. The next year many more houses were made and everyone moved down. Altogether seven villages, 140 households, 740 people. I joined a work-team and learned to plough the earth with yaks pulling the plough. At the end of 1971, I was asked if I would like to study in Peking, where Chairman Mao works. Everybody said I should go. I saw a bus for the first time after I got to Lhasa and went by bus to Chengtu, and a train for the first time when I went from Chengtu to Peking. Of course I didn't know that there were such things. They are very good.'

Asked what he wanted to do in the future, he replied: 'Go home and tell my people about the government and the Communist Party and how we are part of a very big family. Help my people to become like those in other parts. The year before I left all our people grouped together in a People's Commune. In a short time I will go back and help to make life still better.'

Sceptics may justifiably ask what proof we have that what Malakun related is true, and our answer must be: 'None.' But our conviction, based on long experience, is that people such as he are virtually incapable of lying. The effort to explain is so great that deceit is impossible. One could almost feel the cogs turning in his mind to understand what we wanted to know and then going into reverse to record what he knew of what we wanted to know. What was amazing, as we felt it at the time, was that a bridge of a thousand or two years, from a social-economic viewpoint, could be spanned within a couple of years once the right approach and the right method was found. A fact hard to swallow, perhaps, is that the Teng people, from living in a state of primitive communism, have passed over the intervening stages of slavery, serfdom, feudalism and capitalism, to land bang on their feet in socialism. They have leaped forward from being one of the most insecure units of society to become one of the most secure.

As a religion, for those who want it, Lammaist Buddhism still exists, but it is dying a natural death. The young people do not want to spend large parts of their lives inside monastery walls; tens of thousands of young lamas have left the monasteries – as we know from the visits to the Tibetan communities in the non-Lhasa–Tibet provinces – to settle down on the communes and get married. Secular education has opened their eyes to the hoaxes of reincarnation. Economics also played a role. For instance the *hala*, or *puhua* as the Hans call it, a badger-type animal which stores big quantities of stolen grain in underground hide-outs to see it through the long winter, was considered to be the reincarnation of by-gone lamas – and therefore sacrosanct. Its skins now form an appreciable sideline revenue for many communes where the *hala* is now hunted, and the amount of harvested grain has increased proportionately. In certain counties in Tsinghua province, one third of the total butter production went to nourish the local lamassery lamps. Most of that now goes into people's stomachs in the form of the excellent and nourishing buttered tea, or to pay for farm machinery in the county towns.

The Tibetans and other national minorities receive privileges in many respects. The annual revenues of the autonomous regions rarely equals their annual expenditure and the difference is made up by the wealthier provinces. Family planning is not propagated because the appalling living conditions and absence of health services in the past led to stagnation or decline in population growth. This is serious in the frontier areas, where there is a direct link between population decline and the advance of the deserts. Big efforts have been made for health and education – in Tibet the only education in the past was theological study in the lamasseries. That 20,000 Tibetan cadres were running their own affairs by 1973 reflected an enormous effort in education and technical training. The Han 'invasion', apart from the P.L.A., whose job it is to defend China's frontiers, has been in the form of educators and technical cadres for building up industry – there are now two big sugar refineries in the

Lhasa area alone – and power stations, and running them until such time as Tibetans can run their own industry as they now run their administration. In the Chuang Autonomous Region in Kwangsi, from 900 cadres of Chuang nationality in the first years after liberation, the number has increased to 78,000 and they entirely run their own affairs. From the Korean minorities in the north-east to the Yi in the south-west, from the Tibetans, Mongols and others in the north-west to the Li and Miao on Hainan island in the extreme south-east, we found the national minority peoples have been helped in every imaginable way to stride forward from Middle Age darkness into an advanced social system – helped to run their own affairs as completely as possible and to be integrated into the Chinese nation as free and equal partners of the Han majority people.

CHAPTER SEVENTEEN

EVALUATING THE PAST

In May 1967, when the Cultural Revolution was at its stormiest, a bullet-headed youngster with a Red Guard armband on his sleeve swaggered into Rewi Alley's Peking apartment. With a jerk of his chin towards the pottery shards, bronzes, ivories, scrolls and other treasures accumulated during decades of work and travel in the back country, where every sandstorm uncovers fresh relics, the Red Guarder said: 'Better chuck all this old junk out.' Roaring 'Down with your pants,' Rewi Alley reached for his belt. An offspring of one of his adopted sons, the lad had come from a remote province to give the Cultural Revolution in Peking a push from behind – intent on applying too literally the campaign against the 'four olds' (old ideas, old culture, old habits and old ruling-class customs). There were enough young zealots around with similar misinterpretations to cause the government to close museums and place ancient monuments under armed guard.

Fortunately, the treasures which Rewi Alley uses to illustrate facets of China's past remained intact. The campaign against the 'four olds' was aimed at the Confucian-inspired sanctity of age and authority behind which Liu Shao-ch'i and his followers sheltered to advance their policies. In a more specific way, the campaign was also used against well-known reactionaries of the old order to uncover illegally hoarded treasures in the form of gold bars and foreign currency, arms, radio transmitters, Kuomintang uniforms and decorations and, far more significantly, title deeds to properties taken over during land reform and detailed records of former tenants' debts, with compound interest calculated in many cases up to the month of the seizure. Like White Russian émigrés in European capitals, and the dispossessed in all revolutions, a tiny handful of upper-class Chinese still pinned their hopes on the miracle of a Kuomintang come-back. Confiscated evidence of this was displayed during the Cultural Revolution in special exhibitions in Peking, Shanghai and other former strongholds of the privileged.

It was the period when many students and young people from the cities were taking advantage of free transport and peasant hospitality to wander all over China and discover the country-side, while their opposite numbers from the countryside descended into the cities, doubtless with lurking suspicions that they were dens of iniquity that had spawned revisionism and 'capitalist-roaders'.

In urging an attack against the 'four olds', Mao was laying down a challenge to any automatic obedience to authority based on age, classical learning and custom, a legacy of Confucianism which had permeated the educational system and dominated some approaches to scientific research. (It was later seen to have even resisted the cleansing winds of the Cultural Revolution in some fields.)

Confucius, the name a latinized version of K'ung Fu-tzu (Master K'ung), was never regarded too highly by modern Chinese revolutionaries. The May the Fourth (1919) Students' Movement, which was inspired partially by the dissemination of Marxist ideas following the success of the Bolshevik revolution and which paved the way for the founding of the Chinese Communist Party two years later, started by attacking Confucius. A young student leader, Mao Tse-tung, was one of its members. Retrograde ideas, such as insistence on filial piety, the automatic authority of age, scholarship and officialdom as the cornerstones of society, came under heavy fire. Similar concepts which fitted in with K'ung Fu-tzu's campaign to restore the declining slave-owning society were castigated by Mao in some of his earliest published works. It was a theme to which he has returned from time to time ever since. Such attacks were motivated by the fact that every reactionary force throughout the centuries, including the Kuomintang in Mao's time, exploited the Confucian restorationist ideology to reinforce their dictatorial rule and justify their demands for blind obedience from the masses.

The idealistic precepts of Confucianism, despite the many pious appeals for brotherly love within the ruling class and the less publicized advocacy of the merits of slave–master relations, could never be a comfortable bed-fellow of the doctrines of the class struggle. Confucius as the ideologist of restoration was an obvious target, and it was natural to link his name with Lin Piao and Liu Shao-ch'i when the latter were accused of the similar heresies of seeking to restore capitalism in China.

The campaign launched against K'ung Fu-tzu in the latter half of 1973, which gathered force during 1974, was centred around the point that he was an apostle for the restoration of slave society, a hoary reactionary in his own day and age, resisting the advance of the landlord–serf stage of society which historically speaking was an advance on slavery. He is accused of having tried to turn back the wheel of history, the accusations being backed with extracts from his writings and his activities when he was an important official of the ancient state of Lu, now part of Shantung province. The campaign is used as a vast educational movement to familiarize hundreds of millions of Chinese for the first time with the real content and background of the precepts which have been taken for granted for some 2,500 years (Confucius lived between 551 and 479 B.C.) and to draw a parallel with contemporary leaders who also wanted to turn back the wheel of history by resisting the advance towards communism.

As an example of the millennia-long continuity of Chinese history, Chufu, once the capital of the ancient state of Lu, is without parallel. In the shadows of the excellently maintained great golden temple to the honour of the old sage are the tombs of seventy-six successive heads of the K'ung clan – direct linear descendants of K'ung the Master. A break in the continuity will occur only if the ruling head of the clan dies and is buried in Taiwan, whence he was taken by the Kuomintang. According to other members of the K'ung clan who still populate the Chufu area, this was done to prevent such a 'prestigious cultural monument' from falling into communist hands! As seventy-six generations of his ancestors had withstood many vicissitudes to remain in the locality, it is easy to believe that the reigning head of the K'ung clan was abducted by force, as his nearest relatives claim. To contemplate a burial so far from the tombs of his ancestors must be a chilling thought! This, at least, is the opinion of K'ung clan members who populate three communes in the outskirts of Chufu city – and who have been most active in denouncing the retrograde philosophy of the restorationist.

What the old sage would say about the educational principles being taught these days at the Teachers' Training College just west of the walled city, which bore his name until very recently, must remain a matter of conjecture. His theories that a gentleman did not work with his hands; that the scholar's books should be carried by a slave trailing behind; that the masses were innately stupid; that the rule of law being consolidated in his lifetime should be abandoned in favour of the old rule of rites – all those taboos that his teachings laid on people's minds to inhibit their creativeness – have been turned upside down. But his influence on human thought in China for two and a half millennia, and in Japan, as the nearest and most important country to be swayed by his philosophy, is not denied in Mao's China any more than the influence of Jesus Christ in the West is denied by Marxists.

Chufu, however, has preserved its own special quiet and flavour, with avenues of ancient cypresses radiating out from the old drum tower, with its big bronze drum still intact, to the places dedicated to old K'ung. Many family relics from the original K'ung mansion were lost to generations of plunderers before liberation, but there is still an impressive array of magnificent bronzes of the second millennium B.C., portraits of dukes in Ming and Ch'ing Dynasty times, a statuette of a later head of the clan listening to a favourite opera. The People's Government paid for the upkeep not only of the ducal mansion, but also the huge Confucian temple, the walled-in area of cypress forest around the sage's tomb, and the general approaches to the historic spots of the old city.

The temple to Confucius is on the scale of the palace-museums of the Old Imperial City in Peking, a museum in itself, the exhibits constantly added to by ancient bronzes and prehistoric relics unearthed locally during irrigation and other works of reconstruction. There are well-preserved Han (206 B.C. to A.D. 221) Dynasty stone carvings and a copy of a whole set of musical instruments of the orchestra of the state of Lu, as used in the time of Confucius. Musical scholars from Peking have come to study the past and make the melodies and chants of that era come to life again. The tomb of Confucius is situated in what used to be the capital of the ancient state, its walls enclosing an area one and a half times that of Chufu city itself, to accommodate comfortably the tombs of the seventy-six hereditary dukes.

Wherever one travels in China one is conscious of this combination of respect for the old – homage to historical continuity and all that contributes to man's understanding of his own evolution – with a meticulous attempt to separate the progressive from the retrograde.

For example, during a never-to-be-forgotten boat trip from Chungking to Wuhan, through the fabulous Yangtze gorges, an attentive stewardess, when not occupied with the banalities of room and table service, divided her time between pointing out the impressive development of industry and housing on both banks of the Yangtze and indicating the historic monuments past which we glided in a very comfortable passenger steamer. Just before nightfall on the first day, we dropped anchor at Wanhsien, with its lovely grey building leading up from the steep banks, new constructions blending perfectly with the old, in order to pass through the first of the three gorges – the Ch'u Tang – in daylight. During the late afternoon, stewardess Tzu Hung-li, fresh-faced, with stiff, short pigtails and tireless in her attentions, pointed out a succession of curved-roof pagodas, rising one above the other up several hundred feet of steep cliffs on the southern bank to a splendid structure on the summit, a single architectural complex, gleaming white in the rays of the setting sun against the emerald of the tree-covered cliffs. It was the 'Magic Stone' pagoda, Miss Tzu informed us, to mark a Chinese version of the 'Goose That Laid the Golden Egg' morality fable. Legend had it that from a hole in the rock at the summit enough grain emerged every morning to feed a handful of hermit monks who had taken up their abode there. One of them had the bright idea of chiselling out a bigger hole to get more grain. He chiselled away and, like the man who killed the goose to get all the golden eggs at once, found there was no more grain. The pagodas remain as monuments against greediness.

Early next morning, as the broad river started narrowing to squeeze itself into the first gorge, great whorls in the chocolate waters testifying to the inner turbulence that bore us along at speed to a gap where hazy blue mountains stood like giant sentinels, it was to a beautiful sun-lit temple on the northern bank that Miss Tzu drew our attention. It had been built innumerable centuries earlier to the memory of Chang Fei, one of the three main personages in *All Men Are Brothers*, the famous fourteenth-century novel by Lo Kuan-chung. Chang Fei, Miss Tzu told us, had been assassinated by two traitors at the spot where local people had erected the temple.

If Tzu Hung-li was too busy with professional duties, there were fellow-passengers with guide-books in hand to point out historical or legendary landmarks, or to explain the origins of names of towns and counties. (One of the first counties after leaving Chungking had been named Chiang Chou (Longevity) three centuries earlier on the recommendation of an official scholar. Forced to spend the night at the county seat because of bad weather, he had found himself as the honoured guest at a birthday party in which seven generations participated to honour the 150th birthday of an old chap who presided over the ceremonies, downing the wine with the rest of them.)

The most famous sight, the notorious 'Come to Me' rocks, however, had disappeared. Situated as they were in one of the narrowest channels – only 150 feet wide – the only way of avoiding being wrecked on them was to steer straight for the rocky outcrops with the huge 'Come to Me' characters painted in white at the summit, so that the rushing waters would bear your craft aside on a course parallel to the rocks. If you steered to avoid the outcrop you were certain to be swept sideways by the current and be dashed to destruction against the sharp-teethed rocks that lined the gorge.

Liu Hung-yin, the captain of our 'East Is Red No. 32' passenger boat, who had been on the Yangtze run for thirty-three out of his forty-six years, said he could not remember how many wrecks he had personally witnessed in the Kuei Min Kuan, or Demon's Gate Pass, as the 'Come to Me' rocks section of the gorges was known. 'The most spectacular was when a Kuomintang troop transport with about a thousand troops on board was travelling upstream,' he said. 'The captain steered correctly for the rocks, but the troops must have panicked. They all rushed to the shore-side of the boat, which overturned. Not a single person was saved.'

Rewi Alley, who had made the trip frequently in the old days, recalled that boatmen and travellers wore their oldest clothes and left valuables behind if they had to make the trip. 'Steamers would stop when a junk went down, but you would never see a sign of life – everything was sucked straight under the rampaging current. The trackers who were hired in the old days to pull junks upstream fought their way inch by inch along the tow-paths. If anyone missed his footing – and it happened all the time – he was flicked off into the river. Nobody would stop pulling because it was useless and, with one man's hauling power less, the rest of the team and the junk were already in danger. They worked naked, for a tiny pittance – a bitter, dangerous trade with about the shortest life expectancy of any.'

Captain Liu steered our boat comfortably over the spot, through Demon's Gate Pass. In the early days after liberation, P.L.A. men had set to work to widen, straighten and deepen the gorge and blow most of the 'Come to Me' rocks to smithereens. Tackling the bigger rocks first, then the sides of the gorges, they worked away until the navigation hazards were eliminated. Some of the 'Come to Me' rocks still poke their heads above water in the dry season but in calmer and wider waters they were easy to navigate around – at least so Captain Liu assured us, inviting us to make a dry-season trip to see for ourselves. The son of a poor peasant tenant-farmer who could not feed his family, Liu Hung-yin started life as a cabin-boy at the age of thirteen and later graduated to be an apprentice-sailor. Incredible as it sounds, he had never received a cent of pay in his nine and a half years of boat service before liberation, considering himself lucky to have a deck to sleep on and the left-overs from officers or rich passengers' tables to satisfy his hunger.

'It is difficult for foreigners to understand what our life was like,' he said. 'Apart from the miserable living conditions, relations between officers and men were terrible; the gap between the living standard of the captain and the other officers, and between the officers and men, was unbelievable. Now we all live and eat together on an equal basis and have friendly, comradely relations. I've noticed you taking pictures of the old temples and the pagodas and that's fine. Everyone admires them. They are beautiful and we are proud of them – they were built by man a long time ago. But don't let anyone persuade you that these were "good old days" just because beautiful temples were built. For the mass of the people they were terrible old days. In my village, which is now part of a commune and where my father has a decent house, people say: "In the old society poor people were transformed into ghosts, now they are honoured and educated as real people." Had it not been for the revolution, I would still be eking out a non-life, beaten up by anyone who had a stick handy, kicked around like a dog. It was the revolution that pulled me up on to my feet and gave me the chance to study and learn navigation. I am able to serve the people in a way I know – handling a boat up and down the Yangtze. If I speak like this, it is because we have the occasional passenger who sticks his feet up, admires the views and temples and sighs about the "old days". We know how to honour the old,' he concluded, 'but also how to appreciate the new.'

This was proved to be true when some young zealots who wanted to attack ancient monuments as symbols of feudalism were restrained by the local people. Destruction and damage to ancient monuments in China has usually been at the hands of foreign invaders or local warlords. A typical example is at Changteh, in North Hopei, the summer-resort palace of the early Ch'ing emperors. A magnificent bronze temple, together with priceless images, was destroyed and smelted down for munitions by the Japanese shortly after their entry into the Second World War. They shot the deer which grazed in the walled-in forest for food. Later the Kuomintang quartered a division of troops there for three years from 1946 onward, cutting down the trees to build pill-boxes, smashing up doors and windows for fuel and in general completing the depredations started by the Japanese. Since liberation the few scattered pine trees that remained from what had been a magnificent forest have been reinforced by more pines, poplars, elms and cypress trees, so that it has become once again one of the loveliest spots in China. The most famous of all the Ch'ing palaces, the Yuan Ming Yuang in Peking, was burned down by the Anglo-French expedition at the time of the Second Opium War (1856–60).

Indeed while the 'four olds' were being attacked on the ideological front, excavation works continued in many parts of China to uncover past glories, including the search for the tomb of Ch'in Shih-huang, the first Ch'in emperor. The building of his tomb at Lintung, near Sian (once Changan), the first capital of the Chinese empire, is said to have involved the labour of 700,000 men for eleven years! Just as elderly Chinese like to contemplate good, solid coffins near their bedsides in their declining years, so the emperors liked to have tombs to contemplate, no less palatial than the palaces from which they reigned. The fabulous Ming tombs, an hour's drive north of Peking, one of the largest of which was excavated after liberation and is now a favourite sight-seeing spot for foreign tourists, are a spectacular example of this dual attitude towards the past. The exhibition of the finds is an example of the respect paid by the People's Republic to historical treasures.

One finds this blend of respect for old values and traditions, while rejecting retrograde old concepts, in the approach to arts and crafts. The drive to industrialize is not permitted to bulldoze traditional handicrafts out of existence.

We found an interesting example of the cautious approach to modernizing handicrafts at the famous old ink factory of Hu Kai-wen, at Sihsien, the ancient name to which Hweichow city in Anhwei province has now reverted. The ink used for the brushes which make Chinese calligraphy an art in itself comes in small, oblong slabs, usually with delicate landscapes or historic scenes embossed on both sides. Enough ink is rubbed off on the stone ink slab, to which water is added from a special water pot, to form that jet-black ink so much admired on Chinese scrolls.

China now produces – and exports – excellent fountain pens, and there are all kinds of modern bottled inks to go with them. But alongside this there are the sixth- and seventh-generation descendants of the eighteenth-century master craftsman, Hu Kai-wen, still making ink slabs in the finely carved moulds cut in the days of the old master. Some of the moulds still in use date back to the Ming Dynasty (1368–1644), when an old craftsman named Tsao was famous for his mould-making. The fact that such names have been handed down testifies to the appreciation of superb handicraftsmanship in general and of the making of ink slabs as an art form in particular.

Machinery was installed to avoid muscle-straining work such as the 2,000 strokes with heavy iron bars which pairs of workers used to deal to every mixture, considered essential to obtain the right consistency before the black paste was poured off into the moulds. But essentially the process remains on the old handicraft basis. The fine engraving of wooden blocks to vary the landscapes or other themes is still done by hand, as is the painting of the embossed patterns. The slow natural drying process is still watched over for the month considered necessary to give the slabs the special quality for which the factory is renowned not only in China, but in Japan and among Chinese all over the world. A high proportion of the annual production in fact goes for export.

One finds this same meticulous respect for tradition at Shaohsing, in Chekiang province, in the manufacture of the high-quality rice wine which bears its name. The Chinese serve it either hot in small porcelain cups, or cold in glasses. Shaohsing wine can easily pass for a fine sherry. Many small wine-producing enterprises were combined to form a state wine factory which has retained the traditional wine-making process and maintained the high quality. The rice is soaked and steamed and worked over for fifteen days before being put into big ceramic jars for a fermentation period of another seventy days, and then on to the presses for the extraction process. The finished product goes into porcelain jars with specially processed Shaohsing earth packed around the stopper and neck to ensure that the jars remain watertight. Certainly there are other ways to keep the air out, but that is the traditional way. An ancient custom in well-to-do families was to bury a few jars of Shaohsing wine at the birth of a male child, then to resurrect them for a wedding feast or some other auspicious occasion. As with the ink slabs, a good proportion of the rapidly expanding production of Shaohsing goes for export.

In writing about Shaohsing wine, it would be inappropriate not to recall our visit to the jade factory at Chichuan (Wine Spring) in Kansu province. For a couple of thousand years, poets have sung the praises of the green-jade wine cups made there. The old Han period disc-plate jade cutter is still being used, as it has been used for 2,000 years, but it is now driven by electric power. Nothing better has been found for cutting the massive jade blocks quarried in the area. A co-operative of seventy-two workers was turning out beautiful wine cups from jade and a jade-like stone in the forms that have delighted connoisseurs and wine-bibbers for so many centuries.

In an ancient pottery in the outskirts of Sandan, and also in Kansu, where painted pottery has been made since Neolithic times, we found however that the main work in 1973 was making refractory bricks for lining iron and steel furnaces, with table pottery made as a relatively small sideline, the principal pottery product being large, black glazed jars used in commune households for storing grain 'in case of war' and for salting down vegetables for the winter. It was difficult not to have a sneaking hope that no industrial use will be found for jade.

A rather more meaty illustration of respect for tradition was a story that went the rounds of Peking in 1957, shortly after the merger of state and private enterprises. It concerned Mao Tse-tung and one of several Peking restaurants, well-patronized because of their succulent *huo kuo* (fire-pot) mutton. Finely-sliced mutton is dipped into boiling bouillin, flavoured with a variety of sauces to the taste of the diner, in the *huo kuo*, a circular metal dish with a chimney in the centre for charcoal. Cooked within a matter of seconds, it is a very popular dish, especially in winter. After the merger, this restaurant was cleaned up and enlarged. The former proprietor stayed on as assistant manager, and a manager was appointed by the state. Everything went well for the first few days. Old clients returned and new ones filled the increased table space. The manager quietly observed everything with an eye on how better to serve the people.

After about a week, he said to his assistant: 'I notice that the most time-consuming job is cutting each pound of meat into a hundred slices. If we reduce this to eighty slices per pound, the customers will never know the difference, we'll have a 20 per cent saving in labour costs and we'll serve the people better by reducing the price.' The former proprietor had his doubts: 'People are used to a hundred-slice mutton and I don't think it will work.' The conscientious manager was insistent and so the eighty-slice method was introduced. Clients held the meat with their chopsticks the standard few seconds in the boiling bouillon, but it was tough. Old clients started deserting the restaurant, concluding that state control meant no more tender meat. An inquiry was made as to why the clientele was dwindling. The story came to Mao's ears and he is reported to have said: 'Restore the hundred slices. If socialism isn't good for hundred-slice mutton it's good for nothing.' The story may be apocryphal, but the fact that it circulated among high-level cadres shows that this was an approved attitude against monkeying around with well-proven traditions. The continued excellence of the food in Peking restaurants tends to prove that the 'traditionalists' triumphed in the gastronomic field.

The excellence of the old handicraft traditions are being carefully preserved and developed in the arts and crafts workshops. Old ones have been enlarged and new ones have blossomed into life all over China, including the communes. Chinese hands are in no danger of losing their cunning, whether in manipulating the old disc jade-cutter or the electric-powered, dentist-type drills used to pierce jade, ivory and other precious materials in delicate filigree work. Under the watchful eyes of veteran craftsmen, for whose experience and skills there is unlimited demand, a new and exceptionally talented generation of jade and ivory carvers, of workers in lacquer and cloisonné, in silver and other metals, in embroidery and carpet-making, is taking over the traditional arts and crafts for which China is famous. They provide an inexhaustible source of revenue for the export trade, untroubled by competition from any other country. Thanks exclusively to the skills of hundreds of thousands of pairs of hands and a genuine feeling for artistic expression, China has a reserve treasury which no other country can match. Workers in this field are encouraged to branch out into new lines and art forms, to experiment with new materials, and to retain and improve on all that is best in the old techniques.

We found one of the most spectacular successes in making 'something from nothing' in the Wheat Straw Products Section of the Harbin Arts and Crafts Workshop. Stalks of ordinary wheat straw, which would normally rot in the fields after the grain is harvested, are steamed, split open and pressed flat with an ordinary laundry iron and then used as a raw material for such things as feathers for life-size peacocks, or moulded relief effects in portraying mountains and buildings with a gleaming, bronze-like finish, impossible to relate to such humble raw material. There are 370 workers – 90 per cent of them women – in this section alone. Their products are exported to the U.S.A., France, Japan – forty countries in all – and earned 700,000 yuan in 1972. The figure is rising rapidly. As the raw material costs nothing and the total wage bill was just under 200,000 yuan, the Wheat Straw Products Section was making a good contribution to the national revenue, especially if one considers the potential as the idea catches on. It was a pioneering speciality of Harbin at the time of our visit.

Rice straw, we discovered, was not suitable because it was not as robust. We asked where the idea came from. 'The poor peasants in this area used to use wheat straw for hats and soles of slippers,' replied Chung Chiao-hua, the middle-aged woman running the section. 'So it was proved that it was a strong material. And at the New Year the poorest of the peasants who had no money for paper used patterns from flattened-out straw to replace the traditional paper cuts pasted up on the windows.

At first we copied that, glueing the straw on flat surfaces, then went on to moulded, semi-flat effects and finally complete objects, such as birds, squirrels and so on.' From trial products made by four workers of peasant origin in 1960, the section was turning out over a thousand types of products by 1973. It was rather awesome to watch lines of young women, each with a flattened bit of wheat straw pinned to their bench, peeling off curled straw shavings with a razor-sharp scraper, which other girls picked up with pairs of tweezers, dipped into a glue pot and stuck on as feathers to most realistic-looking pheasants – a stuffed bird on a table in front of them serving as a model. In a showroom there was a wheat-straw squirrel on a wheat-straw tree, the whole about 6 feet by 3 feet, priced at 900 yuan.

In the courtyard, alongside an ancient disc-saw eating into a huge block of jade, was a pile of buffalo and cow-horns, which in another workshop we watched being transformed into figurines of heroes and heroines from folk tales and operas, birds and animals, classical lanterns and chains and a whole range of art objects that one would swear were made of amber and jade, except for the difference in weight. 'Another of our specialities,' said Wu Chen-yi, the manager of the whole Arts and Crafts Workshop, a well-built man in his early thirties, with a sensitive face and stubby, artist's fingers. 'We started using horn in 1964, at first for combs and spoons for medical work. Later we made a careful study of its characteristics and found it had beautiful natural colours. It needed only careful selection for each specific object, good cutting and polishing. If you give it the same attention given to the more precious materials you can do all sorts of things with it. We started using it for figure-carving – characters from old legends and fairy tales – and we found it very malleable, capable of producing most life-like portraits. It is especially good for such things as prawns and fish, and objects carved from horn are now very popular export items for south-east Asia, Japan and Canada.' The natural colours could be changed within limits by heating.

'There is no tradition in Harbin for this type of arts and crafts,' explained Wu Chen-yi as we walked through the different workshops. 'We were able to bring in some veteran craftsmen from other centres and created our tradition as we went along, based on a solid national tradition of craftsmanship and love of artistic expression.'

There had been no such tradition in Harbin because until the end of the nineteenth century it was a small wheat-marketing and fish-drying centre, later developed by Tsarist Russia as a headquarters of the Chungchang, the Chinese Eastern Railway – a new and foreign city as far as the Chinese were concerned, not one to inspire traditional arts. The setting-up of the first arts and crafts workshops had taken place in 1958, the year of so many astonishing births in all fields of human activity. The initial nucleus of a handful of veterans and a few hundred art-minded middle-school students – about 300 in all – making paper flowers and doing some embroidery had expanded to 4,200 workers by 1973, grouped according to their specialities, each group organized as a co-operative enterprise and their activities and marketing co-ordinated under the Harbin Arts and Crafts Company.

Another of the Harbin innovations which we discovered by a visit to an exhibit of some 600 items was 'heat-painting' on wood – delicate creams, beiges and browns, obtained on wood surfaces by using an ordinary flat iron at different heats on landscape patterns traced by artists on the sandpapered surface. Under the Company's watchful eye – keen to note the tastes of foreign importers – more than thirty types of objects were produced, each in an infinite variety. At the different ateliers we were urged to advise and criticize, given the lack of experience of workers and cadres! Had they been using up raw materials – even the humble wheat-straw – to turn out standardized busts of national leaders, we might have had a few words to say, but as they had got away to a flying start in creating beautiful things that everyone from children to art collectors could appreciate, we had nothing better to offer in the way of advice than 'press on'.

At the Shanghai Jade and Carpet Factory, however, when a similar request for criticism was made, we did comment on the unimpressive effect of certain arts and crafts exhibits sent abroad because of the predominance of contemporary political themes of transitory importance, compared to the ageless value of traditional Chinese art, and that it seemed that lack of inspiration had affected the skill of the craftsmen. Hung Te-yung, a member of the revolutionary committee of the Jade Carving Factory, a massive, bespectacled elderly man, replied: 'True, for a time there were some very political themes. Exhibits sent abroad were selected according to the requirements of the time. They reflected modern thinking. But during the Cultural Revolution there were some influences of the ultra-left that have since been corrected.'

This was a factory that grouped some of China's finest artisans. No wheat-straw and cow-horns here, but exclusively jade, ivory and coral, with precious stones – emeralds, sapphires and turquoises as well as the common jasper and agate – used as embellishments. Apart from ivory, some of which was imported from abroad, the materials abounded in China. In 1955, the first jade-carvers' co-operative had been formed by seventeen craftsmen. In 1958 it expanded into the Shanghai Jade Carvers' Factory with 200 workers, and employed over 600 craftsmen at the time of our visit in 1972. Its products could certainly be found in the most exclusive art shops of Paris, London and New York.

In the Peking Arts and Crafts Workshop, apart from jade and ivory carvings, specialities included carved red lacquer, silver filigree work, small translucent perfume bottles, painted from the inside by the use of mirrors, and very fine brushes and cloisonné work of which Peking has had the exclusive monopoly for a good 500 years. 'It requires very fine, delicate and precise work,' explained Liu Hsueh-ming, a genial member of the revolutionary committee in his late thirties. He initiated us into the intricacies of setting multi-coloured fragments of enamel into mosaics separated by hair-thin copper wire fillets. 'We have preserved the traditional art but developed new patterns, colours and paints,' explained Liu Hsueh-ming. 'Until a few years ago, there were only a dozen shades of colours. Now there are a hundred. There is also a big development in pattern and design, some reflecting modern trends, the needs of a socialist society, others preserving forms of the Ming and

Ch'ing Dynasties.' As an example of catering to modern requirements he cited the manufacture of prize trophies for the two
most recent Asian ping-pong championships.

The faces of the old craftsmen were a study in themselves –
their deep concentration when they picked up a piece of raw
jade or ivory, turning it round in their hands, eyeing the shape
and grain before deciding the object into which the material
could best be transformed with a minimum of waste; their
pursed lips and frowns and screwed-up eyes – usually behind
spectacles – as they critically examined the work of apprentices
or young workers; their appreciative nods and smiles when their
strict standards were met. We asked one sixty-three-year-old
veteran, Chin Shieh-chuan, a wisp of a man with a deep-lined
face, what he thought of the younger generation of workers and
apprentices.

'These young people have good points,' he said. 'They bring
enthusiasm into their work and some new ideas. They "dare to
speak, think and act", as Chairman Mao advises. We older
workers have a low level of education, but the younger people
help the veterans. In technical things we help the younger
people. It is a good sort of partnership. When I was an apprentice, if I had dared open my mouth about anything, I'd probably have been beaten to death.' His mouth set in a bitter
straight line, even at the thought of the old days. It turned out
that he had started work at the age of ten. 'The life of an
apprentice was hell no matter what the job was,' he continued.
'But if you were working with expensive materials like jade and
ivory, where a mistake caused serious losses, it was even worse.
If the master craftsman made a mistake, he would blame the
apprentice and you would get a terrible beating from the owner.
If you dared open your mouth to tell the truth, you'd be beaten
up by the craftsman as well. There were no set hours – from
dawn to dusk in summer and deep into the night in winter. No
wages at all, no medicine if you got sick. When you finished
your apprenticeship, the usual thing was to be thrown on to the
streets, as I was. Although I was a skilled filigree worker, I
eked out a living as a pedlar until after liberation. By accident
I heard that some of the people I had worked with were going

to set up a handicrafts co-operative and that the government was going to give it a start with money and materials. I was delighted to get back to my old trade. Later on several other co-ops with different specialities joined together to form this factory.'

Chin Shieh-chuan had the status of 'veteran craftsman' and earned 100 yuan per month. Married late in life, he had one son, to whom he had passed on his skills. 'But he joined the P.L.A.,' the old chap said. 'Young people have a mind of their own these days.'

When we asked if he thought there was any danger of industrialization replacing the handicrafts, he looked at us dumbfounded. 'Never,' he replied. 'Machines are good for making trucks and trains, ships and planes and all sorts of things our country never made before. But when it comes to turning out a nice figure or bit of jade or ivory filigree work, you have to have human hands and eyes.'

To our question whether the young people paid due deference to his age, he replied: 'They respect me for what I am, for what I know, for what I can do and for what I can tell them about the past. It's not like the old days of bowing down to people just because they are old. Why should they respect me if I was an old exploiter who got rich by starving and beating up his workers? In this factory young people respect the old for what they are and we respect the young for what they will be and do our best to help them develop all that is best in our old traditions of craftsmanship.'

CHAPTER EIGHTEEN

THE CHALLENGE TO YOUTH

On 14 April 1971, we were present in a reception room at the Great Hall of the People in Peking when a nineteen-year-old American hippie in a floral shirt, his shoulder-length hair kept back by an embroidered band across his forehead, got to his feet and, to the anguished horror of some present, said: 'I'm curious to know what premier Chou thinks about the hippie movement which excites the youth of the U.S.A. today.' Manager Steenoven of the U.S. table-tennis team of which the hippie was a member, very conscious of the dramatic implications of this first venture into ping-pong diplomacy, paled. He had thought Glenn Cowan was joking when he talked of raising the question at a reception premier Chou En-lai was giving to U.S., British, Canadian, Nigerian and Columbian table-tennis teams, invited to China after the 1971 world championships in Nagoya, Japan.

U.S. team members had been briefed on the importance of making a good impression in Chou En-lai's presence, as the first harbingers of new U.S.–China relations. Until Cowan got to his feet there had been the protocol polite exchanges such as 'welcome' from Chou En-lai and 'thank you' from the leaders of the five teams. When Cowan drawled out his question, manager Steenoven and other U.S. team-members either looked at the floor or glared at the happily smiling Cowan.

'First, I'm not very clear about it,' replied premier Chou, batting no eyelids, 'so I can only say something rather superficial. Perhaps youth in the world today are dissatisfied with the present situation and want to seek the truth. Through this there come changes in ideology which are likely to assume various forms. Such forms cannot be said to be final because in their search for truth youth must go through various processes.

'It should be permitted for young people to try out different kinds of activity. When we were young we did the same. Therefore I understand the thinking of young people. They are very curious about things. One can see this same aspect in the young people of other countries who come here. They are not dressed like you but they have something in common – long hair for instance. I have met Japanese youth who also have long hair – but they may not be of your grouping.'

'What is going on in their minds,' replied Cowan, 'is deeper than what is seen from outside. I believe it is a new way of thinking. Not many people are familiar with it but a few are, and understand it.'

'Through the development of mankind,' continued Chou En-lai, 'through the progress of mankind, universal truth is bound to be found in the end. It is the same with the laws of nature. We agree that young people should want to try out various ways of getting at the truth. But one thing is that you should always try to find something in common with the great majority of mankind, and in this way the majority can make progress and achieve happiness. But if through one's own practice it is clear that what one is doing is not correct, then one should change. This is the way of acquiring knowledge.'

By this time manager Steenoven was sitting back relaxed and purring as if he had fathered the whole thing. Chou En-lai was obviously engrossed in the subject.

Cowan commented: 'Men's ideas change through a change of spiritual growth,' to which premier Chou replied: 'But the spiritual must be transformed into material force before one can change the world. And one must have the agreement of the majority of the people – that is the law of development. As we are speaking of philosophy, I would like to quote from Chairman Mao: "From the masses to the masses." That is the guiding line to transform theory into practice.' Table-tennis teams from five countries and a bevy of accompanying journalists listened to this rare exposé of China's attitude to some of the problems of modern youth with rapt attention. And Glenn Cowan was the hero of the day!

Chou En-lai was not just giving some avuncular advice to

foreign visitors, but confirming a policy of official encouragement to youth boldly to seek new ways, as was evidenced during the Cultural Revolution when tens of millions of young people went on the move from their homes and schools all over China – even being provided with free transport for a time – discovering their country for themselves, encouraged to take an active part in the Cultural Revolution and to identify themselves with its objectives. Youth was faced with thousands of new tasks, from reclaiming deserts to discovering new forms of energy. Life is a challenge, progress is a challenge and it is to youth to pick up the gage, not for fame and fortune, but to serve the community.

During the Cultural Revolution, the *only* revolution that this generation of Chinese youth has lived through, new values and new understanding emerged. The class struggle and its basic political concepts were clarified at all levels. The advice to students – a large number in their second, third and fourth year at university – to go to the countryside and be educated by the peasants must have been secretly sneered at by many. But living with the peasants, listening to tales of the old days, gave them an understanding of what the revolution was all about which they could acquire in no other way. This nation-wide touching-down to earth by tens of millions of young people has been built into the consciousness of the present generation of Chinese youth. The Cultural Revolution itself was a green light from Mao for youth to assert itself and get ready for the succession in leadership.

Among the new values learned during the Cultural Revolution was the fact that a production team's experimental group which invents a more efficient way of using human excreta in the compost heap is to be as much honoured as a group of scientists who score a world first in bio-chemistry by synthesizing the manufacture of insulin; the scientists accept that this is a perfectly just appraisal of comparative values.

When we asked our Yangtze stewardess, twenty-year-old Tzu Hung-li, whom we discovered to be following a correspondence course in general education, what she was studying to do later, she said, wide-eyed: 'But I am studying only to do my work better. It's not so easy to serve people as they need. Those who come on our steamer are usually cadres shifting from one job to another. The river trip gives them a chance of a few days' rest. It's my job to see that they can rest in the best possible conditions. Also that they get the sort of food they like. I need to learn more about history and literature so that I can explain about all the historical sites better and make the trip interesting as well as comfortable and restful.'

That is a very typical example of China's version of 'getting on in the world'. With a score or so of young people whom we have seen grow up, children of intimate friends known from babyhood, this is a generalized attitude, strongly affirmed during and since the Cultural Revolution. They want to do what they are doing well because it is this that wins them the greatest community approval. This is part of a revolution in values, a rejection of Confucian concepts. Those who worked with their hands used to be despised – it was only those who worked with their brains that had social status. Now young people are proud to say: 'My father was a worker. My father was a poor peasant.' The attitude to the status of work itself has radically changed. If the 'dictatorship of the proletariat' has any meaning, it is logical that this should be so.

Recently we found an acquaintance of ours in a European socialist country, a political scientist with wide international experience, working on a thesis investigating why young people in his country were turning to the West for inspiration in various fields, economic, political and cultural. His theory was that the family, as the basic unit of society, had acquired a consumer instead of a producer outlook. 'In the old days they worked on their farms, producing what they ate. Conversation around the table centred on problems of production. Now they are part of huge productive units where what they do has little relation to what they eat. They get money wages and the conversation around the table is about what they are going to buy with their money. They have acquired consumer instead of producer mentality. From that point on they think of moving to the nearest city, where they can earn more money and buy more radios, refrigerators, washing machines and all sorts of gadgets.

Once they get a taste for these, they find that Western models are always superior. They get an interest in the technology and culture – and finally the politics – of the society that turns out better-quality goods. All this is very dangerous.' When we asked what was the answer, he shook his head gloomily: 'There is none.'

We explained that this was exactly the reverse of what was happening in China, where, now that the women-folk were working in fields and factories, meal-time conversations tended to centre around the day's activities on the unit in which husband and wife – and their children – were working or studying; that the trend of population movement was from city to country-side; that the superior quality of foreign goods was regarded as a challenge, for the young people especially, to produce goods of equal or superior quality; and that the idea that the main aim of daily activities was to amass consumer goods was regarded as very 'backward thinking' in China. 'Wait till they start earning real money and acquiring tastes for something better than electric torches and thermos flasks. Human nature is the same the world over,' was his pessimistic reply.

A Western friend who had been in China for over a quarter of a century, married to a Chinese woman and with a grown-up daughter adopted from babyhood, made the point: 'Face in China never really depended on material wealth. The get-rich-quickies even had to buy some sort of façade of doing good things – become patrons of something or other. Selfishness and a parade of riches was never a gateway into social acceptance. On the other hand, the honest doctor, dentist, teacher and so forth, if he was poor, could always count on financial support from the people in his area.'

As their house was always filled with his daughter's young friends, we thought they would be good people to ask about youth problems.

'They don't have any particular problems,' was the reply. 'They know they'll have jobs. They usually like what they're doing. If they want higher education and have what it takes – and I don't mean money – they'll get it. They know that it doesn't matter what you are doing, but that doing it well gets you the approbation of society, which is what counts most for them. The different concept of who the "people" are has brought about a transformation of values. It is the poor and former downtrodden who are now recognized as "the people". So what used to be considered very menial and demeaning work has now been elevated to "honourable labour".'

We asked if their daughter and her friends accept the 'Serve the People' idea as their lifetime credo.

'But it is so clearly the obvious thing to do,' our friend replied. 'It is a continuation of traditional morality to which Mao has given revolutionary content. In the old days Confucian precepts applied only within the ruling class. Now it applies to the people as a whole, with emphasis on the real people – those on whose productive labour society as a whole depends. The kids get a great kick out of the appreciativeness of the commune farmers when they give a hand at harvest time, or mend some bits of farm machinery. It's the sort of thing that makes their day. The idea of service to the community has deep roots. In such a closely packed society, and with the black poverty of the old days, life was unbearable unless there was some degree of tolerance, of considerateness and of mutual help among the poor, who formed the overwhelming majority of the people. Another important thing is that education these days prepares them for life as it is. There is no contradiction between what they learn at school, in a technical as well as a moral sense, and the world they move into after schooling. In fact they start moving into that world outside while they are still at school.'

This is correct. Although the periods varied according to the schools visited, even in primary schools pupils put in a certain amount of time each term working in factories or communes – or both. At the Chen Ning Road Primary School in Nanking, for instance, pupils did two weeks each of agricultural or factory work every term, in addition to which they had two small factories, one for making wooden boxes, another which had an annual output of 100,000 wire brushes for cleaning rifles. Similarly at the Peking Affiliated Middle School No. 2 pupils spent one month a year in actual production in industry and another month in agriculture. The school was also linked with the

Peking Metal-Working Factory, from which workers came to lecture on technical subjects and to which pupils went for their month a year practical work. In addition the school had metal-working and carpentry shops – and a small atelier for making diodes.

Following the Cultural Revolution, teaching methods had been revolutionized and aimed at preparing pupils for life in the outside world. In one classroom we visited, pupils were busy with tweezers and soldering irons making electric circuits from a design on the blackboard. The teacher in charge said: 'Before, we used to spend six months' teaching the general principles of electricity. Now they learn theory and practice at the same time. Instead of drawing circuits from blackboards and studying theory from books, they build the circuits right here in the classroom and cover the six months' theoretical course in one month, combined with practice.' It was a good illustration in action of 'Learn what you do. Do what you learn. Conduct scientific experiments.' We were shown some better and simpler electronic circuits the pupils had invented themselves and also a tiny 100-watt heater for welding antennae on to diodes.

'Emphasis is on self-reliance and hard struggle,' explained one of the members of the revolutionary committee. 'And they take that spirit with them after graduation. If they go to a farm, for instance, they start off by building wheelbarrows and all sorts of farm implements. Some went to mountainous areas to settle down for a while. There, if a plough breaks down in the busy season, much time is lost while it is sent to the commune centre for repairs. Our students started taking over repairs on the spot. This had a great effect on the commune members. We have had letters from former pupils thanking the school for having trained them well and saying how much this is appreciated by the peasants.'

The higher up the ladder of learning a student goes these days, the closer is his contact with life outside. At the Shanghai Fu Tan University, for instance, we found the science departments had organic links with over sixty factories. Technicians came from those factories to lecture or to take refresher courses; students did working spells in the factories. The physics department was affiliated to an electronic components plant, the optics department to an electric-lighting sources plant and another making optical instruments. The chemical faculty had set up its own petro-chemical plant within the university. In the electronic workshops, we found that over 100,000 integrated circuits – over twenty varieties – had been made in the year before our visit and the most sophisticated work on micro-miniaturization of transistor circuits was being done – part of it under state contracts. Students were encouraged to find short cuts and to be bold in experimentation, not just to repeat what was known.

The effect of all this, as we found in our travels, is that the enthusiasm of the young people rides highest where the going is toughest, material rewards minimal, but the task in hand a stirring challenge. Reclaiming the Gobi desert is an exciting instance. Under the old order, the sands were advancing and pushing the people back. For generations this had been so. Now the people are advancing and pushing the desert back. A good place to see what is being done is at Minchin county, the centre of which, bearing the same name, was the former 'Chen Fan' (Suppress the Barbarians) frontier city in West Kansu near the border with Inner Mongolia. Minchin county has desert on three sides, and the sands were gradually moving in, smothering fields and villages, forcing people to retreat. In one area of twenty villages totalling 2,300 households in the early 1940s, only 300 people were left at the time of liberation. The counter-attack started in 1952 from the village of Da Ken Yen, half the land there having been lost during the three years since liberation. With the young people in the lead, over 2,000 acres were planted with sand dates, a hardy desert tree, thought at the time to be useful only for its capacity to survive and fix the sands. Later it turned out that the bitter fruit could be converted into an acceptable wine and the leaves could be processed for pig fodder or dried and exported for their medicinal properties.

All eyes were on that first group of pioneers. For the first time in centuries, instead of fighting each other, men of the area were uniting to fight the desert. Ancient irrigation systems and strings of oases had been invaded by the sands while battles were waged for generations in the frontier areas. From the air, looking north, the desert looked like a golden ocean in a state of arrested motion, endless waves of sand as far as the eye could see. In Minchin county alone there were 330,000 sand dunes. The date trees at Da Ken Yen struck root, following which a wholesale assault was launched against the Gobi. Dunes were flattened and the idea caught on of reconstituting nature by carrying in clay as a water-retaining sponge and welcoming bed into which the sand dates could sink their roots and fix the sands. Someone had experimented by covering his grand-mother's grave with clay and sticking some plants into it. They grew. He carried the experiment further by plastering some of the dunes with clay and found that, even if the sand covered it, the clay remained as a stabilizing element. Where the sand date trees struck root, the sand flattened out automatically, and where wells were sunk to tap rivers that had disappeared under the desert centuries earlier the land became fertile again. Supplementing the tough physical labour, small plants were introduced to make concrete sections for wells, one set atop the other as the well-diggers went down to a hundred feet to tap sweet water. Thus they pushed the desert back, consolidating each section gained with trees, pushing forward again with more trees and wells, linking wells with irrigation canals, building roads into the land reclaimed, lining canals and roads with trees. By the time we visited Minchin in 1973 some 230 million trees had been planted since 1952 and 2,650 wells had been sunk – solid tubes of concrete a metre in diameter with mechanized pumps to send the water along the irrigation channels.

As a warning to the local lads to keep on their toes, a group of twenty-three teenage girls formed a work-team, and with a retired old peasant as adviser and team-leader they reclaimed 30 acres of desert, from which they got 40 tons of grain in 1972. Despite the great drought that year, the Minchin county people harvested an average of over half a ton of wheat per acre on thousands of acres of desert where nothing grew before. And by that time they had earned well over a million yuan from the dried leaves of the sand date trees, once thought to be a nuisance. All this was accomplished by much back-breaking work, with the young people always in the vanguard. Their satisfaction was that of creating something out of nothing, turning back the tide of nature, changing the face of the desert, contributing visibly to the national tasks. Populating the frontier areas was one of the ways of preparing against war – but to do that food had to be available on the spot.

In the back country, we found that just the sight of bare hills and deserts was a challenge that young people yearned to take up, especially when the word got round of what had been done at Tachai and Minchin county and scores of other places where nature had been tamed. In Kaotai county, for instance, with a total of 21,330 families, three big protective forest belts had been planted totalling over 100 miles in length, breaking the force of the great sandstorms that used to sweep the area. This sort of thing is going on all over the north-west and has had a notable effect in Peking, where red rain, stained with the sands of the Gobi, used to be a regular feature in the spring. In Kansu province alone, almost one million acres of land had been transformed into forest belts, permitting rice cultivation on another million acres. By terracing former barren hillsides on the Tachai model, 750,000 acres had been reclaimed.

If it is usually difficult to find out what youth wants – what their vision of the future is – it is easier to find out what they do not want. In China, they definitely reject the 'away from it all' Shangri La – and Katmandu – solutions that have attracted many young people from the capitalist West, and also the yearning for the Western 'way of life' that has smitten a section of the youth of the European socialist countries. If they think of travel, it is in terms of travel within their own vast and exciting world. The solutions they are thinking about are those that relate to problems in their own spheres of activity. Students at middle schools and universities keep abreast of activities in the technical field at home and abroad – libraries are surprisingly well stocked with foreign technical magazines, or roneoed extracts if there are not enough copies to go round. They only need to get a whiff of a new idea – something that represents a short cut for science and technology – and working groups are set up to study it, not to win individual face, fame and fortune according to the old concepts, but to make a contribution to building communism.

The young people spend a lot of time in political studies which many of their counterparts in the West think must be terribly boring. But to the best of our knowledge they do not find it so, degrees of enthusiasm varying according to the quality of the person leading the studies. They find it exciting to discover that what they are doing in practice is well founded in theory, not only as expounded in the works of Mao Tse-tung but according to classical Marxist doctrines as studied in the original. Since the widespread study of Marx, Engels, Lenin and Stalin started after the Cultural Revolution, it has been a revelation to young people of our acquaintance that in their day-to-day activities they are giving practical form to the theories of these revolutionary thinkers. It has given a new dimension to their feeling that they are very much part of the world revolution.

When one asks young people about material needs – what they are saving up for – they will often reply that they are saving to buy a bike, a wrist-watch, transistor radio, or perhaps a camera. If you ask if someone is saving up to get married, the usual reply is: 'I'm too young to think about that' – as the social pressures are for late marriages, partly as a reaction to child marriages of the old days, partly as a measure to reduce population growth. If someone is contemplating marriage the reply is: 'My girl has a good job and so have I. We don't need to save for that.' Expensive marriage feasts, gifts and so forth are no longer in fashion. In many cases these days, young people tend to find their partners in the factory, commune, brigade or other organization where they work together. The sort of qualities they seek in each other are those that emerge in daily activities, in their work, study and attitude towards their fellows.

What do such young people get out of this new life that they are building up? It was a question put to both of us when we toured Australia and New Zealand – on different circuits but at the same time early in 1973 – speaking to trade-union, student and other groups about China and Vietnam. They certainly get something that steers them clear of juvenile crime, drugs and obsession with sex. They give the appearance of being happy, relaxed and confident. Their future is assured: interesting jobs, no material worries. They find satisfaction in group activities and quickly fit in with whatever is going if they make a move – from school to factory or farm, from city to countryside. They take an active part, according to their interests, in drama and musical circles, or in sport, which assumes greater importance every day. At least twenty international sports teams, including American swimmers and basketball players, were touring China in the summer of 1973 and their activities were televised.

Certainly, unless he deliberately opts to become a hermit, it is impossible for a young person to suffer from loneliness. Human contact is not something lacking in China. Wherever young people go, they integrate with the youth of the enterprise or educational establishment, joining groups whose members have similar tastes and interests. The generation gap which existed in many fields before the Cultural Revolution no longer exists. The fact that there are usually an equal number of students and professors on the revolutionary committees that run the universities; that each veteran worker takes one or two apprentices or young workers under his wing; that young people have a proportion of the places in management in all enterprises; that avenues are wide open for the initiatives of youth in all fields; that while youth respects the skills, activities and revolutionary pasts of the middle-aged and elderly, the latter respect the superior education and grasp of ideological theory by the young – all this contributes to bridging the age gap.

The Cultural Revolution did much to restore the confidence of young people in themselves. Now they have the glory of having fired the first shots in two mighty revolutionary movements which shook the country to its foundations: the May the Fourth Movement in 1919; and the Cultural Revolution, which started in mid-June 1966, when Peking Radio broadcast the *ta tze pao* of Peking University students, announcing that: 'Revolutionary teachers and students at Peking University have exposed the capitalist-roaders in Peking University pursuing a capitalist line.' The status of youth as one of the leading forces is consecrated in a revision of the Communist Party's constitution, unanimously adopted at the Tenth Party Congress, which now states that leading bodies in future would be elected 'in accordance with the requirements for successors to the cause of the proletarian revolution and the principle of combining the old, the middle-aged and the young'.

The old veterans, Mao Tse-tung at eighty, the other survivor of the original twelve founder members of the party, vice-president Tung Pi-Wu, at eighty-seven, Political Bureau member Chu Teh, 'Father of the Red Army', also eighty-seven, and premier Chou En-lai at seventy-five, have with their comrades formulated the idea of the old and middle-aged revolutionaries coming together with able and proven representatives of the younger cadres, who will collectively take over more executive responsibility with them and thus carry out the ideals of the Cultural Revolution, also smoothing the path ahead for the succession that in time must come. Will today's generation of Chinese youth be the first in the world to proclaim a communist state, where the principle 'from each according to his ability and to each according to his needs' is universally applied? It would be a bold man who would predict the tempo of things to come, although the shape is already defined. Mao's trumpet blast in a reply to poet Kuo Mo-jo on 9 January 1963:

> '... time presses,
> Ten thousand years are too long;
> Seize the day, seize the hour!'

certainly strikes an echo in the hearts of Chinese youth, impatient as youth anywhere to press on to final goals.

MORE ABOUT PENGUINS
AND PELICANS

Penguinews, which appears every month, contains details of all the new books issued by Penguins as they are published. From time to time it is supplemented by *Penguins in Print*, which is our complete list of almost 5,000 titles.

A specimen copy of *Penguinews* will be sent to you free on request. Please write to Dept EP, Penguin Books Ltd, Harmondsworth, Middlesex, for your copy.

In the U.S.A.: For a complete list of books available from Penguin in the United States write to Dept CS, Penguin Books Inc., 7110 Ambassador Road, Baltimore, Maryland 21207.

In Canada: For a complete list of books available from Penguin in Canada write to Penguin Books Canada Ltd, 41 Steelcase Road West, Markham, Ontario.

BOOKS ON TRAVEL
PUBLISHED BY PENGUIN BOOKS

BOOKS ON WORLD AFFAIRS AND
CURRENT EVENTS
PUBLISHED BY PENGUIN BOOKS

BOOKS ON WORLD AFFAIRS AND
CURRENT EVENTS
PUBLISHED BY PENGUIN BOOKS

BOOKS ON CHINA
PUBLISHED BY PENGUIN BOOKS